T0091902

Praise for *Data Quality*

"The promise of the 'data economy' (i.e., data is the new oil), combined with the naive belief that AI can turn a company's data into gold, is leading many enterprises to experiment with adopting AI. But early adopters are learning that one of the primary causes of AI failure is poor-quality data being fed into AI models (garbage in, garbage out). This highlights that raw data is insufficient and that it must be refined to create value. Consequently, implementing data-centric AI is rapidly becoming a best practice at both start-ups and established technology companies. This book provides a pragmatic approach for enterprises to acquire and manage good-quality data based on proven best practices. If you are a C-level executive or an AI practitioner seeking to deploy AI at scale to drive value creation, I highly recommend this book."

—Anik Bose
BGV managing general partner and founder, Ethical AI Governance Group
(EAIGG) (United States)

"Prashanth Southekal has nailed the 'why' and the 'how' about data quality's relation to analytics in this highly readable book. To be an economically viable company in today's transparent, global, and competitive world, business leaders must champion the data quality and analytics journey and embed them in decision support systems as an operational core competency. The companies that advocate data quality and analytics integrate them in their DNA to outsmart their competitors in strategic and tactical decision making that yields sustainable success."

—Gary Cokins
President, Analytics-Based Performance Management LLC;
co-author, *Predictive Business Analytics* (United States)

"Good data is a source of myriad opportunities, while bad data is a tremendous burden. Data is now exposed at a much more strategic level (e.g., through business intelligence systems), increasing manifold the stakes involved for individuals and corporations, as well as government agencies. There, the lack of knowledge about data accuracy, currency, or completeness can have erroneous and even catastrophic results. In this book, Dr. Southekal provides very detailed and thorough coverage of all aspects of data quality management and best practices to improve data quality that would suit all ranges of expertise from beginner to advanced practitioner."

—Michael Taylor
AI chief data scientist, Siemens Mobility (Singapore)

"Dr. Southekal has a way of distilling complexity into practical applications for global leaders who span multiple industries and market types. He leverages his relationships to gain more perspective on data management. His book, *Data Quality: Empowering Businesses with Analytics and AI*, builds on his prior successes and hits the mark once again. 'Improving data quality should be a top priority for all business leaders.'"

—Victor Ojeleye
Planning & Reporting Manager, FP&A,
Cargill Protein North America (United States)

"Data quality is a fundamental building block of success in today's digitally agile world. It creates disruption in long-established industries, but also allows traditional companies to innovate and drive more efficient and effective decision-making practices. Data quality utilization will grow revenues and reduce risk through better-connected intelligence. Dr. Southekal has created a book that explains the why, what, and how of data quality. Written in a structured, logical approach that allows all industries and leaders to fully understand the importance of getting their data quality correct for true value generation, *Data Quality: Empowering Businesses with Analytics and AI* is a must-read."

—Matthew Small
Managing director, Data Value Creation Ltd (United Kingdom)

"Prashanth provides an in-depth and scientific perspective on a very critical topic for businesses and organizations today. He addresses the complete lifecycle related to data quality, provides detailed explanation in each chapter, and starts from what data quality is to how to capture DQ issues proactively, govern the data, comply with regulations, and secure and sustain DQ practices. There are key callouts depicted in the insight boxes within each chapter. With the future trends indicating the shift toward right data from big data, data quality is a concept that needs to be ingrained in a company's business fabric. The book is a very practical guide to data quality that will be part of my toolkit."

—**Ramdas Narayanan**
Vice president, Bank of America (United States)

"Data-driven organizations understand that useful data is not simply found and organized by itself. In this book, his third, Dr. Prashanth Southekal shows business leaders the foundations needed to create a company that wants data- and analytics-led decisions to be part of their strategy. For data leaders and practitioners, this book will not only guide you but will also trigger new thoughts and ideas."

—**Mark Stern**
Vice president of Analytics and BI, BetMGM (United States)

"Data is growing and almost every company is a data company. The majority of organizations want to be in the data-driven space, utilizing and monetizing data through advanced analytics and AI. Although the thought process is great, when it comes to practical implementations most companies are struggling to get value out of their investment. In the consulting space we are seeing repeatedly the need for getting the basics and foundation right. Dr. Southekal's book *Data Quality: Empowering Businesses with Analytics and AI* is empowering business and data leaders and giving practical guidance on how to build good-quality data to get the most value from analytics and AI projects."

—**Rathi Subbaraj**
Senior manager, Dufrain (United Kingdom)

"The most thorough and comprehensive book I've seen on data quality. It covers the entire lifecycle of data management in the current enterprise, AI, and analytics landscape. The book contains a wealth of valuable strategic and tactical elements, as well as best practices for getting the most value from data for the business. A must-read for anyone looking to leverage the value of enterprise data."

—**Tobias Zwingmann**
Managing partner, RAPYD.AI (Germany)

"In today's world, where almost every company is dealing with petabyte-scale data, data quality is something that should be ingrained in all phases of the data lifecycle. In this book Dr. Southekal takes you on a journey of data quality and its lifecycle. It provides an in-depth perspective and the right approach to manage DQ. This book provides a detail explanation of the DARS approach, the DQ lifecycle and its difference phases, multiple dimensions of DQ, data decay, best practices, and a lot more. Dr. Southekal hits the mark again, and this book should be part of the toolkit for all levels of DQ and data practitioners."

—**Ujjwal Goel**
Director, Data Architecture & Data Engineering, Loblaw (Canada)

"The economy of data has been a trending subject for some time now. But the poor quality of the data affects the decision-making ability and the performance results. Most of the publications in this space refer to the physical flaws in data quality, like data downtime, whereas the author extends the definition to the logical flaws in data, which are much harder to spot and resolve. Dr. Southekal created a playbook for delivering business value from data, with prescriptive recommendations based on best practices for data governance and management practices, all based on the proprietary evaluation framework for data quality."

—**Inna Tokarev Sela**
CEO, Illumex AI (Israel)

"Dr. Southekal has done it again: given the data science community a gem of a framework (DARS: Design-Assess-Realize-Sustain) that they can apply to maximize ROI from their data and analytics initiatives. *Data Quality: Empowering Businesses with Analytics and AI* does a phenomenal job explaining nuanced concepts in a language that can be very easily understood by both technical and business audiences."

—**Swapnil Srivastava**
VP and Global Head of Analytics, Evalueserve (United States)

"Like his previous two books, *Data Quality: Empowering Businesses with Analytics and AI* is yet another great read for enterprise data leaders. In this book, Dr. Southekal first sets up a framework to understand and measure the quality of business data (the Define and Assess phases); he then provides a guidebook to implement data quality programs (the Realize and Sustain phases). In today's AI-driven world, this book will help business leaders build a solid data foundation."

—Li Kang
Head of Strategy, CelerData (United States)

"With accelerating change, decision-cycle times are narrowing, placing increased pressure on organizations to make faster and effective decisions to drive the biggest impact. In this environment, data quality issues can amplify the impact and costs of incorrect decisions. In this book, Dr. Southekal provides a comprehensive approach, practical frameworks and best practices to defining and addressing data quality issues. This is a must read, full of important and practical information, for all data professionals."

—Sanjeev Chib, CPA, CA
VP (Product) and managing director, Data Solutions, Moneris (Canada)

"Southekal's *Data Quality* goes well beyond delivering a thoughtful, useful, and usable text on the virtues and value of quality data; it offers accessible and actionable insights into how serious organizations can get measurable value from their data investments. His 'Define, Assess, Realize, and Sustain' framework offers both a guide and a roadmap to making 'data' the asset it can and should be for the digital and digitizing enterprise. I am impressed by its clarity. It's comprehensive without being overwhelming. Check it out."

—Michael Schrage
Research fellow, MIT Sloan School Initiative on the Digital Economy;
Author, *Recommendation Engines* and *The Innovator's Hypothesis*,
MIT Press (United States)

"There are often misnomers when it comes to understanding how valuable data can be to driving an organization forward. Unfortunately, in some cases, data is an afterthought, only because the people managing it either don't invest or they don't know how to go about deploying a great data program. Dr. Southekal's latest book spells it out for you in a way that is simple to understand for all business users looking to improve their data products. If you are a product owner/manager looking to improve your data product, then I recommend adding this to your knowledge bank. I certainly will."

—Diane Robin
Senior technical product owner, Data & Analytics, Talentnet (Canada)

"If you want to know about empowering business with analytics and AI, this is the book for you – the transformation of business through 3Ds (enabling data-driven decisioning). The aspects highlighted in the book could be familiar ('been there, done that'), even anecdotal at times; however, this book helps to highlight and join the dots in the successful integration and management of good-quality data within an enterprise using the DARS framework. I am recommending this book because there is no other in the market that captures or attempts to transform business by purposefully empowering it with its data lifecycle, lineage, security, profile, architecture, and governance, thereby helping a business to leapfrog into the next phase of its evolution and resilience. To quote Prashanth, 'Data is a business asset only when it is *consciously captured and deliberately managed* such that quality data is available to run and sustain the business.'"

—**Tarun Jacob George**
CEO, Tata Insights and Quants (India)

"In a 'data is the new oil' economy, Dr. Southekal illustrates the requirements, pitfalls, and payoffs of 'refining' data for today's business leaders. In the race to create and capture value, many organizations suffer from the 'capture it all, figure it out later' mindset. For leaders seeking to develop a sustainable competitive advantage, the Define-Assess-Realize-Sustain process is essential to maximize value and, more importantly, avoid the many potential perils of acting on insights derived from improper data management."

—**Mike Stratta**
CEO, Arcalea (United States)

"This book by Dr. Prashanth Southekal is a great take on data quality. The book presents aspects of data quality in very easy-to-understand concepts and language. It talks about various frameworks and practical tools that can be adopted to implement and improve data quality in an organization. The concepts are well supported by various statistics that give a very practical and analytical view of data quality. Thank you, Prashanth, for making data quality so easy to understand."

—**Arihant Garg**
Partner, KPMG (India)

"The ability of enterprises to become data driven, achieve data monetization, drive digital transformation, and embrace the power of AI hinges on one thing and one thing only: *data quality*. For companies to deliver and achieve value from its *data assets*, data quality coupled with data management and governance is key. As a data practitioner for well over two decades, I have seen how data quality has played a role in achieving and sustaining long term success from data. This book provides a practical, simple, and insightful guide to manage data quality across its lifecycle (*why* to *how*). It is a must-have book for C-level executives, business leaders, and AI practitioners embarking on the journey to deliver value from data."

—Santosh Raju
Global head Industry & Horizontal Solutions, Microsoft Practice,
HCL Tech (United Kingdom)

"A very well-constructed book written from a practical perspective that demystifies business-driven data quality, taking a much-needed broader approach focused on achieving business operational efficiencies and revenue optimization driven by analytics. It goes beyond the early industry focus on data profiling to encompass business process change and drive Master/Reference Data Systems of Record frameworks. Prasanth brings thought leadership in driving data quality as a top priority for organizations and a primary driver of a targeted business approach versus a component of an enterprise data governance or data management approach.

—Peter Kapur
Head of Data Governance, Data Quality and MDM,
Waste Management (United States)

"Would you like to arm yourself with the best source of information to improving the bottom line of your organization by leveraging data analytics? Look no further and take the opportunity to read the book *Data Quality: Empowering Businesses with Analytics and AI* by Dr. Prashanth Southekal. Dr. Southekal has a way of teaching the value of data to business owners that allows anyone to see how they can easily improve business performance. His expertise is easily adaptable to any industry."

—Hadia Lugo
Director of Financial Planning & Analysis (FP&A),
Duke Energy (United States)

"Data as a strategic asset to drive business performance is being increasingly recognized as a key tenet across many industries. In order to become a data-driven enterprise, quality of data is of utmost importance. I found Dr. Southekal's DARS (Define, Analyze, Realize, and Sustain) approach highly systematic and effective to define and implement a data quality program with both strategic and tactical considerations. His emphasis that data governance works best when implemented early in the data lifecycle is a great insight. Without good-quality data, any attempt to leverage AI/ML is just hype. I highly recommend this book as it provides an excellent, easy-to-practice framework and techniques for practitioners."

—Dr. Venkatraman Balasubramanian, PhD, MBA
SVP and Global Head, Healthcare and Life Sciences,
Orion Innovation (United States)

"There is no dearth of organizations talking about the need for data quality but very few are actually able to make systemic and process level changes to address and action the wide landscape of data in most modern enterprises. The recommendations put forth by Dr. Prashanth Southekal in this book – DATA QUALITY: EMPOWERING BUSINESSES WITH ANALYTICS AND AI provides a practical and incremental way to tackling the behemoth sized problem"

—Kamayini Kaul
VP, Global Head Information Insights and Analytics
CSL Behring

Data Quality

Data Quality

*Empowering Businesses
with Analytics and AI*

PRASHANTH H. SOUTHEKAL

WILEY

Published by John Wiley & Sons, Inc., Hoboken, New Jersey.
Published simultaneously in Canada.

For general information on our other products and services or for technical support, please contact our Customer Care Department within the United States at (800) 762-2974, outside the United States at (317) 572-3993 or fax (317) 572-4002.

Wiley also publishes its books in a variety of electronic formats. Some content that appears in print may not be available in electronic formats. For more information about Wiley products, visit our web site at www.wiley.com.

Library of Congress Cataloging-in-Publication Data is Available:

ISBN 9781394165230 (Hardback)
ISBN 9781394165254 (ePDF)
ISBN 9781394165247 (ePub)

Cover Design: Wiley
Cover Image : © amiak/Shutterstock

SKY10039518_120822

Contents

Foreword   xvii

Preface   xix

    About the Book   xix
    Quality Principles Applied in This Book   xx
    Organization of the Book   xxi
    Who Should Read This Book?   xxiii
    References   xxiii

Acknowledgments   xxv

PART I: DEFINE PHASE   1

Chapter 1: Introduction   3

    Introduction   3
    Data, Analytics, AI, and Business Performance   5
    Data as a Business Asset or Liability   6
    Data Governance, Data Management, and Data Quality 7
    Leadership Commitment to Data Quality   10
    Key Takeaways   12
    Conclusion   13
    References   13

Chapter 2: Business Data   17

    Introduction   17
    Data in Business   18
    Telemetry Data   21
    Purpose of Data in Business   22
    Business Data Views   24
    Key Characteristics of Business Data   31
    Critical Data Elements (CDEs)   32

Key Takeaways   34
Conclusion   35
References   35

Chapter 3: Data Quality in Business   37

Introduction   37
Data Quality Dimensions   39
Context in Data Quality   51
Consequences and Costs of Poor Data Quality   52
Data Depreciation and Its Factors   54
Data in IT Systems   56
Data Quality and Trusted Information   59
Key Takeaways   60
Conclusion   61
References   62

PART II: ANALYZE PHASE   63

Chapter 4: Causes for Poor Data Quality   65

Introduction   65
Data Quality RCA Techniques   66
Typical Causes of Poor Data Quality   71
Key Takeaways   78
Conclusion   79
References   80

Chapter 5: Data Lifecycle and Lineage   81

Introduction   81
Business-Enabled DLC Stages   82
IT Business-Enabled DLC Stages   86
Data Lineage   88
Key Takeaways   90
Conclusion   90
References   91

Chapter 6: Profiling for Data Quality   93

Introduction   93
Criteria for Data Profiling   95
Data Profiling Techniques for Measures of Centrality   98
Data Profiling Techniques for Measures of Variation   100
Integrating Centrality and Variation KPIs   109
Key Takeaways   112

Conclusion   112
References   112

PART III: REALIZE PHASE   **113**

Chapter 7: Reference Architecture for Data Quality   **115**

Introduction   115
Options to Remediate Data Quality   116
DataOps   118
Data Product   120
Data Fabric and Data Mesh   123
Data Enrichment   126
Key Takeaways   131
Conclusion   132
References   132

Chapter 8: Best Practices to Realize Data Quality   **133**

Introduction   133
Overview of Best Practices   134
BP 1: Identify the Business KPIs and the Ownership of
        These KPIs and the Pertinent Data   136
BP 2: Build and Improve the Data Culture and Literacy
        in the Organization   138
BP 3: Define the Current and Desired State of Data Quality   142
BP 4: Follow the Minimalistic Approach to Data Capture   145
BP 5: Select and Define the Data Attributes for Data Quality   148
BP 6: Capture and Manage Critical Data with Data
        Standards in MDM Systems   152
Key Takeaways   155
Conclusion   158
References   158

Chapter 9: Best Practices to Realize Data Quality   **161**

Introduction   161
BP 7: Rationalize and Automate the Integration of Critical
        Data Elements   162
BP 8: Define the SoR and Securely Capture Transactional
        Data in the SoR/OLTP System   168
BP 9: Build and Manage Robust Data Integration Capabilities   173
BP 10: Distribute Data Sourcing and Insight Consumption   181
Key Takeaways   186
Conclusion   189
References   189

PART IV: SUSTAIN PHASE   **191**

Chapter 10: Data Governance   **193**

Introduction   193
Data Governance Principles   195
Data Governance Design Components   197
Implementing the Data Governance Program   202
Data Observability   203
Data Compliance – ISO 27001, SOC1, and SOC2   205
Key Takeaways   206
Conclusion   208
References   209

Chapter 11: Protecting Data   **211**

Introduction   211
Data Classification   212
Data Safety   216
Data Security   218
Key Takeaways   220
Conclusion   220
References   221

Chapter 12: Data Ethics   **223**

Introduction   223
Data Ethics   224
Importance of Data Ethics   224
Principles of Data Ethics   225
Model Drift in Data Ethics   226
Data Privacy   228
Managing Data Ethically   230
Key Takeaways   235
Conclusion   235
References   236

Appendix 1: Abbreviations and Acronyms   **237**

Appendix 2: Glossary   **241**

Appendix 3: Data Literacy Competencies   **245**

About the Author   **249**

Index   **251**

Foreword

Once they built a building in downtown San Francisco. It was right in the middle of downtown. They cleared the space for the building. They started driving steel beams into the ground. It was hard work drilling into the ground for the beams. At some point they said that the beams were in the ground "good enough."

Then they built a multi-story building on top of the beams. They built very luxurious living quarters in the building. The building took its place among the skyscrapers in San Francisco. They started to sell the units at very expensive prices.

Then one day one of the tenants of the building dropped a marble on the floor and it did something odd; the marble rolled across the floor. The building was tilting. The builders had not placed the foundation on bedrock because the ground was so difficult to penetrate. And the steel girders they put in looked sturdy enough. But they weren't.

Slowly the building was tipping over. And at this point trying to go back and reposition the girders was not an option.

Someday – in the hopefully distant future – the skyscraper is going to fall over.

You don't want to be on Market Street or Chinatown when that day comes. Nothing good is going to happen then. And you certainly don't want to be in the building when it tips over.

The same phenomenon is happening today but in a different arena. Today we have a world of glitzy technologies – AI, ML, business intelligence, blockchain, and a whole host of other venues. These technologies are glitzy and have great appeal. But all of these new technologies have a fatal flaw. All of these new technologies depend on a solid foundation of quality data. Just like the San Francisco building that was not built on bedrock, these new and swank technologies will only work if they operate on reliable data.

At the end of the day, it is back to the old principle: GIGO – garbage in, garbage out. AI and ML simply do not work if they are trying to operate on faulty data.

The problem is that nobody wants to address the issues of data quality. Data quality just does not have the sizzle that the newer technologies have. And that is a tragic mistake, because the new and sexy technologies do not function well or at all if they don't have the proper and correct data to operate from.

The original pioneer of data quality, Larry English, would be proud to see this work from Dr. Prashanth Southekal. Many years ago, Larry sowed the seeds of the notion of data quality. Larry would be amazed to see how those seeds have grown in a lush green and verdant field.

One of the things I really like about this book is its completeness that any data, analytics, and AI practitioner would benefit from. Dr. Southekal has covered all the bases, including important data quality best practices in the areas of data management, and data governance – and it is a lot of work to cover all the bases. Some of the highlights of the book include:

- Definitions—what they are and why they are important in business
- Data lineage—a subject overlooked by many authors
- The system of record—another important concept missed by most authors
- The acknowledgment that the volume of data plays an important role in shaping what can be done
- Data governance—what it is and how to do it
- Protection and security—essential to any modern organization
- Ethics—anther subject missed by most authors
- Ownership of data and stewardship

And this short list only scratches the surface of this book.

This book is essential reading for everyone who wants to build technology that relies on data. If you are going to be building massive structures, you need to know how to build solid foundations. Otherwise, you are sowing seeds of disaster.

—Bill Inmon, "Father of the Data Warehouse"
Denver, Colorado, United States
October, 2022

Preface

ABOUT THE BOOK

Every company today is a data company as data is redefining business models and enabling new revenue streams, reducing costs, and mitigating business risks. Today, data is often the primary product for nearly every business, and analytics and AI (artificial intelligence) form the core business model element in many companies. IDC predicts that by 2023 more than half of all GDP worldwide will be driven by products and services from digitally transformed enterprises. A McKinsey report says data-driven organizations provide EBITDA (earnings before interest, taxes, and depreciation) increases of up to 25% (Böringer et al. 2022), and a study conducted by Boston Consulting in 2022 found that the first 9 of the top 10 innovative companies in the world are data firms (Manly et al. 2022). Overall, data today is considered the key enabler of innovation and productivity in business.

To derive business results from data, quality data is essential. But most industries are plagued with poor data quality. An *Harvard Business Review* study found that just 3% of the data in a business enterprise meets quality standards (Nagle et al. 2017). Research analyst firm Gartner found that 27% of data in the world's top companies is flawed. To provide organizations a competitive advantage from data, this book, *Data Quality: Empowering Businesses with Analytics and AI* provides readers with practical guidance and proven solutions to derive quality business data. While there are many books on data quality in the market, the book has three key elements that will make it unique in the marketplace:

1. The book is for practitioners written by a fellow practitioner. It is based on my data, analytics, and AI experience, while consulting for over 80 companies including big brands such as GE, SAP, P&G, Apple, and Shell. In addition, this content has been reviewed by senior data and technology leaders from many leading organizations worldwide.

2. The book is relevant in today's context. Today, companies operate under stiff competition, expanded business networks, increasing regulatory compliance, and emerging technologies such as cloud computing, big data, machine learning (ML), artificial intelligence (AI), blockchain, IoT (Internet of Things), and more. This book caters to managing quality business data in the current AI and analytics landscape. Every effort has been made to ensure that the contents are well researched, the chapters are logically and coherently organized, the topics are relevant for today's context, and the book is written in a simple, clear, and precise manner.

3. The book is technology agnostic. Many data quality books available in the market are IT product–centric. This book looks at the technical concepts without any reference to proprietary vendor technologies. The primary objective of this book is to enable improved business performance from data. Any business leader who is keen to derive quality data can use this book, regardless of which IT and data products they utilize.

 QUALITY PRINCIPLES APPLIED IN THIS BOOK

To ensure that the book is useful to the readers, it is written with four key principles in mind.

1. **Data consumption.** This book is written to improve the chances of utilizing data for better business performance. Improved business performance from data can happen under three key circumstances: (1) when there is quality data, (2) where the focus is on the utilization or consumption of data, and (3) when the purpose of data is to improve and optimize the performance of the business in operations, compliance, and decision making. In short, in this book the focus will be on acquiring and managing **quality data to improve operations, compliance, and decision-making capabilities in business.**

2. **Root cause analysis and continuous improvement.** Data quality management is not a one-time exercise. It is a continuous improvement initiative to identifying and fixing the root causes. This is important because if you are not solving the right issue, you will never be able to eliminate the real problem. Hence this book focuses on techniques to identify the root causes of data quality issues. In addition, the book discusses **16 common root causes** that degrade data quality in business.

3. **Best practices.** This book focuses on industry best practices to improve data quality. Specifically, it offers **10 perspective recommendations or best practices** including the required capabilities to improve the quality of data in business. In addition, numerous insights nuggets which are evidence from research and case studies are provided throughout the book.

4. **Relevance.** This book caters to managing **quality data in the current business and AI and analytics landscape.** AI can improve business performance with automation based on insights derived from analytics only if there is quality data. Essentially, there is no AI without data and no data without AI.

 ORGANIZATION OF THE BOOK

So, how can a business enterprise, acquire and manage good-quality data? What is the methodology to acquire and manage quality data? Against this backdrop, the book looks at a four-phase DARS approach for companies to manage high-quality data. DARS, which stands for **Define-Assess-Realize-Sustain**, is a combination of strategic and tactical elements to deliver the greatest value to the business from data. It is a playbook that offers prescriptive recommendations based on proven best practices in data quality management and governance.

This book has four parts, which are mapped to the four phases of the DARS framework. The first phase, the **define phase**, clearly defines data quality, including the characteristics or dimensions of data quality. The objective of this phase is to bring the readers to a common understanding of data and data quality. The second phase, the **assess phase**, is determining the data quality levels. This phase also includes root cause analysis, where the root causes of data quality problems are identified. In the **realize phase**, the data quality is improved by following industry best practices across the entire data lifecycle. Finally, the data quality that is realized should be sustained to ensure that all benefits continue to live on. This is covered in the last phase, the **sustain phase**.

The process of remediating and improving the data quality with the DARS framework is akin to improving a person's health. The first step is **defining** health, given that health could be physical, spiritual, mental, and so on. Once the specific health category is identified, say physical health, we need to define its characteristics or dimensions. In physical health, the dimensions could be strength, flexibility, endurance, and more. Once we have the physical health parameters and its baseline, the next step is to **analyze** or understand the problem by going into the root causes, given that often problems are stated in symptoms or what is seen. For example, one of the symptoms or effects of poor physical health is fatigue. This fatigue issue has to be analyzed and assessed to determine the root cause(s). A glycated hemoglobin (A1C) test might then indicate that the root cause of fatigue is Type-2 diabetes. So the treatment of the problem is to fix Type-2 diabetes and not simply addressing fatigue. The next logical step is **remediation** of the Type-2 diabetes that is causing the fatigue. This could be achieved using a combination of different methods such as medication, lifestyle changes like healthy eating (with vegetables, fruits, and whole grains), meditation, and exercising regularly. Once these remedial actions are in place, the person needs to put the right controls in place including regular medical checkups so that the measures taken are **sustained**.

In this backdrop, this book, *Data Quality: Empowering Businesses with Analytics and AI*, has 12 chapters which are written in a logical and sequential manner. The organization of the 12 book chapters in each of the four DARS phases is shown in Figure P.1.

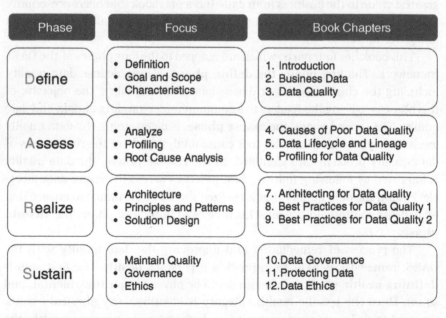

Phase	Focus	Book Chapters
Define	• Definition • Goal and Scope • Characteristics	1. Introduction 2. Business Data 3. Data Quality
Assess	• Analyze • Profiling • Root Cause Analysis	4. Causes of Poor Data Quality 5. Data Lifecycle and Lineage 6. Profiling for Data Quality
Realize	• Architecture • Principles and Patterns • Solution Design	7. Architecting for Data Quality 8. Best Practices for Data Quality 1 9. Best Practices for Data Quality 2
Sustain	• Maintain Quality • Governance • Ethics	10. Data Governance 11. Protecting Data 12. Data Ethics

FIGURE P.1 Book Organization

WHO SHOULD READ THIS BOOK?

The book will explain the core concepts of data quality management and governance and the methods to realize and sustain good-quality data for improved business performance. It will also provide organizations a step-by-step methodology to realize and sustain quality data. However, there are no prerequisites needed to read and apply the concepts mentioned in this book. It is intended for anyone who has a stake and interest in harnessing the value of business data – business and IT teams. The audience could be the chief financial officer (CFO), chief data officer (CDO), chief information officer, accountant, geologist, IT developer, procurement director, claims analyst, data scientist, sales manager, data governance analyst, underwriter, HR manager, credit manager or any other business or IT role. In short, *this book is for anyone who wants to achieve and sustain quality business data.*

REFERENCES

Böringer, J., Dierks, A., Huber, I., and Spillecke, D. (January 18, 2022). Insights to impact: Creating and sustaining data-driven commercial growth. McKinsey & Company. https://www.mckinsey.com/business-functions/growth-marketing-and-sales/our-insights/insights-to-impact-creating-and-sustaining-data-driven-commercial-growth.

Manly, J., et al. (December 2022). Are you ready for green growth? Most innovative companies 2022. Boston Consulting Group. https://www.bcg.com/en-ca/publications/2022/innovation-in-climate-and-sustainability-will-lead-to-green-growth.

Nagle, T., Redman, T., and Sammon, D. (September 2017). Only 3% of companies' data meets basic quality standards. *Harvard Business Review.* https://bit.ly/2UxaHO4.

Acknowledgments

Data Quality: Empowering Businesses with Analytics and AI reflects over two decades of my data, analytics and AI consulting, research, and teaching experience. Writing a book is harder than I thought and more rewarding than I could have ever imagined. I could only cross this finish line because of great teamwork. There are many people who have positively impacted this project. Writing this book was a unique learning and collaborative experience, and it has been one of my best "investments" to date. Throughout the project, I had the privilege of having discussions with top data and analytics researchers and industry experts who were instrumental in giving a better shape to this book.

First and foremost, I thank Bill Inmon – the "father of the data warehouse" for writing the foreword for the book. Bill is an industry veteran and thought leader who is acutely aware of the importance of quality data for the business to thrive in the global marketplace. I have always looked up to Bill and his work right from my university days, and I am truly honored to have him write the book's Foreword.

I'm indebted to the entire Wiley team, including Sheck Cho, Samantha Wu, and Susan Cerra for their editorial help, keen market insights, and support and coaching during the project. Special thanks to Michael Taylor, Tobias Zwingmann, Christophe Bourguignat, Sreenivas Gadhar, and Tony Almeida, for taking the time to review the book and giving valuable feedback. I am also extremely grateful to my consulting clients and my students at IE Business School (Madrid, Spain) for providing me opportunities to learn and understand the nuances of managing data, analytics, and AI initiatives. In addition, I thank the advisors of my firm DBP-Institute (DBP stands for Data for Business Performance), Gary Cokins, Suresh Chakravarthi, and Sana Gabula for offering the right guidance and support while writing this book.

Finally, writing a book required many hours away from my family activities over the course of two years. My wife, Shruthi Belle, and my two wonderful kids, Pranathi and Prathik, understood how important this book is for me and to the data, AI, and analytics community and bestowed me with terrific support, motivation, and inspiration.

Prashanth H. Southekal, PhD, MBA
Calgary, Canada
October 2022

Data Quality

PART ONE

Define Phase

## CHAPTER ONE

Introduction

 ## INTRODUCTION

Today, intangible assets – which are not physical in nature and include things like data, brand, and intellectual property – have rapidly risen in importance compared to tangible assets such as land, machinery, inventories, and cash. In 2018, intangible assets in the S&P 500 hit a record value of $21 trillion and made up 84% of all enterprise value. This is a massive increase from just 17% in 1975 (Ali 2020). IDC predicts that by 2023 half of all GDP worldwide will be driven by products and services from digitally transformed enterprises (IDC 2019). Overall, as technology becomes more pervasive with 5G, artificial intelligence, robotics, the internet of things (IoT), quantum computing, analytics, blockchain, and more, organizations are looking at ways to develop, maximize, and protect the value of intangible assets, especially data, as all these digital technologies are underpinned by data.

Against this backdrop, data – an important intangible asset – is considered a critical business resource as it enables organizations to maximize productivity. Today, four of the top five companies in terms of market capitalization are data companies (Investopedia 2022). In 2019, Brain Porter, CEO of Scotiabank, Canada's leading bank, said, "We are in the data and technology business. Our product happens to be banking, but largely that is delivered through data and technology" (Berman 2016). AIG and Hamilton Insurance Group announced a joint venture firm – Attune, a data and technology platform to harness data and artificial intelligence (AI) capabilities to simplify business processes, trim the amount of time to get insurance, and reduce expenses. Oil field services company Schlumberger captures drilling telemetry data from simulators and sensors to improve drilling performance in oil wells. Moderna's COVID-19 vaccination success story is attributed to data and analytics (Asay 2021). To summarize, data is a key driver for improved business performance today, and many enterprises across various industry sectors have demonstrated that data is a key enabler for improved business performance with enhanced revenues, reduced costs, and lowered risk.

Basically, the data economy – the ecosystem that enables use of data for business performance – is becoming increasingly embraced worldwide. Data has enabled firms such as Netflix, Facebook, Google, and Uber to acquire a distinct competitive advantage. According to Peter Norvig, Google's research director, "We don't have better algorithms than anyone else, we just have more data" (Cleland 2011). In 2021, the market capitalization of Google was more than the GDP of Mexico or Saudi Arabia. Fundamentally, companies that are data-driven demonstrate improved business performance. A report from MIT says that digitally mature firms are 26% more profitable than their peers (MIT 2013). McKinsey Global Institute indicates that data-driven organizations are 23 times more likely to acquire customers, 6 times as likely to retain customers, and 19 times more profitable (Bokman et al. 2014). The industry analyst firm Forrester, found that organizations that use data to derive insights for decision making are almost 3 times more likely to achieve double-digit growth (Eveslon 2020). According to NAIC (National Association of Insurance Commissioners), the implementation of Big Data has resulted in 30% better access to insurance services, 40–70% cost savings, and 60% higher fraud detection rates (NAIC 2021). According to McKinsey & Company, when implemented effectively, data and analytics can yield returns amounting to 30–50 times the investment within a few months in an oil and gas company (McKinsey 2017).

However, most organizations struggle to convert data for improved business performance. There are many reasons for this, and one of the most important is lack of high-quality data. According to Experian Data Quality, a boutique data management company, inaccurate data affects the bottom line of 88% of organizations and impacts up to 12% of revenues (Levy 2015). According to McKinsey, an average user spends two hours a day looking for the right data (Probstein 2019). A report by the *Harvard Business Review* says that just 3% of the data in a business enterprise meets quality standards (Nagle, Redman, and David 2017), and a joint study by IBM and Carnegie Mellon University found that over 90% of the data in a company is unused.

DATA, ANALYTICS, AI, AND BUSINESS PERFORMANCE

> You cannot separate data from AI, and you cannot separate AI from data. The end product of all AI solutions is data and that data will be used again by AI.
>
> **INSIGHT**

Data is the foundation for enabling artificial intelligence (AI) and analytics, and ultimately improved business performance. But what exactly is AI and analytics? Although there is no one universally agreed definition, AI refers to the simulation of human intelligence including cognitive processes by machines, especially computer systems. It is based on the principle that human intelligence can be defined in a way that a machine can easily mimic it, make decisions, and execute tasks, both simple and complex. AI is used extensively across a range of applications today, with varying levels of sophistication from recommendation algorithms in Netflix to Alexa chatbot to self-driving cars to fraud prevention to personalized shopping and more.

> Analytics is asking questions to gain insights for decision making. No questions means there is no analytics.
>
> **INSIGHT**

AI generally is undertaken in conjunction with analytics where the analytics algorithms take the data and look to discern useful patterns to facilitate decision making. Basically, AI looks at patterns or predictions about future states using data and analytics algorithms. In other words, pattern recognition and decision making from data are the foundation for AI. If the patterns and decisions are to be reliable, the data should be of high quality. AI is important in business because it can give enterprises insights into their operations.

In some cases, AI can perform tasks even better than humans, particularly when it comes to repetitive and rule-based tasks. In terms of business performance, AI and analytics support three broad and fundamental business needs: automating business processes, gaining insight on business performance through data, and engaging with stakeholders including customers, employees, vendors and other partners associated with the business. To summarize, successful AI relies on patterns, and patterns that are derived from analytics need quality data.

 ## DATA AS A BUSINESS ASSET OR LIABILITY

While data can be a valuable business asset by offering tangible business results, it has some serious limitations and can become a huge liability if not managed well (Southekal 2021). How can an intangible asset like data become a liability for business? There are four common scenarios where data can become a liability for the business:

1. Collecting data without a defined business purpose will result in huge data volumes, ultimately resulting in increased complexity and cost due to data management. In 2018, according to Deloitte, the average IT spending in a company was 3.3% of the top line and trending upwards at an average of 49% every year. One important reason attributed to these increased IT expenses is the processing of huge data volumes. In addition, if the data is captured without a defined purpose, it will remain unused. Forrester found that up to 73% of data in a company is never used strategically, and research by IBM and Carnegie Mellon University has found that 90% of the data in an organization is unused data or "dark data" (Southekal 2020).

2. Data takes up vast amounts of energy to store, secure, and process, resulting in an increase in the carbon footprint for the business. This makes it less attractive for investors considering their growing interest in ESG (environmental, social, and governance) commitments these days. In 2018, data centers consumed roughly 1% of total global electricity. By 2025, according to Swedish researcher Anders Andrae, the energy consumption of data centers is set to account for 3.2% of the total worldwide carbon emissions and consume 20% of global electricity (Southekal 2020).

3. Cybercriminals are drawn to organizations that have large volumes of data. Many cybercrimes and data breaches in the last few years are associated

with organizations that have large databases. These cybercriminals do not care whether or not the data is dark data, and they acquire all the data they can get their hands on. Following its 2017 data breach, Equifax spent $1.4 billion on modifying its technology infrastructure.

4. Managing data also entails privacy compliance. As noted in *Fortune*, Facebook lost $35 billion in market value following the Cambridge Analytica data scandal. In addition, the scandal resulted in the permanent closure of Cambridge Analytica. While it was data that was responsible for the success and growth of Cambridge Analytica, it was the same data that resulted in its collapse and ultimate closure.

Data is a asset only if it is managed well; if not, data is a liability in business. Just capturing and storing data doesn't make an organization data-driven.

INSIGHT

Overall, data is a valuable resource and has the potential to become a valuable asset for business enterprises. However, just capturing and storing data does not make data a valuable enterprise asset, nor does it make a company data-driven. Data is a business asset only when it is consciously captured and deliberately managed such that quality data is available to run the business. If data is not managed well, data can become a huge liability that threatens the very existence of the firm.

 DATA GOVERNANCE, DATA MANAGEMENT, AND DATA QUALITY

The preceding sections discussed the importance of managing data for empowering business. But what exactly is data management, and how is it related to data governance? Often in the process of achieving quality data, the terms *data governance*, *data management*, and *data quality* are used interchangeably. Although each of the three domains are different, a company must implement all three of them in order to gain the most value from data.

- **Data management** covers principles, practices, programs, systems, and processes a company must undertake to operationalize the data in its lifecycle: that is, from creation to deletion. It is the practice of collecting, keeping, and using data securely, efficiently, and cost-effectively as per the data strategy, of the organization. Gartner says that data management consists of the practices, architectural techniques, and tools for achieving consistent access to, and delivery, of data across the spectrum of data subject areas and data structure types in the enterprise, to meet the data consumption requirements of all applications and business processes (Gartner 2022).
- **Data governance** is a sub-discipline of data management. Data governance comes into play when there is data and that data comes from data management. Data governance is the organizational structures, data owners, policies, rules, process, business terms, and metrics in the end-to-end lifecycle of data. The data lifecycle includes collection, storage, use, protection, archiving, and deletion, and data lifecycle will be covered in detail in Chapter 5. The role of data governance to achieve and sustain quality data will be discussed in detail in Chapter 10.
- So, what are the success criteria of the data governance function? The key criteria of the success for the data governance function are availability of **quality data** for business. Fundamentally, data is considered to be of high quality if the data is fit for use in operations, compliance, and decision making (Southekal 2017).

Basically, data management and data governance work together to improve data quality. For example, the company's business strategy and the data strategy may state that high product quality will come from high data quality attributes of the products and the associated production processes. In achieving this, data management will help the company ensure completeness in the product data attribute, removing inaccuracies and duplications, integrating product data attributes from multiple IT systems and spreadsheets in a single unified view, and so on. In this regard, the company identifies the pertinent IT systems impacted by how the product data is managed and works to achieve high-quality product data.

Business strategy drives data management, and data management drives data governance, and the outcome of the data governance is quality business data.

INSIGHT

This effort to enable high-quality product data is a collaborative effort led by the data governance team. Data management will help the company ensure the availability of product master data. The data governance team will work with relevant business stakeholders to define the criteria of quality product data, that is, the IT team who will help in implementing the data integration procedures for unifying product into one single view, the data security team on the data sharing and access control mechanisms, and so on. Overall, the data governance team formulates business rules to maintain and manage the state of quality data. Without the help of data management and data governance teams, organizations cannot trust their data, and therefore cannot guarantee the quality of their data. Business vision and strategy drive data management, and data management drives data governance. The outcome of the data governance function is quality data for improved business results. Figure 1.1 shows the relationship between data management, data governance, and data quality.

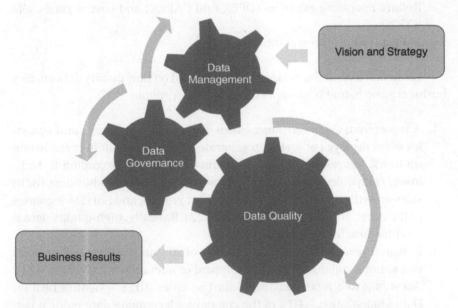

FIGURE 1.1 Data Management, Data Governance, and Data Quality

LEADERSHIP COMMITMENT TO DATA QUALITY

Most business leaders today understand the role and importance of quality data to fuel business. But they often have other business priorities to focus on, and data-quality initiatives work well only if the business support is available. For example, why should the CRO (chief revenue officer) spend their time improving sales data quality instead of working on training the sales team, forecasting and tracking sales, setting sales goals, and more issues related to leads and increasing sales? Why should the CFO (chief financial officer) worry about data quality instead of spending time on reviewing financial performance of the company? Why should a business leader be concerned about data quality instead of focusing their time and effort on other core business initiatives? What is the impact of data quality in improving business performance? Fundamentally, every business entity has three main objectives:

- Propel growth in revenues and profit
- Reduce operating expenses (OPEX and CAPEX) and cost of goods sold (COGS)
- Mitigate risk and protect the business

Let us first look at the evidences from the field on how quality data enables business growth, that is, enhances the top line – revenue.

1. A report from CGT (Consumer Goods Technology) says, data and analytics when deployed at scale can generate a 5 to 10% uplift in revenue and up to 6% increase in EBITDA margins (CGT 2021). According to McKinsey, companies that are using data-driven business-to-business (B2B) sales-growth engines report above-market growth, and EBITDA increases in the range of 15 to 25% (Böringer 2022). Basically, high-quality data is essential to achieve business growth.
2. Research reveals that the combination of AI and Big Data technologies can automate almost 80% of all physical or manual work (Forbes 2021). According to a report on "Big Data Use Cases 2015 – Getting Real on Data Monetization," 40% of the companies leveraging data enjoy a better understanding of consumer behavior (52%), better strategic decisions (69%), and cost reductions (47%). Moreover, the organizations have reported an average of 10% reduction in costs (Tableau 2019)
3. Without data quality, companies not only miss out on data-driven opportunities, they also waste resources and the productivity of employees.

According to McKinsey's 2019 Global Data Transformation Survey, an average of 29% of the total enterprise time was spent on non-value-added tasks because of poor data quality and availability (McKinsey 2020b) shown in Figure 1.2.

Lack of data quality and availability can cause employees to spend a significant amount of time on non-value-added tasks.

Time spent on non-value-added tasks due to poor data quality and availability
Estimated % of total employee time

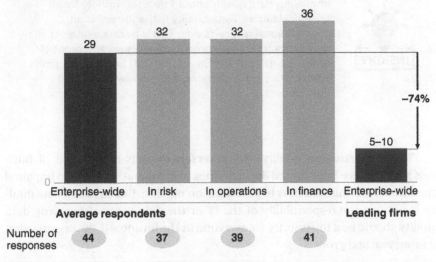

FIGURE 1.2 2019 Global Data Transformation Survey of McKinsey

Apart from increasing revenues and reducing expenses, data is also used to protect the business by reducing risk. As businesses increasingly collect more granular data about consumers, regulators need greater insight into what data is available to the industry, how it is being used, and whether it should be used by insurers at all. This means there is a risk in carrying data, and regulatory compliance is essential for running the business. In 2014 Home Depot reportedly paid out at least $134.5 million to credit card companies and banks as a result of a data breach. In 2021, retail giant Amazon's financial records revealed that officials in Luxembourg issued a $877 million fine for breaches of the General Data Protection Regulation (GDPR) (Hill 2022). At the same time, regulatory compliance is just not on privacy data. It also applies to data types that concern life and environment. For example, when Nexen, an oil company based in Alberta, Canada, spilled over 31,500 barrels of crude oil in July of

2015, the Alberta Energy Regulator (AER) ordered immediate suspension of 15 pipeline licenses issued to Nexen due to lack of maintenance data records. This means that every business leader needs to know how to collect, store, and protect data in accordance with operational and regulatory mandates to run the business, and this business risk can be prevented only when the data is of high quality.

Improving data quality should be a top priority for all business leaders. Data quality management is an organizational responsibility. This is because good-quality data propels business growth in revenues and profits, reduces expenses (OPEX and CAPEX) and cost of goods sold (COGS), and mitigates risk, thereby protecting the business.

INSIGHT

To summarize, low-quality data adversely impacts many areas of business performance from missed opportunities to increased spending to impaired operations, to enhanced risks to poor decision making. But ensuring data quality is not just the responsibility of the IT or the data teams. Improving data quality should be a top priority for everyone in the business if the organization is to survive and grow.

 KEY TAKEAWAYS

So, what did we learn in this chapter? These are the key takeaways.

- Every company today is a data-driven industry as data cuts across the entire business value chain. But unfortunately, firms have been plagued with poor data quality that is affecting their business performance.
- As analytics and AI will have a profound impact on business performance, it is imperative for firms to have good-quality data.
- The terms *data management*, *data governance*, and *data quality* are sometimes used synonymously. But they are three separate disciplines and they need to work together. Quality data is the outcome of solid data governance and data management practices.

■ Improving data quality should be a top priority for all business leaders. Data quality management is an organizational responsibility. This is because good-quality data propels business growth in revenues and profit, reduces operating expenses (OPEX) and cost of goods sold (COGS), and mitigates risk.

 CONCLUSION

Today, just capturing and storing data does not make data a valuable enterprise asset, nor does it make a company data-driven. Data is a business asset only when it is consciously captured and deliberately managed such that quality data is available to run and sustain the business. If data is not managed well, it can become a huge liability that can threaten the very existence of the firm. When data is managed well with appropriate data management and data governance practices, there will be high-quality data for AI and analytics. This quality data will power the AI and analytics solutions and offer significant improvements in business performance including increased revenue, reduced expenses, and mitigated risk.

REFERENCES

Ali, A. (November 2020). The soaring value of intangible assets in the S&P 500. https://www.visualcapitalist.com/the-soaring-value-of-intangible-assets-in-the-sp-500/.

Apte, P. (February 2022). How AI accelerates insurance claims processing. https://venturebeat.com/2022/02/02/how-ai-accelerates-insurance-claims-processing/.

Asay, M. (August 2021). How Moderna uses cloud and data wrangling to conquer COVID-19. https://www.techrepublic.com/article/how-moderna-uses-cloud-and-data-wrangling-to-conquer-covid-19/.

Balasubramanian, R., Libarikian, A., and McElhaney, D. (March 2021). Insurance 2030: the impact of AI on the future of insurance. https://www.mckinsey.com/industries/financial-services/our-insights/insurance-2030-the-impact-of-ai-on-the-future-of-insurance.

BCG. (2021). Overcoming the innovation readiness gap. https://www.bcg.com/en-ca/publications/2021/most-innovative-companies-overview.

Berman, D. (July 2016). Shaking up Scotiabank: three exclusive insights into CEO Brian Porter's revolution. https://www.theglobeandmail.com/report-on-business/shaking-up-scotiabank-three-exclusive-insights-into-ceo-brian-porters-revolution/article31094316/.s.

Bokman, A., Fiedler, L., Perrey, J., and Pickersgill, A. (July 2014). Five facts: how customer analytics boosts corporate performance. https://mck.co/2Ju0xYo.

Böringer, J., Dierks, A., Huber, I., and Spillecke, D. (January 18, 2022). Insights to impact: Creating and sustaining data-driven commercial growth. McKinsey & Company. https://www.mckinsey.com/business-functions/growth-marketing-and-sales/our-insights/insights-to-impact-creating-and-sustaining-data-driven-commercial-growth.

CDO. (January 2022). Designing and building a data driven organization culture – a best practice case study. https://www.cdomagazine.tech/cdo_magazine/editorial/opinion/designing-and-building-a-data-driven-organization-culture-a-best-practice-case-study/article_96fdad00-6349-11ec-bd2c-ef6d18bc1631.html.

CGT. (2021). "Learn how Tyson Foods' appetite for data is customer-driven. https://consumergoods.com/learn-how-tyson-foods-appetite-data-customer-driven.

Cleland, S. (October 2011). "Google's infringenovation secrets. https://www.forbes.com/sites/scottcleland/2011/10/03/googles-infringenovation-secrets/?sh=7099cd1130a6.

Evelson, B. (May 2020). Insights investments produce tangible benefits – yes, they do. https://www.forrester.com/blogs/data-analytics-and-insights-investments-produce-tangible-benefits-yes-they-do/.

Forbes. (April 2021). Utilizing AI and big data to reduce costs and increase profits in departments across an organization. https://www.forbes.com/sites/annie brown/2021/04/13/utilizing-ai-and-big-data-to-reduce-costs-and-increase-profits-in-departments-across-an-organization/?sh=6269df516af7.

Gartner. (March 2022). Data management (DM). https://www.gartner.com/en/information-technology/glossary/dmi-data-management-and-integration.

Heale, B. (May 2014). Data quality is the biggest challenge.https://www.moodys analytics.com/risk-perspectives-magazine/managing-insurance-risk/insurance-regulatory-spotlight/data-quality-is-the-biggest-challenge.

Hill, M. (September 2022). The 12 biggest data breach fines, penalties, and settlements so far. https://www.csoonline.com/article/3410278/the-biggest-data-breach-fines-penalties-and-settlements-so-far.html.

IDC. (October 2019). Enterprise transformation and the IT industry. https://www.businesswire.com/news/home/20191029005144/en/IDC-FutureScape-Outlines-the-Impact-Digital-Supremacy-Will-Have-on-Enterprise-Transformation-and-the-IT-Industry.

Investopedia. (March 2022). Biggest companies in the world by market cap. https://www.investopedia.com/biggest-companies-in-the-world-by-market-cap-5212784.

Insurance Information Institute, III. (August 2022). Insurance fraud. https://www.iii.org/article/background-on-insurance-fraud.

Levy, Jeremy. (July 2015). Enterprises don't have big data, they just have bad data. http://tcrn.ch/2iWcfM5.

McKinsey. (October 2017). Why oil and gas companies must act on analytics. https://www.mckinsey.com/industries/oil-and-gas/our-insights/why-oil-and-gas-companies-must-act-on-analytics.

McKinsey. (June 2020a). Designing data governance that delivers value. McKinsey Digital.

McKinsey. (June 2020b). Insights to impact: Creating and sustaining data-driven commercial growth." https://www.mckinsey.com/business-functions/growth-marketing-and-sales/our-insights/insights-to-impact-creating-and-sustaining-data-driven-commercial-growth.

MIT. (August 2013). Digitally mature firms are 26% more profitable than their peers. https://bit.ly/2xBTPNe.

Nagle, T., Redman, T., and Sammon, D. (September 2017). Only 3% of companies' data meets basic quality standards. *Harvard Business Review.* https://bit.ly/2UxaHO4.

NAIC. (May 2021). Big data. https://content.naic.org/cipr_topics/topic_big_data.htm.

Probstein, S. (December 17, 2019). Reality check: Still spending more time gathering instead of analyzing. https://www.forbes.com/sites/forbestechcouncil/2019/12/17/reality-check-still-spending-more-time-gathering-instead-of-analyzing/?sh=154dc44228ff.

Southekal, P. (2017). *Data for business performance.* Technics Publications.

Southekal, P. (2020). *Analytics best practices.* Technics Publications.

Southekal, P. (September 2020). Illuminating dark data in enterprises. https://www.forbes.com/sites/forbestechcouncil/2020/09/25/illuminating-dark-data-in-enterprises/?sh=39c4a7f6c36a.

Southekal, P. (April 2021). Can data be a liability for the business? https://www.forbes.com/sites/forbestechcouncil/2021/04/06/can-data-be-a-liability-for-the-business/?sh=63eabd9e3c44.

Tableau. (2019). Big data use cases: getting real on data monetization. https://www.tableau.com/learn/whitepapers/big-data-use-cases-getting-real-data-monetization.

## CHAPTER TWO

Business Data

 INTRODUCTION

Today, data touches every facet of the business value chain. For example, in the insurance sector, data impacts policyholders, agents, adjusters, appraisers, actuaries, and others in offering personalized insurance policies, reduced risk management, optimized support for underwriting decisions, and faster claims processing and settlement and more. In the oil and gas sector, companies use enormous amounts of data for regulatory complacence and to utilize assets better, make more informed decisions to innovate exploration and production, make sense of operational data from the plant floor, improve supply chains, and more. eCommerce and retail businesses use data to optimize their customer service and offer enhanced shopping and channel experiences leading to better customer satisfaction and retention. Overall, data helps businesses to understand customer needs, predict customer behavior patterns, improve the quality of products and services, reduce expenses and costs, mitigate risks, develop new products and services, enhance employee engagement, and more. All these improvements are possible only when there is quality data.

DATA IN BUSINESS

It is often said, no matter what industry you are in, business success and growth come down to three fundamental questions:

1. Who are the valuable or profitable customers?
2. How can one retain (and grow from) these valuable customers?
3. How can one find more of them?

The answers to these fundamental questions, which hold the key to business enterprise success, depend on quality data. There are four types of data a typical business enterprise needs to manage.

1. **Zero-Party Data**

    Zero-party data is data about customer preferences, interests and intent shared directly through surveys, campaign data, social media polls, and so on. This data can help companies provide educational content to create better experiences for prospects and customers and be more effective in the marketing campaigns. In the sales and marketing world, zero-party data is mainly about prospects or leads. In the procurement world, zero-party data is about requests for proposal (RFPs), requests for quotation (RFQs), or requests for information (RFIs).

2. **First-Party Data**

    First-party data is data collected directly by the organization to run its business. This data includes contracts, orders, invoices, purchase history, payment data, email activity, web behavior through cookies, CRM data, claims data, and more. Financial reporting and compliance to accounting standards like GAPP and IFRS are based on first-party data. Not only is first-party data incredibly valuable, generating it is extremely cost-effective. In addition, data privacy concerns surrounding first-party data are minimal because you know exactly where it came from and you own it outright.

3. **Second-Party Data**

    Second-party data is information that is collected, owned, and managed by a partner company through a specific agreement or partnership with the company. It is the first-party data of the company's partners such as agents, distributors, resellers, vendors and so on which is used by the company. Basically, second-party data in a nutshell is someone else's first-party data that can be utilized for one's own business activities.

For example, insurance agents are external entities who are responsible for identifying sales opportunities for insurance plans and overseeing a portfolio of clients. If the data that is created and owned by the agents is used by insurance firms like Allstate and Liberty Mutual, that data can be considered as second-party data. Similarly, in the oil and gas industry, EPC (engineering, procurement, and construction) companies such as WorleyParsons and Fluor typically work on E&P (exploration and production) projects of oil companies like Shell or Chevron. The drawings and the specifications created by the EPC companies become second-party data for the oil companies. In the retail industry, the product marketing and customer data of the distributors and resellers like Ingram Micro and Best Buy are the second-party data of the OEMs (original equipment manufacturer) like Microsoft, Dell, and Samsung.

4. **Third-Party Data**

Third-party data is generally aggregated from many different sources and often includes contact, demographic, location, weather, psychographic and other data gathered from various platforms, mobile apps, websites, and data products. While other three types of data types – that is, zero-party, first-party, and second-party data can be more accurate and contextual, those data types simply cannot match the volume and variety of third-party data. Mortgage companies for example, rely significantly on third-party data such as customer credit history data from credit bureaus while assessing the mortgage application.

Most third-party data is collected through third-party cookies. But in recent years, regulators have been clamping down on the use of third-party data due to issues in consumer privacy, and browsers are discontinuing the use of third-party cookies. Safari and Firefox already limit their use, and Google plans to deprecate third-party cookies and the associated data through its Chrome browser by 2023.

Ideally, an enterprise will use all four of these types of data. Each of the four types has its own advantages and disadvantages. The following table compares the four data types.

Business Data Types	Pros	Cons
Zero-party data (ZPD)	■ Contextual – Relevant for future business growth and partnerships	■ Hard to measure and use as there are no business transactions between the counterparties
First-party data (FPD)	■ Complete and exclusive ownership ■ Reflected in business performance (and financial reporting)	■ Dependent on high-quality data ■ Limited/defined scope and scale
Second-party data (SPD)	■ Low data management costs as the data is managed by the partners	■ Control is outside the business and this can result in potential data integration issues
Third-party data (TDP)	■ Easily and readily available ■ Broad selection of data sets	■ Lacks transparency; risks and data quality can vary wildly ■ General data as this data is also accessible to competitors

The association of the four types of business data to size (or data volume) and their business impact is shown in Figure 2.1.

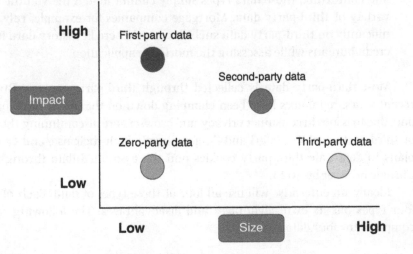

FIGURE 2.1   Types of Business Data

To sum up, zero-party and first-party data are the most reliable in the business as they are originated and captured internally with a specific purpose. The second-party data, which is the data that is coming from partners, is typically less reliable. Third-party data, on the other hand, is a set of data from rather unknown sources and has the least reliability and trust. In addition, third-party data which are offered as data products is risky, as you have to be sure that the third-party data was processed according to data privacy and other regulatory mandates.

TELEMETRY DATA

These four types of data are primarily discussed from a discrete data perspective where the data is created manually by business users. But today an enormous amount of data is generated automatically by billions of IoT (internet of things) devices that are being deployed worldwide for various business purposes. These IoT devices, which could be wireless sensors, actuators, smartphones, cameras, alarms, vehicles, appliances, and more, acquire data at regular points in time. The time-series data from these IoT devices, which are used to observe and monitor the performance of these IoT devices, is known as telemetry data. Companies using IoT or telemetry data benefit in myriad ways, including achieving operational efficiencies, upgrading the customer experience, cost savings, and reduced accidents from proactive equipment maintenance, and more. According to Statista, while the amount of data generated worldwide in 2025 is estimated to be 181 ZB (zettabytes), the amount of data generated just by the IoT devices is expected to reach 73.1 ZB (Statista 2022). This means telemetry data will be about 40% of the data footprint in a company.

Telemetry data is captured with wireless mechanisms, such as radio, ultrasonic, or infrared systems, as it helps businesses to access data that have constraints in location and scale. Nearly any physical object can be converted into an IoT device, as long as it can be connected to the internet. In this regard, there are four types of telemetry or IoT data that are managed in business, and companies such as Datadog and Splunk offer solutions for monitoring and analyzing data generated from various IoT devices. They are of four types – metrics, events, logs, and traces, or MELT for short.

1. **Metrics** data represent the measures of device performance that are often calculated or aggregated over a period of time.

2. **Event** data is related to discrete action happening at a given point in time. Event data are valuable, because it can confirm if a particular action or event has occurred at a specific point in time using the data timestamp attribute. Event data can also include the location data – that is, the geographical location of the IoT device. While events are granular data, metrics are aggregated data.

3. **Logs** are event-based records of anomalies captured in unstructured data formats; logs are essentially lines of text. Logs are invariably associated with events as one event can have many log lines. Logs are very useful as they offer a detailed record of what happened at a particular time.

4. **Traces** provide insights into how the entire IoT system is working at any given point in time. Traces are samples of causal chains of events between different components in the entire IoT ecosystem.

 ## PURPOSE OF DATA IN BUSINESS

Overall, the different types of data discussed in the preceding sections have three main purposes in business – operations, compliance, and decision making (Southekal 2017).

1. **Operations**

   Business operations are a coherent set of activities or business processes that businesses engage in on a daily basis to increase the value of the enterprise so as to earn a profit. These business processes can be core or primary operations like product development, manufacturing, and sales and marketing, or secondary of supporting functions like IT, HR, and finance. The overall operational activities can be optimized to generate sufficient revenues to cover expenses and earn a profit.

2. **Compliance**

   The compliance function ensures that the company adheres to pertinent regulations, standards, laws, and internal policies. Regulations are indispensable to the proper functioning of businesses as they underpin markets, protect the rights and safety of citizens, and ensure the delivery of public goods and services. Specifically, compliance, including regulatory compliance, includes:

   ▪ Data privacy regulations such as CCPA (California Consumer Privacy Act), GDPR (General Data Protection Regulation), and more.

- Financial regulation standards and market conduct from NAIC (National Association of Insurance Commissioners), PCI DSS (Payment Card Industry Data Security Standard), and so on.
- Investor protection regulations such as Solvency (U.S. Solvency, EU Solvency II, etc.), FINRA (Financial Industry Regulatory Authority), SEC (Securities and Exchange Commission), and the like.

3. **Decision Making**

The third purpose of data in business is decision making from the insights that are derived from data and analytics. These insights could be based on descriptive, predictive, and prescriptive analytics (South-ekal 2020).

- Descriptive analytics reviews historical performance using exploratory analytics, associate analytics, and inferential analytics (hypothesis testing) techniques. Descriptive analytics answers the question "What happened?"
- Predictive analytics predicts what is most likely to happen in the future based on techniques such as regression, trend analysis, and other data-driven machine learning techniques. Predictive analytics tries to answer the question "What will happen in the future?"
- Prescriptive analytics recommends the actions one can take to affect those outcomes. Prescriptive analytics is a form of data analytics that tries to answer the question "What do we need to do to achieve this?"

Often in business, data is originated and captured for operations and compliance, Once the data captured reaches a critical size, analytics is carried out. So analytics is the by-product of analytics.

INSIGHT

In fact, when data is originated and captured, it is often for operations and compliance; rarely is data originated and captured solely for analytics. Once the data captured for operations and compliance reaches a critical size, it becomes available for opportunities to glean insights and patterns with analytics for decision making. For example, when a home insurance policy is created for a customer, it is mainly for operations and compliance. Once the home insurance policies that are sold by the insurance firm reach a critical size after the product is sold to multiple customers, one can draw insights such as patterns, inferences, correlations, predictions, outliers, and more, based on relevant business questions.

 BUSINESS DATA VIEWS

The data that is used for the above three purposes – that is, operations, compliance, and decision making – can be viewed from different data management and data governance perspectives. Business data elements or data objects can be viewed from four main perspectives or views, namely:

1. Storage
2. Integration
3. Compliance
4. Analytics

Storage View

Every business has a combination of structured and unstructured data. Some data is structured, but most data is unstructured.

Structured Data

Structured data is highly organized and formatted in relational databases and spreadsheets so that data is easily searchable. A relational database – technically called an RDBMS (relational database management system) – is a collection of data items with predefined relationships between them. The data items are organized as a set of tables with columns and rows. Tables hold data about the objects to be represented in the database. The main advantage of structured data is that the data can be queried efficiently. Examples of structured data include customer name, policy dates, age, customer addresses, credit card numbers, SSN (Social Security Number), VIN (Vehicle Identification Number), and more.

Unstructured Data

Unstructured data includes text, images, and audio and video files. These data have no predefined format or organization, making it much more difficult to collect, store, process, and analyze. While structured data is managed in

RDBMS and spreadsheets, managing unstructured data often requires a hierarchical structure referred to as a taxonomy. Recent projections indicate that unstructured data is over 80% of all enterprise data. The main advantage of structured data is that the data can be completely captured in the native state. Since unstructured data does not have a predefined data model, it is best managed in non-relational (NoSQL) databases.

Integration View

Often data in a company is not in one system in one type and format. It is distributed across many systems in various data types and data formats. This data has to be integrated to run the business, be it for operations, compliance, or for decision making. In this regard, there four main types of data from an integration view: reference data, master data, transactional data, and metadata.

Reference Data

Reference data is a set of permissible values that can be used to categorize the business data. Examples include business categories such as product category, account groups, gender, currency, plants, and so on. Technically reference data consists of sets of drop-down values, statuses, or classification schema, and has two key characteristics:

1. The first key characteristic of reference data is its reliance on data standards – internal and external. For example, country codes are defined in ISO 3166, and UoM (unit of measure) codes are in ISO 2022. Other types of reference data such as purchasing organizations, sales offices, and employee positions are internal to the company and follow standards specific to the organization.
2. The second important characteristic of reference data is its impact on the business process. For example, introducing a new product category will invariably result in change to the product management process due to characteristics specific to that product category.

Master Data

Master data are business entities used across multiple systems, LoB (lines of business), business functions, and business processes in the enterprise. Master data is considered the backbone of the enterprise, and is often called the "golden record" or the "single version of truth." According to Gartner, master data is the consistent and uniform set of identifiers and extended attributes that describe the core entities of the enterprise, and are used across multiple business processes (Gartner 2021). In its purest form, master data is the single and authoritative source of business data. Master data falls generally into three types:

1. People, including customers, agents, employees, and suppliers
2. Things, including products, policies, devices, and physical assets
3. Concepts, including contracts, warranties, GL accounts, profit centers, claims, and licenses

Transactional Data

While master data is about business entities (typically nouns), transactional data is about business events or activities (usually verbs). Transactional data is information that is captured from business activities or transactions. In other words, transactional data is data generated by various applications while running or supporting everyday business activities of buying, trading, and selling. Transactional data has five main characteristics:

1. It deals with business resources.
2. It records the financial value.
3. It a compliance document between the counterparties.
4. It has a twofold effect on accounting.
5. It promotes performance management and decision making.

Basically, transactional data is relevant to the external world as it is a compliance or legal record. Transactional data is typically created using the reference and master data to record a specific business event or transaction. Incidentally, the majority of the data that is managed in an enterprise is transactional data. For example, an insurance policy issued to the customer is a piece of transactional data. Sales orders, purchase orders, and vendor invoices are transactional data. Customer interactions data via the social media platforms, which is a function of time, are also transactional data.

In longitudinal data analysis, you analyze the same measurement entity over different points of time. In cross-sectional data analysis, you analyze different measurement entities at a specific point in time.

Against this backdrop, closely associated with transactional data are longitudinal data and cross-sectional data. Longitudinal data or panel data is the data that is collected through a series of repeated observations of the same subject such as customer or products or contracts over a given time frame. Longitudinal data analysis is effectively following the same data entity over time, and differs fundamentally from cross-sectional data that analyzed different subjects (whether customers, firms, or regions) at a specific point in time. Cross-sectional data analysis is done at a single point in time, rather than over a period of time. Cross-sectional studies take fresh data each time analysis is done, whereas longitudinal data analysis follows the same sample of people over multiple time periods. Cross-sectional analysis can be used to analyze many different aspects of business-like revenue, costs, inventory, and more, while longitudinal data analysis is used, for instance, to analyze the revenue of the company in FY2019, FY2020, and FY2021. Basically, in a longitudinal study you repeatedly collect data of the same entity over different points of time, and in a cross-sectional study you collect different data at a specific point in time.

Metadata

Metadata is "data about data." In other words, metadata is used to describe another data element's content. ISO 15489 defines metadata as data describing context, content, and structure of records, and their management through time. Technically called a data dictionary, metadata mainly labels, describes, or characterizes the other three types of data – reference data, master data, and transactional data. Unlike the other three types of data, metadata has no real business utility, and is always married to one or more of the three types of data (reference data, master data, and transactional data).

Basically, metadata is "data about data," and not the data in itself. While metadata is not truly business data, what is the business value or role of metadata? Metadata has two fundamental objectives:

1. Locating and retrieving business data

   Searching is the acid test for data quality. Metadata attributes such as author, timestamp, subject, data type, and more foster better search and retrieval of business data by enabling optimized querying.

2. Enabling the use and reuse of business data

   To use and reuse data, one needs to understand how the data is structured, defined, originated, and captured. Metadata provides details on how the business data is structured, defined, organized, and more to facilitate data security and interoperability, especially for data exchange. In addition, metadata can be used to flag security settings, validating data access, and controlling the distribution of business data.

In this regard, ISO/IEC 11179 is an important standard for managing enterprise metadata. When data elements are well documented according to ISO/IEC 11179, finding and retrieving them from disparate databases as well as sending and receiving them via electronic communications are made easier. Basically, the purpose of ISO/IEC 11179 is to make data understandable and shareable by addressing:

■ Semantics of data
■ Representation of data
■ Registration of data

Metadata is further is classified into three types:

1. Technical metadata, used to describe the data structures. Examples are field length, type, size, and so on.
2. Business metadata, used to describe nontechnical aspects of the data and their usage. Examples are report name, document name, class, XML document type, and others.
3. Log metadata, which describes details on how, when, and by whom the data object was created, updated, or deleted. Examples are timestamp-related attributes such as created date and changed date.

The relationships among the four types of data are shown in Figure 2.2.

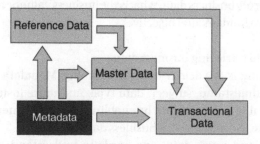

FIGURE 2.2   Relationships among the Four Types of Data

The key characteristics of the three main types of business data are shown in the following table.

#	Parameter	Reference data	Master data	Transactional data
1	Volume of records	Low	Medium	High
2	Life span	High	Medium	Low
3	Frequency of change	Low	Medium	High
4	Utility span	Enterprise-wide and company	LoB and company-wide	Function-wide
5	Consumer diversity	High	Medium	Low
6	Data structure	Structured and semi-structured	Structured	Structured and semi-structured
7	Management location	Master data management system	Master data management system	Application systems

Compliance View

The third way to view business data is from a compliance perspective. From the compliance view, data can be classified based on its level of sensitivity so that appropriate controls on data protection are set up for safeguarding the data. Data based on compliance can be of four types.

1. **Open Data**

   Open data or public data is when the unauthorized disclosure, alteration, or destruction of that data would result in little or no risk to the company and its partners. Examples of public or open data include press releases, product brochures and specifications, financial statements, location addresses, and so on. In this regard, many governments provide online access to data collected and created by them in a standards-compliant way that is openly available, simple to access, and convenient to reuse.

2. **Personal Data**

   Personal data or personally identifiable information (PII) is any data that can be linked to an individual directly or indirectly and if released could result in potential harm to the individual.

3. **Confidential Data**

   Data is confidential or private when the disclosure, alteration, or destruction of that data could compromise the competitive advantage of the company and its affiliates. Access to this data is based on the business roles of the users technically called RBAC (role-based access control). Examples of confidential data include commissions, profit margins, employee salaries, and more.

4. **Restricted Data**

   Restricted or sensitive data can cause potential harm to the company if compromised. Data may also be restricted-use because of confidentiality promises or proprietary information. Examples of sensitive data include privacy data, payment card data, trade secrets, design details, and more.

Analytics View

One of the key objectives of data, is to measure and monitor business performance using analytics. From the analytics point of view, there are four types of data – nominal, ordinal, interval, and ratio types.

1. Nominal data are used for labeling or categorizing data. It does not involve a numerical value and hence no statistical calculations are possible with nominal data. Examples of nominal data are gender, product description, customer address and the like.

2. Ordinal or ranked data is the order of the values, but the differences between each one is not really known. Common examples here are ranking companies based on market capitalization, vendor payment terms, customer satisfaction scores, delivery priority, and so on.

3. Interval data is about finite numerical values with no zero values. This means that if there are zero values, the entity will not exist. For example, the number of employees in a company is interval data. If the number of employees in a company is zero, that means the entity – that is, the company – practically doesn't exist.

4. A ratio scale has all the properties of an interval scale with a meaningful zero. For example, the zero value in the company's profit means the company did not make any money, but the company can still exist even with zero profit.

Basically, interval and ratio level data types represent numeric or quantitative values. They are amenable to statistical techniques, and these two data types are grouped together as continuous or numeric data.

 ## KEY CHARACTERISTICS OF BUSINESS DATA

As discussed earlier, data of any type is a representation of the real-world category, entity, or event or that is recorded in a meaningful format wherein they could be processed further. However, to fully realize the benefits of data in business, data should be of high quality. Before looking into data quality, let us first understand the characteristics of business data.

- Business data always has latency.

  Business data is a record of past events and circumstances. This lag or latency could be seconds, minutes, and sometimes even days or months. Rarely is data about the future state of the business recorded.
- Business data is collected with a purpose.

  Business data is intentionally collected to serve an immediate business need and is used to record a business category, entity, or event related to operations, compliance, and decision making.
- Data is stored in a medium.

  Once the data is captured, it is stored in a medium or storage device like hard disks – technically called the secondary storage. These days the data storage is in IT systems, which could be in the cloud platforms – or the data can be stored in IT systems in the company's own data center.
- Data is often reused.

  Once the data is captured in the IT systems, it can be reused for the same purpose or for different purposes. For example, once the customer data is captured, that specific customer data record can be reused to market and sell other insurance products like Home, Auto, Life, Travel, and so on.
- Business data is encoded in a specific format.

  The data captured in the digital format is in a specific format. Customer name typically is in text format, date of birth is in DD-MM-YYYY format, SSN (Social Security Number) is in numeric format with a hash-function validation, and so on.
- Data is raw that needs to be "processed" for deriving value

  Often data in the insurance industry is captured in an unstructured format (such as audio, documents, video, and images) without any compliance to a predefined data model. From the analytics perspective, data per se is not very valuable to the business – it is the insights, such as relationships, patterns, categorization, inferences, outliers, and predictions, which are derived from the data that makes data valuable. So, data needs to be processed using the right data structure or data type (nominal, ordinal, or continuous) so that the statistical tools can consume it and produce insights.

■ Business data has legal implications.

Business data has legal implications because the business itself is a legal entity that is subject to laws and regulations in that jurisdiction. For example, a retail or ecommerce company that is collecting data of European customers should comply with GDPR regulations.

■ Business data is interoperable.

Business data is often shared and consumed by multiple stakeholders. This interoperability facilitates seamless portability of data across the enterprise and ultimately reduces the risk and cost associated with data management and data governance. For example, customer data is of interest to the sales and marketing team to sell insurance products, but the same customer data is also of interest for the finance team, especially to the credit and accounts receivables teams. The customer data is the same, but the viewpoints and utility are different.

CRITICAL DATA ELEMENTS (CDEs)

 CDEs at the core enable "data minimization." This means businesses should limit the data collection to what is directly relevant and necessary to accomplish a specified purpose. This includes retaining the critical data only for as long as it is necessary to fulfill that specified business purpose.

INSIGHT

Not all data in a business has equal value – some data elements are so critical that poor management of these data elements might even jeopardize the survival of the firm. Understanding what data is the most critical is essential to the success of the organization. This data is termed "critical data elements" (CDEs). CDEs are defined as "the data that is critical to success" in a specific business area (line of business, shared service, or group function). CDEs could be reference data or, master data, or transactional data. CDEs vary by industry and business needs, but identifying and managing CDEs allows the firm to deliver high-value, high-impact, and high-visibility data quickly and affordably. Common examples of CDEs include customer data, employee data, product margin data, PII (personal identifiable information) data, PCI DSS (Payment Card Industry Data Security Standard) data, and so on.

Creating a list of CDEs is not a regulatory requirement per se, but the process of creating CDEs can start from the regulatory requirements. CDEs also offer numerous benefits by reducing the complexity and effort involved in managing data. CDEs makes it easier for enterprises to manage a smaller number of key data elements to ensure data quality and fit-for-purpose with the appropriate data governance measures. Basically, some pointers to identify a CDE are:

▪ Association with regulatory compliance. For example, managing data elements and the associated data attributes related to privacy, payment and other regulations often qualifies as a CDE.
▪ Data that is shared by multiple stakeholders – internal and external. The automotive industry relies extensively on JIT (just in time) process, which uses the advanced shipping notice (ASN) data issued by the supplier. ASN data is critical as it notifies the customer of details of the shipment so the customer can be prepared to accept delivery at the right time at the right location. This ASN data can be a CDE.
▪ Master data and reference data are used in creating transactional documents which help in running the business. If the quality of master data and reference data is poor, the quality of the large number of transactional data will also be poor. Hence master data and reference data elements can be CDEs.
▪ Key performance indicators (KPIs) measure enterprise performance. For example, if the net profit margin (NPM) is the KPI used to measure enterprise performance and the quality of sales order data to calculate NPM is poor, then the sales order data is a CDE.
▪ CDEs deal with data elements that have significant financial impact risk, such as increased liabilities, costs, revenue opportunities, or profits. For

example, products that are a risk to health, safety, property, or the environment are classified as dangerous goods, and these would be a CDE.

- Data elements that can potentially interrupt critical business process for an extended time period can be CDEs. For example, if the credit department in a bank is dependent on the credit scores from the rating agencies and if that credit data is a not available in a timely fashion to approve the mortgage application, then the credit data is a CDE.

 ## KEY TAKEAWAYS

Following are the key takeaways of this chapter.

- There are four types of data in a typical business enterprise: zero-party data, first-party data, second-party data, and third-party data. Zero-party and first-party data are most reliable in the business as they are originated and captured internally. The second-party data, which is the data that is coming from partners, is typically less reliable compared to the first-party data. Third-party data, on the other hand, is a set of data from rather unknown sources and has the least reliability. In addition, third-party data is risky as you have to be sure that the third-party data was being processed according to data privacy and other regulatory mandates.
- Data in business is used for three main purposes: operations, compliance, and decision making. In fact, when data is originated and captured, it is often for operations and compliance; rarely is data originated and captured solely for analytics. Analytics uses the data captured for operations and compliance.
- Business data elements can be viewed from four main perspectives or views, namely: storage (structured data and unstructured data), integration (reference data, master data, and transactional data), compliance, and analytics.
- Unstructured data (which is text, audio, and video and image files) that does not have a predefined data model is about 80% of the enterprise data. Unstructured data is hard to process as it does not follow a defined data model. But it is easy to capture and if managed well, it can potentially offer great business value.
- Transactional data is relevant to business because:
  - It deals with business resources.
  - It records the financial value.

- It a reliable compliance document.
- It has a two-fold effect on accounting.
- It promotes performance management and decision making.
- While metadata is not truly business data, it has two fundamental purposes.
  1. Locating and retrieving business data
  2. Enabling the use and reuse of business data
- Critical data elements (CDEs) are defined as "the data that is critical to success" in a specific business area (line of business, shared service, or group function). In simple words CDE is the data required to get the job done.
- CDEs are normally reference data and master data.

 ## CONCLUSION

We live in an age where data is a key driver of success in any organization, no matter the industry. From home to life to business, the business landscape is undergoing a vast transformation in today's data-centric, consumer-driven economy. The speed at which different types of data is captured and processed is playing a critical role in the business performance of organizations. The different types of data bring different perspectives and strategies on harnessing the business value from data. However, harnessing this business value involves not only capturing the right type of data, but also managing it effectively based on business needs so that data can be used effectively for operations, regulations, and decision making.

REFERENCES

BCG. (May 2017). Profiting from personalization. https://www.bcg.com/publications/2017/retail-marketing-sales-profiting-personalization.

Gartner. (September 2002). Master data management. https://www.gartner.com/en/information-technology/glossary/master-data-management-mdm.

Southekal, P. (April 2017). *Data for business performance*. Technics Publications.

Southekal, P. (April 2020). *Analytics best practices*. Technics Publications.

Statista. (2022). Volume of data/information created, captured, copied, and consumed worldwide from 2010 to 2020, with forecasts from 2021 to 2025. https://www.statista.com/statistics/871513/worldwide-data-created/.

## CHAPTER THREE

Data Quality in Business

INTRODUCTION

Deriving improved business performance from data is dependent on quality data. But most business enterprises have data quality issues of varying sizes and impacts. Stakeholder needs in most data management programs are varied and vague, and most enterprises lack the data culture, literacy, governance, technology, leadership, and more to address data quality issues. Research published in *Harvard Business Review* reports that just 3% of the data in a business enterprise meets data quality standards (Nagle, Redman, and Sammon 2017). While quality data in business is contextual and multidimensional, defining the context and selecting the pertinent data quality dimensions will help enterprises derive better business performance from data (Southekal 2017). In this regard, DBP Institute, a leading research, consulting, and education firm conducted research to determine the main roadblock for successfully implementing data and analytics solutions in business enterprises. Over 147 industry practitioners across the globe took the survey, and data quality was the second-most-cited reason that is preventing businesses from realizing value from data and analytics (see Figure 3.1).

Which is the #1 roadblock for successfully implementing Data and Analytics solutions in business enterprises?

Culture	46%
Literacy	16%
Quality Data	31%
Others (Pls comment)	6%

147 votes · **Poll closed**

FIGURE 3.1   Key Factors to Derive Business Value from Data

The cost of poor data quality in U.S. business alone moved from $600 million in 2002 to $3.1 trillion in 2020.

INSIGHT

Generally, data quality is an afterthought in most enterprises, and this results in poor business performance. Organizations that have data quality deficiencies struggle to achieve growth, agility, and competitiveness. According to Experian Data Quality, a boutique data management company, inaccurate data affects the bottom line of 88% of organizations and impacts up to 12% of revenues (Levy 2015). In 2002, The Data Warehousing Institute (TDWI) stated that poor data quality costs American business $600 billion annually (Eckerson 2002). This figure has continued to worsen due to the increase in data volume and management complexity in the recent years. According to IBM research, in the United States alone, businesses lose $3.1 trillion annually due to poor data quality (IBM 2020).

While achieving data quality is complex and time consuming, one of the fundamental challenges arises from the many definitions of "data quality." Currently there is no universal agreement on what exactly "data quality" means, and what constitutes the key data quality dimensions. Even though data quality is contextual and determined by the location, time, and other circumstances, it can be defined and measured on different dimensions. The rationale is based on the work of David Garvin, a Harvard Business School professor who emphasized the importance of understanding quality and its various dimensions for business managers in his 1987 research article published in *Harvard Business Review* titled "Competing on the Eight Dimensions of Quality." In this regard, this chapter looks at the definition of data quality, and the key data quality dimensions.

DATA QUALITY DIMENSIONS

 Data is considered to be of high quality if it is fit for use in operations, compliance, and decision making.

INSIGHT

There is no one universal definition of data quality. One of the leading advocates of quality, Philip Crosby, defined quality as "conformance to requirements" way back in 1979 (Crosby 1979). But from the business enterprise perspective, data quality is more about ensuring that the data is useful for business operations. Dr. Thomas Redman believes that "data is considered to be of high quality if they are fit for their intended use in operations, decision making and planning" (Redman 2016). Basically, data is considered to be of high quality in business if it is fit for use in operations, compliance, and decision making (Southekal 2017).

To define data quality comprehensively, it is important to understand the key dimensions of data quality. Based on the work of the Data Management Association (DAMA), this section examines 12 different dimensions of data quality for a business enterprise (Southekal 2017, p. 107). The word "dimension" is used to identify aspects of data elements that can be defined, quantified, measured, implemented, and tracked.

Completeness

Completeness is the degree of usage of the attributes of a specific data element in a specific business process. Given that data origination and capture is an expensive and time-consuming process, data values for all attributes or fields will not be typically managed for any data element in an enterprise.

For example, if a customer master has 600 attributes in the Oracle Sales Cloud CRM application, not all 600 attributes will be populated, as some of the data attributes are not required to run business processes. Practically speaking, data completeness involves striking a balance between the effort it takes to populate the relevant data attributes versus the utility those data attributes bring to the business process.

For example, in the same customer master example, the customer's first name and last name could be mandatory in the CRM application, while the middle name is optional. Any effort to update the middle name will cost time and money for very little business value. So, the customer data record can be practically considered complete, even if the data value for the middle name attribute is not populated. This situation is technically called NULL; NULL indicates that the value for the attribute doesn't exist in the database.

To sum up, data completeness is tied to the business process and the resources available in the company. In Figure 3.2, the vendor payment terms field can be meaningfully populated, provided the finance department is in the position to meet the financial obligations of clearing the vendor invoices as per the payment term conditions and the available cash (which is a business resource) position in the company.

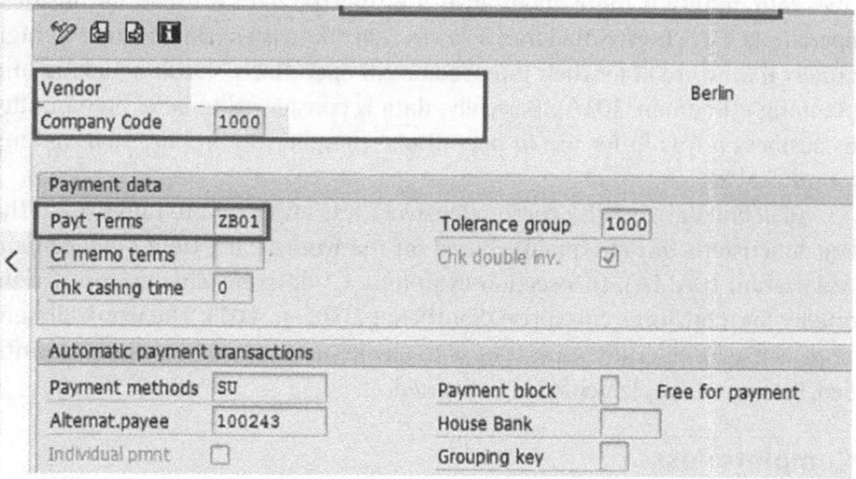

FIGURE 3.2 Payment Terms in SAP Vendor Master

Consistency

Consistency in data is the process of keeping data uniform as in the various IT systems in the enterprise. While data integrity (which will be covered later as a data quality dimension) means that the data is correct, consistency means that the data format is correct, or that the data is correct in relation to other time frames and location. Data consistency in the enterprise IT landscape can be seen from two perspectives:

1. **Data value consistency.** Consistency in this case means that the data values across all tables and databases for a specific data element within the enterprise system landscape (or outside the enterprise system landscape) are the same. For example, the GL (general ledger) account for customer deposits in the CRM system should have the same value in the ERP system as well.
2. **Data traceability consistency.** This deals with the integrity of the data during data movement and transformation, between systems or in the same system. Associated with data lineage, data traceability consistency typically is tied to business rules. One example of data traceability consistency is that purchase orders cannot be issued for the vendor if the supplier contract is closed or not available. Another example of data traceability consistency is when employee status is terminated in the IAM (identity and access management) system, the employee also has no access to the ERP system.

Conformity or Validity

Conformity, also called validity, refers to data that adheres to specifications, data standards, or guidelines, including data type, description, size, format, and other characteristics. For example, the product description can be limited to 40 characters due to the data dictionary or metadata compliance requirements in the IT system. Another example, in many companies is that the product code description follows a *noun-modifier-attribute(s)* format – a common naming convention for describing products. Though this format is not commonly defined in the data dictionary, any data in violation of this format would be considered low-quality due to inconsistencies in the naming standards.

Uniqueness or Cardinality

Uniqueness or data cardinality ensures that there are no duplicate values for a data element. For example, there might be two insurance agents (agents sell insurance products to consumers on behalf of the insurance companies) who are recorded in the system say as Perfect Insurance Inc. and Perfect Insurance Canada, although in fact they are the same business entity.

Technically uniqueness in the data record corresponds to having a unique primary key, and the value this attribute holds can never be NULL. NULL indicates that a data value does not exist in the database. Uniqueness or cardinality in a data element can be described at three levels: high, medium, and low.

1. High cardinality means that a column or attribute contains a large percentage of unique data values. Examples of fields with high cardinality are customer identification codes, email addresses, SSNs, and phone numbers.
2. Medium cardinality values are columns or attributes with values that are not commonly repeated. Examples include postal codes and payment terms.
3. Low cardinality means that the column contains many duplicates. Low cardinality values include states codes and gender.

In enterprise databases or tables, all these three types of cardinalities coexist. For example, in a database table that stores customer bank account information, the "Account Number" column will have very high cardinality, while the customer gender column will have low cardinality (as the column will likely only have "Male" and "Female" as values).

So, what are the business benefits of having high cardinality? How does high cardinality or uniqueness affect data quality? Technically, high cardinality affects business performance in two main ways:

1. Firstly, primary key columns have high cardinality, to prevent duplicate values from being entered. This means it will not be possible to assign two different customers the same customer code as duplicate data create tremendous challenges for effective targeting of customers. Basically, when you have duplicate records, it is more difficult for the system to correctly match data entities like customers to behaviors.

2. Secondly, the primary key field greatly speeds up queries, searches, and sort requests, as database indexing is dependent on the primary key. If the measure of data quality is speed of processing, then it is preferred to query data fields that have high cardinality or uniqueness, and the primary key attributes have high cardinality. In brief, data fields with high cardinality enable faster querying due to database indexing.

Note: Cardinality has two versions: relationship cardinality and data cardinality. Relationship cardinality is associated with designing the database – called data modeling. Relationship cardinality means that whether the relationship between different data attributes is one to one, many to one, or many to many. But the more important definition of cardinality that matters in data quality is the second version, namely data cardinality. Data cardinality is associated with data integrity and query performance. Data cardinality is how many distinct values are present in a particular column or data attribute.

Accuracy and Precision

Accuracy is the degree to which data truly reflects the business category, entity, or event. Accuracy refers to the closeness of a measured value to a standard or true value. Accuracy is closely related to precision, which is the degree to which repeated measurements under unchanged conditions show the same results. For example, if data for the age attribute originates as 17.4 years, but it is captured as 17 years, there is a loss of precision. While accuracy is closeness to the actual or true or correct value, precision is a measure of repeatability.

One can think of accuracy and precision in terms of hitting a bull's-eye. Accurately hitting the target means you are close to the center of the target, even if all the marks are on different sides of the center. Precisely hitting a target means all the hits are closely spaced, even if they are very far from the center of the target. Measurements that are both precise and accurate are repeatable and very near true values. The KPIs to measure accuracy and precision are standard deviation and standard error, covered in the data profiling section in Chapter 6. This is illustrated in Figure 3.3.

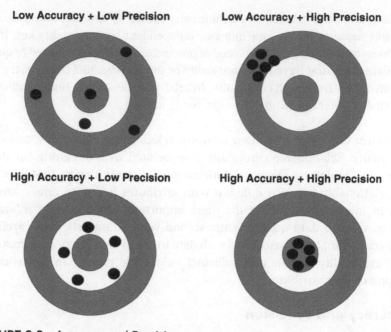

FIGURE 3.3 Accuracy and Precision

Correctness

Correctness is basically having no errors or mistakes in the data. Correctness is the conformance of a data value to the accepted reference. To be correct, a data value must be the right value and must be represented in a consistent and unambiguous form. Correctness is Boolean in nature; something is either correct or not. There cannot be a degree of correctness unlike accuracy or precision. The customer's address needs to be accurate, but the phone number should be correct. If the street name is recorded as "Coventry St." instead of "Coventry Street," then the accuracy and precision of the address data attribute is affected. But, on the other hand, the phone number needs to be correct. If the phone number is recorded as "403-235-3689" instead of "403-235-3688," then even an issue with just one character makes the data record practically useless for business.

Accessibility

The ability to effectively search, retrieve, and use data at all times for business operations can be considered a key characteristic of good data quality.

Data accessibility is the means by which authorized users get access to the data. Access control methods are used to authorize users to access data based on their roles or positions in the business. Data accessibility is very important from the business perspective, especially if business stakeholders need to accurately, securely, and quickly analyze data.

Data Security

Closely related to data accessibility is data security. Data security entails protecting data from destructive forces, including unauthorized users or systems throughout the data lifecycle. Data security also includes the ability to detect cyber threats such as hacking, scams, or malware, by using suitable security tools for data protection, and data security mechanisms are required when data is at rest, in use, and in motion. Basically, data security also ensure that data is available to anyone in the organization who needs access to it.

Furthermore, data security does not always need to be in the actual production system; a production system is an environment that is used by the end users for daily business operations. Sometimes non–production systems (where software development and testing of software programs is done by the developers and IT administrators before moving the changes to the production system) also manage a significant amount of the actual production data. In 2011, research by Stuart Feravich, a respected solution expert, reported that 70% of surveyed enterprises use live or real customer data in non–production systems (Feravich 2011). Data security will be covered in detail in Chapter 11.

Currency and Timeliness

Fundamentally, data quality is time sensitive as the data values continually change during the data lifecycle. Currency (or "freshness") refers to how "stale" the data is, and how much time has elapsed since it was created or last changed at the data source. According to David Loshin, a recognized thought leader in data quality, currency is the degree to which data is current with the world that it models (Loshin 2010). For example, if vendor payment terms are not been updated for years, the data would be termed low quality, as there could be a potential opportunity to renegotiate the contracts with the vendor for better terms and conditions.

Related to currency is timeliness. Timeliness refers to whether the most current data value is readily available when it is needed. From the enterprise IT landscape perspective, timeliness is the rate of dissemination of data.

Timeliness depends on business criticality and impact. For example, online availability of item stock must be immediately available to inventory management, but a four-hour delay could be acceptable for clearing vendor invoices in the vendor invoice clearing system. Due to increasing demands for quick data-driven decisions, timeliness is increasingly seen as a critical dimension of data quality in today's business environment, especially while deriving insights for real-time analytics.

Practically, real-time analytics is near-real-time analytics, given that there is always some delay between data capture and insight derivation.

However, when we say real-time analytics, it means using data as soon as it is available to derive insights for decision making. For some use cases, say an oil refinery real-time insights need to be derived within a few seconds after the data is available while in back-office functions like finance, real-time analytics means insights that are derived in minutes or hours after the data is available. Overall, real-time analytics is contextual or time-sensitive and can be defined as deriving insights using the available data with minimal delay or latency.

Timeliness in data quality has a significant impact on real-time analytics, which can be defined as deriving insights from the available data with minimal latency including data latency and query latency.

Minimizing data latency is typically associated with (a) data ingestion into canonical systems, such as the data warehouse, and (b) querying of data from the data warehouse. In other words, real-time analytics or timely data availability should address data latency and query latency. Data latency is a measure of the time from when data is generated to when it is queryable.

As there is usually a time lag between when the data is collected and when it is available to query, real-time analytics systems should minimize the lag associated in getting the quality data to the data warehouse. Query latency is the amount of time it takes to execute a query on the data in the data warehouse and get the output. Overall, the key to real-time analytics in reducing the latency or the response times in bringing the data to the data warehouse and executing the query faster.

Redundancy or Data Availability

Data redundancy is a condition created within a database or data storage technology in which the data object or element is replicated and captured by two multiple IT systems in different locations. Redundancy is a deliberate and planned mechanism that enterprises use for backup and recovery purposes. The purpose of this replication is to increase the reliability and data availability of the system and thereby improve data quality.

Redundancy is closely tied to duplication, as duplication occurs when the same record is repeated in the same table within the database in the same system. While redundancy, which is at the system level, is a desired characteristic to mitigate risk of data loss, duplication, which is at the individual record level, is not desired. Data duplication can be avoided by using two main techniques.

- Deduplication. In data quality deduplication is used to describe a process where two or more data records that describe the same real-world entity, are merged into one "golden record." The golden record is the best possible record for the organization to be utilized. Deduplication is a process to improve data quality by removing redundant or repetitive data from systems manually or by applying fuzzy logic routines. Fuzzy logic is an approach to computing based on "degrees of truth" rather than the usual "true or false" (1 or 0) Boolean logic.
- Normalization. When you normalize the data, you organize the columns (attributes) and tables (relations) of a database to ensure that their dependencies are correctly enforced by database integrity constraints. Data integrity is a set of rules for normalizing data, and a database is considered "normalized" if it meets the third normal form, meaning that it is free of data insert, delete, and update anomalies.

So, what is the difference between duplicate data and redundant data? Duplicated data exists when an attribute has two or more identical values. But a data value is redundant if you can delete it without the information being lost. In other words, redundancy is desired duplication of data, and one of the tools to assess and measure data redundancy is the cosine similarity. The cosine similarity is a technique used to measure cohesion or similarity between the data elements based on the data attributes.

Coverage (Fit for Purpose)

Fundamentally, data management is complex, time consuming, and expensive. Hence, the ability of data to serve multiple diverse business needs or stakeholders is always desirable. Reference and master data have high coverage (or "comprehensibility"), as they are usually shared in the enterprise, while transactional data has less data coverage as it is specific to the business event associated with the LoB or business function. For example, sales office (a reference data) and customer (a master data) are used by marketing and agents, but the insurance claims data (a transactional data) is relevant for the claims department.

While data coverage promotes data sharing, it is tied to the business process. For instance, a 10% error rate in customer address might be acceptable for telemarketing. But if billing decides to use the same address data to send invoices, this rate might be unacceptable. Overall, data quality can be considered high if the span or coverage of a data element includes multiple business processes.

Integrity

Data integrity ensures that data is recorded exactly as intended, and that when data is retrieved, it is the same as it was when originally recorded. Data integrity ensures that data is not compromised and that the data can be trusted. The two main ways to ensure data integrity are data governance process and database management. Data integrity can be enforced as a part of the data governance process, and this will be covered in a separate chapter in the sustain phase of the DARS model in Chapter 10. Enforcing data integrity using the DBMS (database management system) controls can be implemented in a series of data integrity rules that are implemented when data is captured on the database. From the DBMS perspective the four types of data integrity rules are:

1. Entity Integrity

    Entity integrity ensures that each row of a table (record or tuple) can be uniquely identified. Entity integrity is enforced using the primary key of a table. Basically, for entity integrity there should be a primary key (PK) in every database table as a primary key helps to uniquely identify the record in the database. For example, customer identifier is typically a primary key and this primary key cannot be NULL.

2. Referential Integrity

    Referential integrity ensures that a value in one table references an existing value in another table. In referential integrity, whenever a foreign key (FK) value is used it must reference a valid, existing primary key in the parent table. The foreign key is a cross-reference between tables because it references the PK of another table, thereby establishing link between the tables.

3. Domain Integrity

    Domain integrity ensures that all the data items in a column fall within a defined set of valid values. Each column in a table has a defined set of values, such as the set of all values for zip code (five numeric digits in the United States). Basically, when you limit the value assigned to an instance of that column (an attribute), you are enforcing domain integrity. Domain integrity is enforced by adopting the data dictionary or metadata standards: that is, choosing the correct data type and length for a data attribute supported with dropdown lists, check lists, and radio buttons.

4. Business or User Integrity

    Business integrity ensures that the database enforces business rules. This is done at the application level. For example, business rules can be set such that a home damage insurance claim can be cleared only when the damage evaluation report is submitted by the appraisers.

From the data quality perspective, data integrity ensures that data remains intact and unaltered. It also describes data that can be traced and connected to other data, and ensures that all data is recoverable and searchable. Figure 3.4 gives a holistic view of the 12 data quality dimensions for a business enterprise.

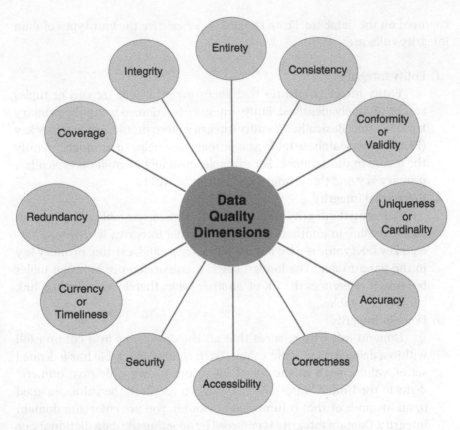

FIGURE 3.4   Data Quality Dimensions

The implementation of the 12 data quality dimensions involves improving data literacy, implementing a strong data governance process, leveraging the technical capabilities of the DBMS, and more. The following points should be noted regarding the implementation of these 12 data quality dimensions:

■ The 12 dimensions should be applicable to most enterprises for business performance and should serve as a baseline to understand data quality. This list has 12 data quality dimensions that are evolving, given that data management capabilities, regulatory processes, market needs, and so on are also evolving. All these data quality dimensions are desired attributes for data quality. For example, duplication is not included in the list as it is an undesirable data quality attribute. (Of course, the desirable attributes like uniqueness and cardinality that are presented here prevent data duplication.) Fundamentally, data quality is contextual in nature, and these dimensions should be considered based on context.

- Realizing a high level of data quality for each of these 12 dimensions takes time and effort. It could take months just to determine the current level of data quality. Hence, the 12 data quality dimensions should map to specific business requirements and KPIs, if any steps are taken to improve data quality.

- Compliance to all these 12 data quality dimensions is not mandatory for an enterprise, but compliance does improve business performance. Improving all 12 data quality dimensions will include a trade-off between time, cost, and quality. For example; updating the customer's middle name for 500,000 customers might improve the completeness dimension for the telemarketing department. While it might meet the technical requirements, it will cost a lot of time and effort for relatively few business benefits.

 ## CONTEXT IN DATA QUALITY

The above 12 dimensions of data quality are relatively static in nature. Applying these data quality dimensions to measure and assess data quality might not provide the compute state of data quality given that data moves and has a lifecycle. As mentioned before, business data is used for three main purposes – operations, compliance, and decision making, and data is often originated and captured for operations and compliance. At this juncture the data quality is defined and deterministic and the data format is often in the native and proprietary format. But when data is used in analytics to derive insights for decision making, the focus shifts from operations and compliance, to deriving insights for performance improvement, innovation, experimentation, productivity and more. This means businesses work on hypotheses and often the data is not always available. The fundamental characteristic of hypothesis testing or significance testing is the supposition or proposed explanation made on the basis of limited data as a starting point for further investigation.

Data is often originated and captured for operations and compliance, where the data model and data quality are defined and deterministic. But when data is needed for analytics to derive insights, the focus shifts from defined data models to hypotheses where often the data is not available or the data is limited. Basically, depending on the nature of questions you ask for deriving insights for analytics, at some point in time data will give up. While you could strive for high-quality first-party data for operations and compliance, expecting high-quality first-party data for analytics for all the use-cases or scenarios might not be realistic.

For example, let us take a gas station which has a car wash facility. Typically, the gas station captures the sales in point of sales (PoS) systems where the sales order has details on the product such as quantity, unit of measure (UoM), price, and so on along with the customer details, and this is an operational activity. But if the hypotheses for insight derivation is WARM WEATHER DRIVES CAR WASHES, the data quality would be poor as the weather data is usually not captured in the PoS transactional systems as part of regular operations. This means, the gas station will have poor-quality data for analytics even though for operations and compliance the data quality is very good. Another example is a retail store manager who believes increased inventory leads to increased sales. To validate this hypothesis with insights, they need the inventory details and if the inventory data is not available then the data quality will be considered poor. Overall, the data-quality metrics for master data and reference data are relatively static. However, data-quality metrics for transactional data are contextual as the transactional data is dynamic. The discussion will be further continued in the data observability section in Chapter 10.

CONSEQUENCES AND COSTS OF POOR DATA QUALITY

So, what are the consequences of not complying with these 12 data quality dimensions? What would happen if the data quality in the enterprise is poor, given that many enterprises have poor data quality ultimately impacting business performance? Chapter 1 covered this topic to some extent. To further explain this, based on the work of David Loshin, there are four categories where poor data quality impacts business performance (Loshin 2010).

1. **Financial impacts.** Financial impacts due to poor data quality results in increased operating costs, decreased revenues, missed opportunities, reduction or delays in cash flow, and others. For example, if GL (general ledger) accounts are not assigned to the right product categories, then it is difficult to assess which product segments are profitable and which are not.
2. **Marketplace impacts.** These impacts are associated with missing expectations in the marketplace due to compromises in business-defined integrity. This ultimately results in decreased organizational trust, low confidence in management reporting, and delayed or improper decisions.
3. **Productivity impacts.** Productivity impacts operational efficiency due to increased workloads, decreased throughput, and increased cycle time, to name a few. As a simple example, what is the impact if the product description does not adhere to the noun-modifier-attribute format or the conformity data quality dimension? Inconsistent product description results in duplicate product master records. This means the same physical product that is codified in different ways results in product assignment to different GL accounts in the contracts, purchase orders, invoices and other transactional documents. This "domino effect" ultimately results in increased workloads to the staff as reconciliations and data clean-up is needed during reporting and analytics.
4. **Risk and compliance impacts.** Risk and compliance impacts due to poor data quality can increase exposure to compliance and financial risks, thereby decreasing the ability to execute in the marketplace. Key impacts include credit assessment, cash flow, capital investment, government regulations, industry expectations, internal company policies, and so on. As an example, how does the payment term data element (used in vendor masters) affect compliance and business performance? The vendor payment terms not only determine the due date for clearing vendor invoices, but also improve the cash flow and the working capital requirements of the enterprise.

The 1-10-100 rule states that prevention is less expensive than remediation. Being proactive is better than being reactive; prevention is always better than remediation.

INSIGHT

The above business consequences have an impact on the growth, cost, and risk; and a good data quality principle is to follow the **1-10-100 rule**. The 1-10-100 data quality rule was developed by George Labovitz, Yu Sang Chang, and Victor Rosansky to assess and prevent the impact of dirty data (Labovitz Chang, and Rosansky, 1993). The 1-10-100 rule states that $1 equates to the amount it costs to assess data. If this step is not followed the amount increases to $10. This $10 signifies the cost that businesses inure to remediate the data. In the third and final phase, the initial $1 rises dramatically to $100, and this figure represents the amount of money businesses will have to pay when they have failed to clean the data. The **1-10-100 rule** is illustrated in Figure 3.5.

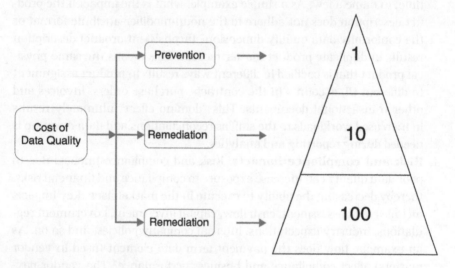

FIGURE 3.5 Data Quality 1-10-100 Rule

▪ DATA DEPRECIATION AND ITS FACTORS

Generally, any business asset – tangible or intangible – tends to depreciate over time. From the accounting perspective, depreciation is the decrease in value of assets so that the company allocates an asset's cost over the duration of its useful life. Technically, for intangible assets such as data, brands, and intellectual property, the process of allocating costs over time is known as "amortization." Given that data is considered an intangible asset, the term *amortization* is more appropriate when it comes to data quality degradation.

Data decay or degradation refers to a gradual loss in the quality of data. In terms of the data quality dimensions just described, when any of those data quality dimensions are compromised, data is said to be decaying or degrading. Information management researchers Scott Tonidandel, Eden King, and Jose Cortina indicate that **in a typical enterprise, data degrades between 2% and 7% every month** (Tonidandel, King, and Cortina 2015).

According to Gartner, poor quality data costs an average organization about $14.2 million annually, and 40% of business initiatives fail to achieve targeted benefits because of poor data quality. According to Experian Data Quality, 77% of companies believe that their bottom line is affected by inaccurate and incomplete data (Levy 2015). Today businesses are increasingly looking at AI technologies for improved business performance. But if quality data is not available, then these AI technologies will have severe limitations in improving business effectiveness and efficiency. Basically, there is no AI without quality data.

The process of improving the 12 data quality dimensions and preventing data-quality degradation is based on managing three main factors or parameters:

1. **Context.** Context depends on the purpose of data – how a specific data element is used in the enterprise. Ultimately, the context or purpose of the data determines the specific data quality dimension that can be used to most effectively raise the quality level of the data. For example, from the analytics or decision-making perspective, the data quality dimensions that are most critical are currency, accessibility, conformity, and consistency. But from the compliance side, say for SSAE-16 (Statement on Standards for Attestation Engagements) certification, the data security dimension is very important. So, if the main purpose of some data is to make business decisions, there would be relatively little attention paid to security, resulting in the degradation of the security data quality dimension.

2. **Lifecycle.** Data lifecycle (DLC) is a series of 10 stages involved in successful management of data and information. DLC has a significant impact on data quality as it touches systems, applications, business processes, and stakeholder roles and responsibilities. Fundamentally, data is never stationary. When data flows between systems, it is subject to change in values, format, and usage. This affects data integrity, ultimately causing lower data quality in the enterprise. DLC will be covered in detail in Chapter 5.

3. **Data governance.** Successful implementation of any strategic initiative (including data quality initiatives) is a human process. When there are specific goals to achieve, and when the data element is subject to varied forces that could potentially jeopardize data quality, control or governance of data is absolutely essential. Data governance will be covered in detail in Chapter 10.

Fundamentally, the quality of data held in IT systems will deteriorate unless practice steps are taken to manage data quality. There has to be a deliberate effort that requires among other things a vision, focus, leadership, governance, and more to ensure that the data elements are formally managed throughout the enterprise.

DATA IN IT SYSTEMS

Discussing data and its quality levels without talking of IT systems is incomplete because data is originated, stored, processed, viewed and even purged in IT systems. Basically, IT systems manage the lifecycle of data from origination to integration to processing to consumption to closure. In this regard, there are three main types of IT systems where data is managed in business enterprises: OLTP (Online Transactional Processing) systems, Integration or Middleware systems, and OLAP (Online Analytical Processing) systems.

They say there's no AI (Artificial Intelligence) without IA (Information Architecture).

INSIGHT

OLTP systems facilitate fast insertion, updating, and deleting of business data; especially transactional data. They are used for high-throughput inserts to support hundreds of business users concurrently. Invariably, the databases in OLTP systems are relational and the four key database "CRUD" operations, that is, "create, read, update, and delete" are performed by the OLTP system. Basically, the key value propositions of OLTP applications are availability, speed, concurrency, recoverability, and data integrity. ERP and CRM systems are popular examples of an OLTP system. Other examples of OLTP systems include the teller application in a bank, a billing application in an electricity distribution company, and a trading system in an oil company, among others.

The second type of IT systems are the integration or middleware systems. Most enterprises have multiple OLTP systems specific to business functions, and these systems manage different types of data. For example, sales data could be in the ERP system, while the prospect or lead data is in the CRM system. To have a unified and enterprise-centric view of customer data and business processes, these OLTP systems have to be integrated, and this is achieved by integration or middleware systems. Basically, integration systems help to transfer, transpose, and orchestrate data. Transferring data is moving it from one system to another. Transformation of data is the conversion of data from one format into another, say M3 to gallons. Data orchestration is collecting, sequencing, and organizing disparate data. Data integration will be covered as a best practice in Chapter 9.

The third type of IT systems is the OLAP systems. While OLTP systems provide a high degree of data validation and integrity, retrieving data from OLTP systems (especially for reporting) to cater to different needs of the stakeholder is time consuming due to extensive data validation. OLAP also known as the SoI (System of Insights) systems enable users to quickly and selectively retrieve and view data from different points of view. At the core, the three main characteristics of OLAP systems are denormalization, data aggregation, and multidimensionality.

OLTP systems are used to run the business, integration systems are used to integrate the business, and OLAP systems help to understand the business.

INSIGHT

Fundamentally, for quick and easy data retrieval, we need data structures with little data integrity as data integrity is usually done when the data is captured in the OLTP systems. The data structure that is typically used for data retrieval or reads relies on a technical concept called denormalization, and the denormalized data structure is the key characteristic of the canonical databases like the data warehouse (DWH), data lakes, and lake houses. A DWH is a federated repository for all the data (typically historical) that an enterprise's various OLTP systems have collected. In fact, a DWH supports an OLTP system by providing a place for the OLTP system to offload the data it accumulates. These are services if not available that would complicate and degrade OLTP performance. OLAP systems perform descriptive, predictive, and prescriptive analytics. In addition, the OLAP systems are normally complemented by data visualization (DV) tools as DV tools give visual context to data, by displaying data in infographics, dashboards, geographic maps, heat maps, and detailed charts. The key differences between the three types of IT systems are as shown below.

Parameter	OLTP system	Integration systems	OLAP system
Purpose	Run business	Integrate business	Understand business
Focus	Getting data into the system	Manage integration of data	Getting data out of the system
Data source	Granular data generated by one source system	Granular data coming from multiple source systems	Aggregated data and insights from multiple source systems
Data currency	Current	Current and historical	Historical
Data model	"CRUD" model, i.e., create, update, read, and delete	"TTO" model. i.e., transpose, transfer, and orchestrate	Mainly reads data, following the "WORM" model: "written once, read many"
Queries	Relatively standardized and simple queries executed on granular business data	Relatively simple queries executed on metadata	Complex queries involving aggregations
Processing speed	Very fast	Fast	Slow
Storage space requirements	Can be relatively small if historical data is archived	Can be relatively small if the integration messages (called payload) are archived	Large due to the existence of aggregation structures and historical data
Database design	Highly normalized with many tables	Not applicable as data is not designed to support business processes or rules	Typically, denormalized with fewer tables

DATA QUALITY AND TRUSTED INFORMATION

Often the terms *data quality* and *trusted information* are used together. But what exactly is trusted information? Before we look at trusted information, let us try to understand what exactly is information and how is it different from data. Fundamentally, when data is processed, in a given context it is known as information or insights. In simple terms, context + data = information or insights (Southekal 2017). Basically, to trust the information, there has to be trust in context and data.

Trust in Context

Context is the circumstances especially location, roles (organization structure), and time that surround the collection, integration, processing, and consumption of data. In simple terms, context to data primarily comes from three key aspects: when (time), where (location), and by whom (roles), and these three elements are captured in the transactional data. Transactional data holds the key to business trust and context for the following reasons.

1. Businesses are often constrained by resources like capital, time, skills, machinery, and more. Transactional data represents the consumption of these business assets and can provide insight into how these resources are managed.
2. Transactional data, unlike reference data and master data, represents monetary value that could impact your business's bottom line. There might be 500,000 customers (master data) in your CRM system, but how many of these customers placed orders (transactional data) in the last 12 months?
3. Transactional data has a twofold effect in accounting: For every value received, there is an equal value given. This means that compliance to accounting standards like IFRS (International Financial Reporting Standards) and GAPP (Generally Accepted Principles and Practices) is based on transactional data.
4. Transactional data serves as a legal record or binding document in the case of invoices, orders, remittance advice, shipments, and more between counterparties.

5. Transactional data promotes performance comparisons and decision making. Striving for measurement is best when there is quantitative data to process or track. Transactional data is generally quantitative in nature and can help measure business performance using the right KPIs.

Fundamentally, context helps in building trust as it creates the relationship between the data and the actual consumption. For example, an increase in insurance claims on a specific insurance product may be hard to pinpoint when the raw claims data is examined on its own. But, for instance, imposing the hailstorm data and the geolocation data on the claims data can provide the necessary context in understanding the data and insights.

Trust in Data

Essentially, trust in data is associated with sharing third-party data. But fundamentally, trust in data is ensuring high data quality because data high in trustworthiness promotes data sharing and collaboration in the company. While the 12 dimensions of data quality discussed in this chapter provided the foundation in building trust in data, trusting data should also address the following questions.

- Is data captured accurately? Chapters 7, 8, and 9 look at this matter in detail.
- How to measure and validate data quality? Chapters 6 looks at the metrics to measure data quality.
- Is the data well protected? Are there any risks or issues with data? Chapter 11 looks at methods to protect data.
- Is data managed ethically? Data ethics is covered in Chapter 12.

 KEY TAKEAWAYS

Following are the key takeaways of this chapter.

- Data is considered to be of high quality if they are fit for use in operations, compliance, and decision making.

- Most enterprises have data quality issues of varying sizes and impacts. Data quality in business is multidimensional, and selecting the pertinent data quality dimensions will help enterprises better assess business performance from data.
- The 12 different dimensions of data quality for any business enterprise should serve as a baseline for data quality. This list will evolve giving the changing business and AI landscape.
- Every asset – tangible or intangible – tends to depreciate over time. Data decay or degradation refers to a gradual loss in the quality of data. In a typical enterprise, the quality of data degrades 2–7% every month.
- Preventing data quality degradation or depreciation is based on managing three main factors or parameters:
  1. Assessing the context, that is, the role of data in business management
  2. Understanding the transformation of data in the lifecycle
  3. Effectiveness of the data governance process
- Trusted information comes from deriving reliability in both context and data.
- Discussing data and its quality levels without talking of IT systems is incomplete because data is originated, stored, processed, and even purged in IT systems. In this regard, there are three main types of IT systems where data is managed in business enterprises: OLTP (Online Transactional Processing), Integration or Middleware, and OLAP (Online Analytical Processing) systems.

 ## CONCLUSION

It is estimated that enterprise data doubles every four years. According to Eric Schmidt, former CEO of Google, every two days we create as much data as we did from the dawn of civilization up until 2003 (Johnston 2015). This increased volume of data capture will correlate with complexity thereby resulting in more challenges for deriving business performance from data. Given that every business endeavor today rests on sound data quality, ensuring quality data in the enterprise is of paramount importance. Data quality initiatives should be pursued holistically, considering the firm's strategy, goals, business processes, IT systems, and stakeholders' roles and responsibilities.

REFERENCES

Crosby, P. (1979). *Quality is free: The art of making quality certain*. McGraw-Hill.

Eckerson, W. (2002). Data quality and the bottom line. TDWI.

Feravich, S. (December 2011). Ensuring protection for sensitive test data. http://www.dbta.com/Editorial/Think-About-It/Ensuring-Protection-for-Sensitive-Test-Data-79145.aspx.

IBM. (January 2020). Spreadsheets vs. Watson Studio Desktop. IBM Research.

Johnston, N. (2015). *Adaptive marketing: leveraging real-time data to become a more competitive and successful company*. Palgrave Macmillan.

Labovitz, G., Chang, Y.S., and Rosansky, V. (1993). *Making quality work*. Harper Business, 1993.

Levy, J. (July 2015). Enterprises don't have big data, they just have bad data. http://tcrn.ch/2iWcfM5.

Loshin, D. (2010). Evaluating the business impacts of poor data quality. Knowledge Integrity Incorporated, Business Intelligence Solutions. https://www.myecole.it/biblio/wp-content/uploads/2020/11/3_DK_2DS_Business_Impacts_Poor_Data_Quality.pdf.

Nagle, T., Redman, T., and Sammon, D. (September 2017). Only 3% of companies' data meets basic quality standards. https://bit.ly/2UxaHO4.

Redman, T. (May 2016). Data quality should be everyone's job. *Harvard Business Review*.

Southekal, P. (2017). *Data for business performance*. Technics.

Tonidandel, S., King, E., and Cortina, J. (2015). *Big data at work: the data science revolution and organizational psychology*. Routledge Publications.

PART TWO

Analyze Phase

4

Causes for Poor Data Quality

 INTRODUCTION

In the first three chapters we covered the define phase of the DARS model. Specifically, we looked at the definition of data quality, the business case for data quality, the different types of data, the 12 key dimensions of data quality, and more. The next three chapters will look at the second phase of the DARS models: that is, the **analyze phase**. Specifically, this chapter will explore or analyze the key reasons for data to decay or depreciate or degrade.

Data decay refers to the gradual reduction or loss in utility of data for business. In general, there are two types of data decay: physical and logical.

1. Physical data decay is data loss from the storage medium. Examples include server crashes, hard disk corruptions, data records getting purged without a trace, and more. Physical data decay is instantaneous, and often out of one's control. The most common solution to address physical data decay is regular backup of the database or recovery of the system in an alternative or secondary data center.

2. Logical data decay "silent killer of data" is commonly due to the compromises on the different data quality dimensions. Logical data decay reduces the utility of data for business activities. Logical data decay is the main reason for poor data quality in business.

While the physical data decay can be solved easily by periodic refreshing by rewriting the data with backups, alleviating logical data decay is very complex and time consuming. This is because with logical data decay "the silent killer of data" it is often harder to spot the root causes, and the causes can be many, complex, and varied.

DATA QUALITY RCA TECHNIQUES

Root cause analysis (RCA) helps to systematically address the underlying issues or causes rather than just treating the symptoms of the problem.

INSIGHT

In quality management, the terms *problem* and *symptom* are often used interchangeably. But they are actually different. A symptom is a sign or indication of a problem that can be seen and assessed. A symptom happens as a result of a problem. For example, the problem of increased insurance claims is actually a symptom and not a problem per se. The factors or the reasons for the increased claims could be climate catastrophes, inflation, economic volatility, and so on.

Hence the first step to solving a problem is to define the problem precisely and finding the real or the root cause of the problem – and not just the obvious symptoms. Root cause analysis (RCA) is important for two key reasons:

1. Often problems are presented as symptoms and *not* as problems. RCA helps to find the real or the root cause of the problem
2. Even if the problem is well stated, the root cause of the problem should still be identified. If the right problem is not solved, one will never be able to eliminate the real problem that is causing the issue, and this will result in recurring problems.

So, how can one identify the root causes of a problem, especially the data-quality problems? Below are four common tools that can help to identify the root causes of the data quality issues:

1. Affinity Diagram
2. Failure Mode and Effects Analysis (FMEA)
3. Fishbone Diagram
4. The 5 Whys

Affinity Diagram

Categorization is one of the first and fundamental steps in effective management of a problem. The Affinity Diagram is a tool that gathers large amounts of ideas, opinions, and issues and organizes them into homogeneous groups or categories based on their associations or relationships for further analysis. Basically, the Affinity Diagram follows a three-step process.

1. Collect large amounts of data, such as ideas, opinions, and issues on both the symptom and the problem
2. Organize the list into homogenous groups or categories
3. Label those groups or categories for further review and analysis

Once completed, the Affinity Diagram may be used to create FMEA (Failure Mode and Effects Analysis). The Affinity Diagram is as shown in Figure 4.1.

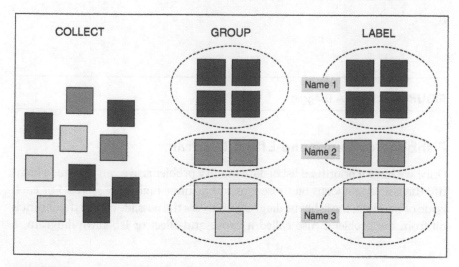

FIGURE 4.1   Affinity Diagram

Failure Mode and Effects Analysis (FMEA)

Once we have a list of data quality issues that are logically labeled and categorized using the Affinity Diagram, we need to look to the impact of these issues on the business. FMEA (Failure Mode and Effects Analysis) is a technique used to identify the data quality problems or the modes of failure. In FMEA, each failure mode or data quality issue is assessed on three key factors:

- Severity (S), which rates the severity of the potential effect of the failure
- Occurrence (O), which rates the likelihood that the failure will occur
- Detection (D), which rates the likelihood that the problem will be detected before it reaches the customer

Rating scales for each of these three factors usually range from 1 to 5 or from 1 to 10, with the higher number representing the higher seriousness or risk or consequence of the issue. The product of the three scores produces a risk priority number (RPN) for each issue and helps to prioritize which problem category must gain attention first – that is, RPN = S * O * D (see Figure 4.2).

Issue Category	Failure Description	Severity (S)	Occurrence (O)	Detection (D)	RPN

FIGURE 4.2 FMEA Diagram

Fishbone or Cause-and-Effect Diagram

Once we have a prioritized list of data quality problems, we can choose to identify the issues and focus on those issues that have high RPN scores. For each issue or problem, the fishbone diagram analyzes the possible causes that branch off from the problem. Also called a cause-and-effect or Ishikawa diagram, a fishbone diagram shows multiple sub-causes branching off of each identified issue or symptom. This model uses the assessment of the 6Ms as a methodology for identifying the probable root cause. The 6Ms include:

1. Man
2. Machine
3. Methods
4. Materials
5. Measurement
6. Mother Nature – i.e., Environment

Figure 4.3 is an application of the fishbone or cause-and-effect or Ishikawa diagram, to determine the causes associated with incorrect customer address.

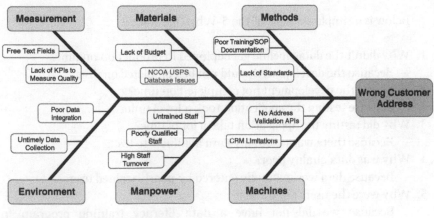

FIGURE 4.3 Fishbone Diagram

The 5-Whys Method

To further deep dive into the individual issues or causes, the 5-Whys methods is very useful. The 5-Whys method uses a series of questions to drill down into successive layers of a problem or even the symptom. Sakichi Toyoda, founder of Toyota Industries, developed the 5-Whys technique in the 1930s. The basic idea is that each time you ask why, the answer or the cause becomes the basis of the next why. The process continues until "Why" is asked five times. The 5-Whys method is shown in Figure 4.4.

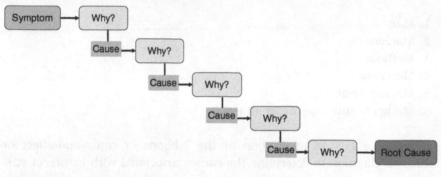

FIGURE 4.4   5-Whys Technique

Below is a simple example of the 5-Whys Technique.

1. Why didn't the data pipeline get deployed in production on time?
   - Because the development could not be completed on time.
2. Why was the development not completed on time?
   - Because testing the application took a lot of time.
3. Why did testing the application take a lot of time?
   - Because there was no quality data available to test.
4. Why was data quality poor?
   - Because data was manually entered by poorly trained users.
5. Why were the users not trained?
   - Because we did not have a data literacy training program in the company.

Now we know that the data pipeline did not get deployed on time because there was no data literacy training program in the company.

Figure 4.5 is an integrated view of applying these four RCA techniques to determine the root cause of a problem.

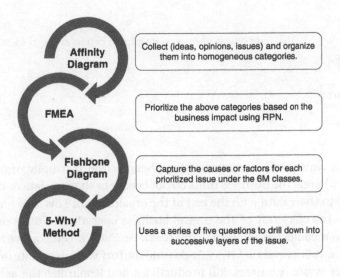

Affinity Diagram — Collect (ideas, opinions, issues) and organize them into homogeneous categories.

FMEA — Prioritize the above categories based on the business impact using RPN.

Fishbone Diagram — Capture the causes or factors for each prioritized issue under the 6M classes.

5-Why Method — Uses a series of five questions to drill down into successive layers of the issue.

FIGURE 4.5 RCA Techniques

 ## TYPICAL CAUSES OF POOR DATA QUALITY

RCA is the first step or the beginning of the problem-solving process. Once the root cause is determined using the four techniques discussed in the preceding section, the next step is identifying the factors and determining the right solution for implementation. Based on extensive literature surveys and referencing some of the work of Arkady Maydanchik from his book *Data Quality Assessment* (Maydanchik 2007), the following are 16 common causes of poor data quality.

Data Silos Resulting from Organization Silos

As mentioned in Chapter 2, business data can be of three main types: reference data, master data, or transactional data. While reference data and master data are typically enterprise-wide and shared, transactional data is specific to LoB and business functions. However, if the reference data and master data are managed by multiple LoBs, the chances of having poor data quality increases as each business unit views a data element from their own unique business perspective. For example, if the finance department decides to own the product master data and maintain the safety stocks to a low data value (to reduce the inventory carrying costs), that safety stocks value would not be very useful to the sales and marketing department as they need a high level of inventory to serve the business.

The root cause of most data silos is organizational silos.

INSIGHT

The root cause of this compromising phenomenon is usually organizational silos, wherein the business units do not believe in sharing data or do not see the need to share data with the rest of the organization. This "silo mentality" reduces the efficiency of the overall business operations, and is mainly attributed to a conflicted top leadership team. As Patrick Lencioni writes in his book *Silos, Politics and Turf Wars*, "Silos and the turf wars devastate organizations. They waste resources, kill productivity, and jeopardize the achievement of goals." He goes on to advise leaders to tear down silos by moving past behavioral issues and address the contextual issues that are present in the enterprise.

Interpretation and Consumption of Data Happen in Different Ways

According to Ted Freidman, Gartner's VP of research, "Data quality is a business issue and not an IT matter. Data quality requires businesses to take responsibility and drive improvements" (Saves 2008). However, within a business, the intended use of data might be very different from the actual use as data is contextual and is always tied to the business process and the role of the data consumer. For instance, the phone number field in the customer master data is usually a shared data element throughout the entire sales process. The customer service representative can use it to contact the customer while the tax analyst can use it for validating the customer jurisdiction code along with the tax codes – even though the telephone number was not originally meant for tax calculation. For example, a telephone number that starts with 212 is assigned to the New York region, but tax analysts might use the number 212 to validate the tax codes as these tax codes are based on jurisdiction. This effectively means that if the telephone number is not maintained, the tax analyst might report poor data quality – even though the telephone number field was never intended to validate and calculate taxes.

Frequency of Use and the Number of Users

Sharing data increases the number of data consumers. But all of those consumers come with varied and implicit needs. For example, the order status in a sales order might provide the sales director the sales pipeline of the business. If the accounting analyst decides to use the same order status to improve the prediction of future sales, the delivery dates and payment terms must also be maintained in the sales order. This is because the accounting analyst needs both the sales and finance data to improve the prediction of future sales.

In addition, when more people use data, the more data elements must be managed and governed. Satisfying the diverse requirements of multiple data consumers invariably results in increased data management and governance, with different data quality dimensions to satisfy. This increase in scope results in increased costs and complexity, ultimately resulting in poor data quality.

Poor Business Case for Data Origination and Capture

Going back to our previous example, one might ask – why can't the delivery dates and payment terms be maintained when creating the sales order, or for that matter, why can't all the data fields just be populated? Populating database tables and fields for adherence to the data quality dimension of completeness does not necessarily guarantee high data quality. Populating the database fields not only takes time and money, most importantly it has to adhere to the business processes or rules. More importantly, usage of the data fields within the database must be tied to business processes and user needs. For instance, if the procurement department decides to update the terms of payment in the vendor master to 45 days, it is important to ensure that the accounts payable and treasury teams in finance are aligned to clearing the supplier invoices within 45 days.

Data Searching and Retrieval Challenges

Sometimes the unavailability of data is perceived as poor data quality. The issue could be due to the data element value itself being missing, or it could be due to the way the search is performed by the users. For example, say that a business user in Sun Life Insurance is trying to search the details of the health insurance product "Simplified" by entering the search parameter "Simplified." But if the product is maintained as "SIM LI AUG 2020" in the IT system, the user will not get any product codes for "Simplified" for the search results. Most of the issues in searching can be attributed to factors such as lack of formatting, inconsistent taxonomy, lack of standards, missing characteristics, poor data governance, database constraints, or even poor training.

System Proliferation and Integration Issues

For most businesses, a system of record (SoR) is the authoritative source for data entities. Data in the SoR is interfaced to target applications where specific business processes are carried out. As an enterprise usually carries a mix of IT systems, it is imperative to have an enterprise-wide data model. The enterprise data model reduces complexity and fosters better collaboration and communication in the enterprise. It brings together diverse applications, teams, processes, projects, and data. But often many firms lack an enterprise-wide data model. The multiplicity of systems can jeopardize data integrity due to differences in semantics, syntax, business processes, timing of the data extracts, system bugs, and more. For example, units of measure (or UoM) often vary depending on which business entity is involved. A customer's age might be quantified in an enterprise's system of record (SoR) with a UoM of "YEARS" but the CRM system, on the other hand, might have the customer's age as "YR."

Even if some data fields are maintained in the source SoR system, the values might change when these data objects are interfaced to target OLTP applications that handle specific business processes. For example, a customer might be described as "BOB SMITH" with an Age as "YEARS" (each). But the sales team might change the age in the CRM system to "MTS" as the insurance premium is calculated based on the age of the customer in months. Each of these values for the age attribute is correct from the individual stakeholder and system perceptive. The differences due to business processes and system proliferation enable the respective departments to contextualize the data to meet their specific needs affecting data integrity. Fundamentally the ACID (atomicity, consistency, isolation, and durability) model and metadata definitions are more vulnerable to compromises during data integration.

Varied Value Propositions between Consumers and Originators of Data

Typically, consumers of data have more issues with data quality than the producers of data. This reflects basic human nature; when you create and own something, you develop a sense of ownership over it and this phenomenon is commonly called the IKEA effect or bias. The IKEA effect, derived from the name of Swedish manufacturer and furniture retailer IKEA, is a cognitive bias in which consumers place a disproportionately high value on products they created. With the name, in the previous example, the problem with the value Age of "YEARS" for the customer is seen by the CRM team as problematic, as they want to use a different value for age, that is, MTS. Also, due to the business process dependencies, the CRM users are not the originators or creators of the data. In addition, data quality problems become visible and even get amplified when data gets propagated to different business functions, stakeholders, and systems.

Data Rules Affect Business Operations

While business rules define things like categories, entities, and events, data rules define database attributes such as field length, type, format, and other technical or metadata aspects. For example, if there is a data rule defined in the IT system that field length for product description is restricted to 30 characters, if some actual product description is 43 characters long, then complete details of the product cannot be maintained. This affects the completeness, accuracy, and correctness data quality dimensions, ultimately affecting data quality. This example shows that data rules impact business performance making the relationship among the data entities and events more complex.

Another scenario where data rules affect business operations arises when an enterprise purchases data from external agencies, that is, the second-party and third-party data. Many enterprises assume that data quality will be high when purchased from agencies such as AC Nielsen, IHS, Bloomberg, and others. But unfortunately, that is not necessarily the case as data vendors suffer from the same aging, context mismatch, field overuse, and other data quality issues.

Data Quality Is Time-Sensitive

Although many business processes are asynchronous and discrete, the timing of data availability (i.e., timeliness and concurrency data quality dimensions) might cause data quality issues. For example, let us imagine a purchase order (PO) is created with INCO (International Commercial) term CIF (Cost, Insurance & Freight). International Commercial Terms are pre-defined commercial terms that make international trade easier by helping traders in different countries understand one another. Between the time that the PO is issued to the supplier and the time that the goods are delivered by the supplier, supplier negotiations could result in the INCO term being changed to CFR (Cost & Freight). Consequently, the accounting teams will potentially have a challenge reconciling the INCO term codes between different documents – that is, the purchase order and delivery.

Inherently, data values change over time. For example, it is estimated that 60% of the phone records in the United States change each year. If the data records related to the telephone fields are not kept current, this affects data quality. Furthermore, the goals and strategies of the companies also change as they evolve; they start, grow, acquire, rename, go bankrupt, and spin-off. If regular data validation is not performed, the quality of data degrades. As mentioned in Chapter 3, in an average company data quality degrades between 2 and 7% every month.

Results of Data Quality Improvements Are Normally Transient

When businesses change and evolve, data quality degrades if it is not controlled. Factors such as business needs, entity relationships, metadata definitions, data structures, and system configurations continuously change over time. Basically, data quality degrades if it is not controlled or governed regularly. The data quality degradation is typically gradual, if checks to measure and control data quality are not maintained throughout the entire data lifecycle. Data governance plays a key role in data quality, and data quality initiatives cannot be successful without effective data governance. Data governance is part of the Sustain phase of the DARS methodology and is covered in detail in Chapter 10.

Data Conversion and Migration Issues

In *Data Quality Assessment*, author Arkady Maydanchik writes, "Databases in business enterprises rarely begin their lives empty" (Maydanchik 2007). Often, data origination and capture start from data conversion or migration from some legacy database. While the main purpose of data conversion and migration is to get data into the enterprise system, data conversion and migration projects are typically a risky, time-consuming, and complex undertaking. To manage the project constraints, often during data conversion and migration, populating the database becomes the main focus and very little attention is paid to the data quality aspects such as the business rules, data rules, and user-interface layers.

Interface Feeds

Interface feeds, i.e., the data integration feeds – especially the ones that are big and regular data exchanges between OLTP systems – are also a big reason for poor data quality. Two main interface feed issues that impact data quality are:

1. System Changes. When the source OLTP system is subject to system changes, updates, and upgrades, the data structures and data models usually change. This in turn impacts the data feeds from the source IT system to multiple target OLTP systems. If the development is in the namespace

of the company, there is no major risk in managing these development objects. But if the custom development is in the product namespace, there is a risk of losing the changes during the product upgrade. In this regard, a namespace uniquely identifies a set of names so that there is no ambiguity when development objects having different origins but potentially the same names are mixed together in one computing environment.

2. Automation. Interface feeds quickly spread poor-quality data, as they are normally automated and work on large data sets. Any bad data quality that gets into the source system will invariably trickle down to the target system(s). These "bad" records will be used in business activities in the target system, resulting in more data getting corrupted. This impact is more severe when the quality of reference data and master data is impacted, as these data elements are used in creating the transactional data.

System Upgrades

Often data elements are used for the wrong purposes, not populated completely, not converted into a form acceptable to the system, and so on. Basically, during manual data entry, users try to force-feed data by adjusting the data rules. Business processes and IT programs rely on these anomalies causing potential data quality issues. For example, as discussed earlier a piece of programming code might exist to take the first three characters of the customer's telephone number to assign the tax code. However, during system upgrades, especially on the COTS (commercial-off-the-shelf) systems, programs are designed and tested against what data is really expected to be and not what data really is.

Manual Errors

One of the biggest sources of poor data quality is the data that is entered, edited, and manipulated by people manually. In this regard, the most common cause of poor data quality is manual data entry. Traditionally, manual entry involved transferring data from various documents into transactional applications, which the record books. Manual data entry normally originates from cumbersome and inconsistent data entry forms, paper-based documents, and other manual processes. Manual errors can also be caused by lack of training or simple carelessness. But in some cases, data curation will take a tremendous amount of time, in an effort to improve the accessibility and timeliness of data quality dimensions. A common example of a place with much room for errors is when multiyear, multimillion-dollar supplier contracts are entered with significant numbers of clauses, terms, and conditions. In a survey by TDWI (The Data

Warehousing Institute), 76% of the survey respondents said, "Manual data entry is the number-one source of poor data quality" (Eckerson 2002).

Poor Database Design

Data integrity cannot be ensured if the database design itself is poor. No amount of data governance will help if the database design is poor and poor database design is very common in custom databases in the bespoke systems. The following aspects, if not appropriately addressed, will result in adversely affecting data integrity. These aspects are:

- **Data normalization.** Normalization is the process of refining tables, keys, columns, and relationships to create an efficient database specifically for querying and searching. It refines the data definitions, eliminates repeating groups, and unnecessary dependencies.
- **Data Integrity.** The main purpose of normalization is to minimize redundancy and remove potential anomalies coming from data insert, update, and delete operations. However, to ensure that the database content is accurate and consistent, data integrity is very important. Data integrity can be enabled with the proper use of the four elements – entity integrity, referential integrity, domain integrity, and business integrity rules, as discussed in Chapter 3.

Improper Data Purging and Cleansing

Data purging is the erasing and removing of data from the storage space. As said before, data is interpreted and consumed in many ways. In most cases the use and users of the data element might not be clearly defined. So, the data purging and cleaning initiative might begin after consulting only a selective group of stakeholders and ignoring a majority of the stakeholders.

 KEY TAKEAWAYS

Following are the key takeaways of this chapter.

- Data decay can be (1) physical such as server crashes, hard disk corruptions, data records getting purged without a trace, and more. (2) Logical data decay which impacts the business more and is common occurs due to the compromises to the data quality dimensions.

▪ Understanding the root causes for the logical data decay will help firms improve data quality and prevent the problem from recurring. Finding the root cause of the problem is important because, if the right problem is not identified and solved, one will never be able to eliminate the real cause. In fact, root cause analysis (RCA) should be the first step or the beginning of the problem-solving process.

▪ By conducting the RCA and addressing root causes, enterprises can prevent data quality issues from recurring, thereby saving time and money for the company.

▪ The most common tools that can help to identify the root causes of data quality issues are:
  1. Affinity Diagram
  2. Failure Mode and Effects Analysis (FMEA)
  3. Fishbone Diagram
  4. The 5-Whys

▪ Based on literature surveys and secondary research, there are 16 root causes of poor data quality. The 16 root cases discussed here are some of the most commonly found ones in the industry, and it is no means a complete list. But the four RCA techniques discussed in this chapter should help to identify the data quality root causes that are specific to the organization.

 ## CONCLUSION

When you have a broken wrist, will painkillers work? You need to get into the root cause of the issue to heal the bones properly. But what do you do when you have a data quality problem? Do you jump straight in and treat the symptoms, or do you analyze deeply to check whether there is actually a deeper problem? Basically, if you only fix the symptoms – what you see on the surface – the problem will almost certainly return, and need fixing over and over again. Root Cause Analysis (RCA) helps to answer the question of why the problem occurred in the first place, to identify the origin of a problem and to find the root cause of the problem, so as to prevent the problem from recurring. The 16 root causes discussed here are some of the most commonly found data quality issues in the industry. In addition, data teams can apply the four RCA techniques discussed in this chapter to further identify the root causes specific to the organization.

REFERENCES

Eckerson, W. (2002). Data quality and the bottom line. TDWI. http://download.101com .com/pub/tdwi/Files/DQReport.pdf.

Maydanchik, A. (May 2007). *Data quality assessment*. Technics Publications.

Saves, A. (January 2008). Firms need data stewards to optimize business initiatives. http://wwwcomputerweekly.com/news/2240084684/Firms-need-data-stewards-to-optimise-business-initiatives.

Southekal, P. (2017). *Data for business performance*. Technics Publications.

CHAPTER FIVE

Data Lifecycle and Lineage

 INTRODUCTION

Data in business has a definite life span and follows a defined lifecycle. The data life cycle (DLC) is the entire period of time that data exists in the organization. This lifecycle encompasses all the stages that the data goes through. The DLC encompasses the end-to-end effective and efficient management of business data with appropriate policies and procedures throughout its lifecycle. A thorough understanding and analysis of the DLC is needed for the following reasons:

1. Data is a reflection of reality in business. Just like a business changes as it evolves, data also changes. The data status changes at different stages of the DLC. A good understanding of the data is essential, and DLC provides that understanding.
2. Know the key stakeholders and what stages in the data lifecycle they add value to data.

3. Understand the risks involved in data management from origination to archival and purging.

In this regard, the data lifecycle can be seen from two main views: business-enabled DLC and IT-enabled DLC.

 BUSINESS-ENABLED DLC STAGES

The DLC is the entire period of time that data exists in the IT landscape of the organization. Most data from a business perspective goes through eight key stages: origination, capture, validation, processing, distribution, aggregation, interpretation, and consumption. The following section discusses the eight key business-enabled DLC stages.

Origination

In most cases, business data originates in an unstructured or native format – text, image, audio, and video – for operations and compliance. The source of origin can be in two main forms: humans or machines. When data is originated by humans, it could be directly from a single person or from a group as a workflow mechanism. When the business processes are discrete, data origination is manual in nature and the data is discrete. Examples are contracts and orders. But some business data is also originated by machines.

When data originates from machines, the rate and the volume at which the data originates is significantly higher than with manual means. Machine-generated data is the lifeblood of the Internet of Things.For example, trackers set up on vehicles for driver behavior tracking is used by the auto insurance companies. The data from IoT devices (smart home devices) is used by utility companies to connect and engage with customers on their utilities consumption. The data from wearable devices reveal the physical and chemical properties of the human body to evaluate wellness.

Capture

Once there is a need to originate data, that data needs to be captured. Whether facilitated by humans or machines, data origination is the process of acquiring new data or updating existing data in a machine-readable format. The data in most cases is formatted and saved in databases of IT systems as structured data. But recently, data has increasingly been captured in unstructured formats in IT systems. Regardless, data capturing can be manual or automatic.

1. Manual data capture (MDC) is appropriate for low-volume data records that need to be captured on an ad hoc basis. Furthermore, MDC is usually performed when human discretion is needed for data capture.
2. When data volume is big, defined, and predictable, data is usually captured automatically into computer systems using automatic identification and data capture (AIDC) technologies. These mechanisms include bar codes, RFID (radio-frequency identification), smart cards, video and audio recognition software, and so on. While some of the data that is automatically captured is intentional, a significant amount of data is "shadowed." A data shadow is a data set that is a by-product of the automatic data capture process. The data in the shadow normally includes data pertaining to authentication, sensors, communication metadata, and more. Because of this high volume of data, AIDC technologies contribute significantly towards increased data volumes.

Chapter 9 looks at these two methods when capturing transactional data.

Validation

Once the data persists in IT systems after capture, it must be validated. Data validation is the process of ensuring that the computer programs in the IT system operate on quality data. Some amount of data validation (especially for structured data) happens during data capture, by ensuring adherence to the data dictionary or metadata. But a significant amount of validation is carried out by the transactional application programs before the data is ready for processing. Furthermore, if the data element is subject to internal or industry standards, validation could be performed manually. For example, the CASS (Coding Accuracy and Support System) software utility developed by the USPS (US Postal Service) validates U.S. postal address to USPS specifications before the address is saved in the system.

Processing

Data processing involves systematic actions such as classifying, sorting, searching, and calculating, such that the data is transformed into meaningful or useful information. Processing is usually the first step in realizing meaningful patterns from raw data. The degree of effective in data processing depends on the data type (nominal, ordinal, or numeric), and data types were discussed in the "Business Data Views" section in Chapter 2. If the data type is numeric, then the effectiveness of statistical processing will he high especially when deriving insights from analytics. In other words, the selection of the data science algorithm depends on the data type. For example, if the independent and dependent variables in regression are of numeric data type, then multiple liner regression is used. If the variables for correlation are numeric or categorical data types, then tetrachoric correlation or Cramer's V correlation is used.

The majority of the data processing takes place in transactional application systems like the ERP and CRM systems where the data is often in a structured format. Processing structured data is fairly straightforward, since the processing logic is managed by the application programs. In contrast, unstructured data requires structuring of the data to the appropriate data model before it can be processed. From a technical perspective, there are various methods of data processing:

1. Single User Programming. It is usually done by a single person for a specific application.
2. Multi-Processing. In this type of data processing two or more processors work on the same dataset simultaneously to produce a cohesive output.
3. Batch Processing. In batch data processing the data is collected and processed in batches, and it is mostly used when the data is homogenous and in large quantities.
4. Real-Time Processing. In this technique, the user has direct contact with the system. This technique is also known as the direct mode or the interactive mode technique and is useful to perform one task.
5. On-Line Processing. This technique facilitates the entry and execution of data directly. This method does not store data for processing. The technique validates data as it is entered to ensure that only right data is captured in the databases. This technique is widely used for web applications.
6. Time-Sharing Processing. This is another form of online data processing that facilitates several users to share the system resources. This technique is adopted when results are needed quickly.
7. Distributed Processing. In this type of data processing, multiple individual IT systems work on the same programs, functions, or systems to provide the required capability.

All these techniques have their use-cases. But if in today's data-centric environment, batch, real-time, online and distributed processing systems are most widely used for data processing.

Distribution

Data distribution or integration is the process of bringing together diverse data from various source systems in different formats for a unified view. Data distribution or data integration covers three key functions: Transfer, Transpose, and Orchestrate.

1. Transfer of data is moving or transferring data from one system to another. For example, transferring sales quotes data from the CRM to the ERP system for order processing.
2. Transpose of data is converting data from one format to another format. For example, transposing price data from Canadian dollars to U.S. dollars as the financial reports need to comply with GAPP requirements in the U.S. headquarters.
3. Orchestration of data is the sequencing of all the data integration tasks in a way that reflects their relationships and dependencies. Data orchestration solutions are based on the concept of a DAG (direct acyclic graph) for the management of data integration jobs and the pertinent documentation.

Data distribution or data integration can be delivered in eight ways and these eight techniques will be discussed in Chapter 9.

Aggregation

This step combines large quantities of data from different sources into one canonical database by consolidating (or "aggregating") large quantities of data. The objective here is for analytics and decision making by providing visibility for businesses to measure and manage performance. The purposes of consolidating data are to reduce duplicates, introduce standardization, perform validity checks, and clean erroneous data, populate missing values, and ultimately present data in a unified (and thereby more valuable) form.

In this context, a Market Pulse survey commissioned by Matillion and IDG found that companies are drawing from an average of over 400 different systems to derive insights at the enterprise level (King 2019). During data aggregation the application's logic is normally skipped, with data movement carried out by extract, transform, and load (ETL) technologies directly from the databases. The products of consolidation or the ETL process are typically data marts, data warehouses (DWH), data lakes and data lakehouses that go on to be used by business intelligence (BI) and analytics systems.

Interpretation

Data interpretation can be defined as the combination of three elements: analysis, synthesis, and evaluation.

1. Analysis ensures that when the information is broken down, it can be traced back to the individual data elements. Also, analysis is on historical performance, unlike analytics, which is both historical and futuristic.
2. Synthesis is the process of building information from data – namely, finding patterns.
3. Finally, evaluation includes combining the outcomes from synthesis and analysis to make judgments for a given purpose.

Consumption

This DLC stage is all about realizing results from data. As mentioned before, business data is used for three main purposes: operations, compliance, and decision making. Data is consumed in operations so that companies can run their daily operations. The use of data for compliance ensures that businesses are abiding by industry standards, security policies, and government laws and regulations. From the decision-making perspective, data consumption includes deriving insights, visualizing data and insights, making decisions, and suggesting recommendations for business actions.

On data visualization, data and insights can be viewed in three different forms:

1. Transactional reports coming from the OLTP systems
2. BI reports, or analytics (predictive and prescriptive) reports coming from the OLAP systems
3. Dashboards coming from both OLTP and OLAP systems

 ## IT BUSINESS-ENABLED DLC STAGES

Each of the above eight business DLC activities are performed in IT systems that involve secure data storage, which includes secure backup, archival, purging, and disaster recovery (DR). Hence, we can add two more functions to the DLC: storage and security. Whenever data is used in business processes, security and storage must accompany it at every stage of the process.

Storage

Data storage is the physical data storage in IT systems. There are two main kinds of data storage: primary and secondary.

1. Primary data storage refers to the memory storage that is directly accessible to the processor, including internal memory (registers), fast memory (cache), and main memory (RAM) placed on the motherboard. Data in the primary memory is volatile and is non-removable.
2. Secondary storage involves storing data for long-term use. Secondary memory structures are non-volatile devices that hold data until it is deleted or overwritten. Common examples of secondary storage devices are magnetic disks, optical disks, hard disks, flash drives, and magnetic tapes.

Storage also covers the archiving and purging of data. Archiving is transferring data from active use to inactive use; purging is permanently deleting data from storage. Because the cost of storage is dropping dramatically every year, and compliance requirements are regularly becoming more stringent, enterprises are archiving data more often than purging it. Overall, once data is no longer useful for production environments, it can be moved to less costly storage, whether that is on premises or in the cloud.

Security

Data security entails protecting data from destructive forces and unauthorized users or systems, in order to maintain its integrity. From the IT perspective, data security encompasses measures on authentication, authorization, and confidentiality, with the ultimate goal of preventing unauthorized access and protecting data from corruption and loss. Data security is applicable whether the data is in motion or at rest. Data security is covered in detail in Chapter 11.

In total, there are 10 DLC activities; eight of them are focused on business and two are IT-focused. The 10 DLC activities – business and IT are shown in Figure 5.1.

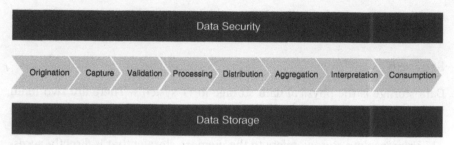

FIGURE 5.1 DLC Activities

 DATA LINEAGE

Closely related to the DLC is the concept of data lineage. Data lineage is the flow of data, from origination to consumption. Data lineage includes all the changes data underwent in the DLC, that is, how the data was transformed, what attributes and values changed, when, and more. According to DAMA, "Data lineage is a description of the pathway from the data source to their current location and the alterations made to the data along the pathway." Basically, data lineage, that is, data's "line of descent" is the process of understanding data as it flows from the source to consumption (DAMA-DMBOK 2017).

Knowing the lineage of data is important because transactional and canonical systems – including the data warehouses, data lakes, and data lakehouses – contain diverse datasets, in different formats that come from a wide variety of sources at a rapid pace. For example, data lakes may contain images, video files, log files, documents, raw text, or files in formats such as JSON, CSV, Apache Parquet, or Optimized Row Columnar (ORC) formats. In this complex data landscape, if one is required to track the origins and the potential changes to the data in the flow, it would be very difficult to do so manually. Basically, data lineage focuses on validating data accuracy and consistency by looking at the upstream and downstream systems in the data flow to discover anomalies and helping to correct them.

So, how do the data lineage solutions work? In general, a solid metadata or data dictionary is the prerequisite for proper management of data lineage practices. There are different data lineage techniques such as pattern-based lineage, data tagging, parsing, and so on. All these techniques look at both the metadata and the actual data itself to trace the data issue. Overall, effective data lineage encompasses the relationships, virtual datasets, transformations, extracts, and queries for full visibility on where critical data objects are – especially the ones that affect the business KPIs.

Why is data lineage important? What value does it offer to the business? Data lineage can help to visualize the end-to-end journey of data in the entire DLC. Given that data integration is a significant part of data engineering, data lineage provides the audit trail of the data in the entire DLC. Data lineage not only helps you fix issues, it also enables you to ensure the integrity of data by tracking changes, how they were performed, and who made them, and so on. Regulations such as GDPR, CCPA, and Solvency II have data lineage requirements. Specifically, data lineage helps in:

1. Better understanding the impact of data on regulations

    The accounting and regulatory framework in companies needs to show evidence of how data flows when used in reporting and analytics. Data lineage provides insights into the impact of the changes on data. Data lineage adoption is an important step to meeting compliance with regulations such as the U.S. Health Insurance Portability and Accountability Act (HIPAA), the U.S. Sarbanes-Oxley Act (SOX), and the EU General Data Protection Regulation (GDPR).

2. Visualizing the dataflows

    As every enterprise becomes more data driven, collaboration between finance, risk, and IT departments in the organization is very important. Data lineage can uncover the data flows with great visuals and thus create a greater transparency to relevant stakeholders.

3. Audit trials

    Today, in the reporting environment there is a shift from using reports with aggregated data towards reports that are granular or detailed. Businesses are often challenged to trace final reporting figures back to the initial source of the data and to identify the data transformation along the DLC.

4. ML impact

    Data lineage provides insights on the impacts of machine learning (ML) due to model drift. *Model drift* refers to the performance degradation of ML model due to changes in data and relationships between input and output variables.

Overall, data lineage enhances the control of the data transformation and reporting processes. This in turn will result in improved quality of data and improved quality of the discussions not only, with the regulators and accounting auditors, but also with internal business stakeholders.

KEY TAKEAWAYS

Following are the key takeaways of this chapter.

- Data quality is fundamentally a business problem and not an IT problem.
- Data in business has a defined life span and follows a defined lifecycle. The data lifecycle (DLC) is the entire period of time that data exists in the organization to serve business objectives.
- A proper understanding of the DLC is needed for three key reasons:
  1. Data is a reflection of reality in business. A good understanding of the DLC provides the manner in which data changes at different stages in its life.
  2. To know the business and IT stakeholders and at what stages in the DLC they add value to data.
  3. To understand the risks involved in data governance and data management, from origination to archival and purging.
- DLC, which has 10 functions, can be split into two ways: eight business functions and two IT functions.
- Closely related to DLC is data lineage. Data lineage is the flow of data, from origination to consumption. Data lineage includes all the changes data underwent in the DLC, that is, how the data was transformed, what attributes and values changed, when, and more. Data lineage helps to visualize the end-to-end journey of data in the entire DLC.

 CONCLUSION

At the core, data quality is a business problem and not an IT problem. With increased amounts of data captured, businesses should understand the root cause of data quality issues and manage the data in its entire lifecycle. Data lifecycle (DLC) covers the origins of data and where the data transforms and moves over time thereby helping firms understand the lineage of data and its impact. Apart from tracing errors in the relevant systems, DLC and data lineage help firms minimize the risk of data breaches and prevent sensitive and critical data from being misused.

REFERENCES

DAMA-DMBOK. (August 2017). *Data management body of knowledge.* 2nd ed. Technics Publications.

King, T. (November 2019). Companies are drawing from over 400 different data sources on average. https://solutionsreview.com/data-integration/companies-are-drawing-from-over-400-different-data-sources-on-average/.

## CHAPTER SIX

Profiling for Data Quality

 ## INTRODUCTION

In the previous chapters, we discussed the fact that data is a valuable business asset that can transform business performance when the quality is high. While many companies are plagued with poor data quality, not many have a good understanding of the level of data quality. However, before you fix the data quality, you need to have a good understanding of where you stand so that you know what to fix. So, how can one can one objectively assess the quality of the data set? The solution to objectively assess the quality of the data is by profiling the data with the right KPIs (key performance indicators).

A key performance indicator (KPI) is a measurable value that demonstrates how effectively the measurement entity is achieving its key objectives. While designing KPIs in data quality, three key rules are recommended (Southekal 2020):

1. Why do you want to know? How much do you want to know? What is the value of knowing and *not* knowing?
2. Who owns this KPI? Knowing the KPI's ownership is the key to realizing change.
3. Is the KPI owner close to data? If the KPI owner is close to data, that means they are close to the business processes and implementing the change will be much easier.

Broadly, data quality issues, especially logical data decay issues, can be either visible or hidden. Visible data quality problems are easy to see, and solving them creates tangible and quick value creation for the company. But, as you go deeper, visibility quickly decreases. Problems become harder to identify and describe, and eventually the issues become invisible. Invisible problems, which often are substantial, are the root cause of many of the data quality problems. But because of their invisible nature, they often go undiagnosed, despite having a significant impact on business performance. Basically, the visible costs of poor quality are just the tip of the data quality iceberg compared to the deeper invisible costs lurking below the data quality waterline. This is illustrated in Figure 6.1.

FIGURE 6.1 Data Quality Issues

In this regard, data profiling is the discipline for discovering data quality issues – both visible and hidden. Specifically, data profiling is the process of holistically examining, analyzing, and creating useful metrics on the business data to support the discovery of data quality issues, risks, and overall trends. The purpose is to uncover root causes of many data quality issues related to metadata, data structure, data integrity, security, accessibility, timeliness, missing values, and other data quality dimensions.

So, what is the business value of data profiling? Fundamentally, data profiling has two main benefits.

1. Firstly, assessment in any field is a key component of learning and understanding. Assessment of data quality helps in evaluation, making judgments about performance, and improving upon it.
2. Secondly, data profiling helps to save money by implementing an important 1-10-100 quality rule. As discussed earlier, $1 spent on prevention will save $10 on correction and $100 on failure costs.

CRITERIA FOR DATA PROFILING

Data profiling provides visibility for businesses to measure and manage performance. But when there are so many different data types, what data should be profiled? Basically, measurements drive business behavior, results, and the organization culture (Southekal 2020). However, the most critical aspect in measurement is identifying the entity, that is, the data element for measurement. Should it be reference data (on business categories), master data (on business entities), or transactional data (on business events)?

Overall, compared to reference data and master data, transactional data is more suited for measurement and for improving the business performance. Why? Here are five main reasons why the transactional data should be considered for data profiling or assessment.

1. Businesses are often constrained with resources like capital, time, skills, machinery, and more for running their operations. Hence organizations consume these resources very judiciously. Transactional data represent the consumption of business resources and provide insights to the business on how these resources are managed.
2. Transactional data represents monetary value, thereby impacting the financial position of the business. Reference data and master data elements

do not carry any financial value. For example, there might be 500,000 customers (master data) in the CRM system, but how many of these customers actually gave orders (transactional data) in the past 12 months, given that purchase orders issued by the customers bring revenue to the company?

3. Transactional data has a twofold effect in accounting, that is, for every value received, there is an equal value given. This means compliance to accounting standards such as IFRS (International Financial Reporting Standards) and GAPP (Generally Accepted Principles and Practices) is based on transactional data. Reference data and master data elements do not have much compliance needs except on data privacy, so measuring transactional data is measuring the level of compliance.

4. Transactional data is also a binding document for counterparty relationships. Every transaction is between two parties, and the counterparty is the other party in the transaction. Transactional data serves as a legal record, as in the case of invoices, orders, remittance advice, shipments, and more between the counterparties. Hence measuring transactional data helps to assess the relationships businesses have with different stakeholders – internal and external.

5. Lastly, transactional data promotes performance comparison and decision making. Striving for measurement is appropriate where values associated with the data attributes are quantitative, and transactional data attributes are typically quantitative in nature. Specifically, assessment KPIs like the centrality KPIs and variation KPIs need numeric nature, and transactional data offers attributes that are numeric or quantitative in nature. This enables transactional data to acquire the statistical capabilities required for computation, comparison, and decision making.

So, once the transactional data type is selected based on the above five criteria, how can businesses leverage the transactional data to measure and manage business performance? There are many types of transactional data in a company, but not all of them provide the same business value. So, what are the recommendations to select the right transactional data element that has a high correlation toward improving business performance?

Firstly, the transactional data selected should be strongly tied to one or more of the three strategic goals of the enterprise, that is, to increase profitability, reduce expenses, or reduce risk. In other words, the transactional data selected should provide a strong business impact. Research has shown that having a well-defined goal can help in taking control of the business's direction and increase the chances of achieving business targets (Southekal 2020). Performance frameworks such as Balanced Scorecard (BSC) and Goal-Question-Metric (GQM) can be leveraged in formulating a concrete KPI-driven goal statement (Southekal 2014).

Secondly, the selected transactional data element should be under the influence and control of the business. For example, the price of crude oil is a piece of transactional data for an oil company, as price is a function of time. But the crude prices are determined by global supply, demand, and geopolitics over which businesses have no or very little influence and control. So, trying to measure the crude oil prices would have very little business utility. On the other hand, the company has a good control on the purchase orders issued to the vendor, as it can directly control and influence decisions pertaining to the items, quantities, price, vendor, and so on, so measuring the performance of the purchase orders that are under the influence and control of the organization is preferred.

Thirdly, the selected transactional data should lend itself to be optimized; it should enable itself for continuous measurement of the business processes. In other words, the transactional data selected should not be on the non-operating activities, that is, activities that are outside the company's usual activities. If the transactional data does not get factored in the operating income or EBIT (earnings before interest and taxes) calculation, measuring it might not be very useful. Today, the rules of business are changing very rapidly. If businesses are slow to adapt the insights from data and analytics quickly and efficiently, they will ultimately fail. Hence measuring business performance on transactions should not be a one-time event; it should be a continuous process so that the business becomes optimized.

Fourthly, if there is a conflict in the selection of one transactional data from multiple transactional data elements, the selected transactional data should be the one with the highest co-efficient of variation (CV) as CV offers scope for improvement. CV is the measure of the relative variability and will be discussed in detail in the following sections. Technically, CV is a measure of the dispersion around the mean. In business terms the CV determines the amount of volatility or variability. Business hates variation. A high CV offers an opportunity to reduce variability business process, reduce cost, and improve quality.

In this context, profiling of data, especially the transactional data with the right KPIs, has two main measurement areas: centrality measures and variation measures. The following section discusses these two areas in detail. To explain these measurement concepts and associated KPIs better, we will use a sample sales order data set of a transportation company as shown below.

Sales Order Identifier	1	2	3	4	5	6	7	8	9
$ Amount in '000s	2	4	3	3	1	6	4	24	7

Before going further, we discussed in Chapter 2 that the data types from an analytics or measurement perspective can be broadly classified into three types:

1. Nominal for text and categorical data
2. Ordinal for ordered or ranked data
3. Continuous for numeric or quantitative data

These data types are important because the statistical techniques to calculate or compute the measure of centrality and variation are dependent on the data type.

 ## DATA PROFILING TECHNIQUES FOR MEASURES OF CENTRALITY

A centrality KPI or a central tendency KPI is a single number that best represents an entire data set where the data set can either be a sample data or the entire population. Technically centrality is a single number that represents the center point or location of the given data set. The three common measures of centrality are:

1. Mode
2. Median
3. Mean

Mode

The mode is the most frequently occurring value on the list. In the given sales order example, the mode is 3 because the sales amount occurs twice which is more than any other number. The mode is the least used of the measures of central tendency even though it can be used when dealing with any data type – nominal, ordinal, or numeric data.

Median

The median is the middle value in a list ordered from smallest to largest or vice versa. In the above sales order example, the data when arranged from smallest to largest will be 1, 2, 3, 3, 4, 5, 6, 7, 24. The middle value in this list is the fifth data element, which is 4. So, the median of the sales data is 4. The median is a very useful measure of central tendency for skewed distributions or distributions with outliers. For example, the median is often used as a measure of central tendency for income distributions, which are generally highly skewed.

Mean

Technically, there are three types of mean: arithmetic mean, geometric mean, and harmonic mean.

The arithmetic mean is determined by adding the numbers and dividing the sum by the number of numbers in the list. This is what is most often meant by an average. In the above example, the arithmetic mean or the average of the sales order value = $(2 + 4 + 3 + 3 + 1 + 6 + 5 + 24 + 7)/9 = 54/9 = 6$, that is, \$6,000. While the arithmetic mean takes into consideration all the values of the data set, the mean value can easily get distorted if the data set contains outliers or extreme values.

Along with arithmetic mean, there are two others types of means – geometric mean and harmonic mean. The geometric mean is calculated as the nth root of the product of all values, where N is the number of values. If the data contains only two values, the square root of the product of the two values is the geometric mean. For three values, the cube-root is used, and so on. For example, if the data values are 3 and 8, the geometric mean is the square root of $(3*8) = 4.90$. If the data values are 2, 3, and 5, the geometric mean is $(2*3*5)^{1/3} = 3.1$.

The harmonic mean, also known as weighted average mean, is calculated as the number of values divided by the sum of the reciprocal of the values. For example, if the data values are 3 and 8, the harmonic mean is $2/(1/3 + 1/8) = 4.36$. If the data values are 2, 3, and 5, the harmonic means is $3/(1/2 + 1/3 + 1/5) = 2.9$

Now that there are three different ways of calculating the average or mean of a data set. Which one should be used? Even though the arithmetic mean is the most commonly used mean, it assumes that each data value is independent. But the arithmetic mean may not be appropriate in cases where the outliers are included in the analysis.

On the other hand, if the values are dependent on each other and have large fluctuations, it is better to use the geometric mean. Applications of the geometric mean are common in finance, where it is frequently used when dealing with percentages to calculate growth rates and returns on a portfolio of stocks. Harmonic mean is often used in calculating the weighted-average values such as the price-earnings ratio because it gives equal weight to each data point. However, if the data contains negative or zero values, then both the geometric and harmonic means cannot be used.

Overall, of the three types of mean, arithmetic mean is the most popular mean. This is because, one of the key assumptions of statistical analysis is that data values are independent and arithmetic mean meets this condition. Also, the arithmetic mean is simple to calculate, and very easy to understand, and most importantly includes all the values in the data set for its calculation. So, going forward, the term *mean* is assumed to be the arithmetic mean unless stated otherwise.

As seen above there are three different values for the measure of centrality. The arithmetic mean gave a value of 6, the value from the median was 4, and the mode was 3. But, which one do we actually use as one central value? Fundamentally, using the results or the values of the three KPIs depends on the assumptions and dependencies. The following table summarizes the three measures of centrality and the relevant assumptions and dependencies.

	Pros	Cons
Mean	▪ Applicable to continuous or numeric data ▪ Provides a unique value ▪ Values are independent in nature	▪ Value is affected by outliers, that is, extreme values ▪ Data should be continuous or numeric ▪ Geometric mean and harmonic mean cannot be used if one of the values in the data set is zero
Median	▪ Unaffected by outliers, that is, extreme values ▪ Provides a unique value	▪ The value obtained does not reflect the entire data set ▪ Data should be continuous or numeric
Mode	▪ Good for all three types of data: nominal, ordinal, and continuous or numeric	▪ Value does not reflect the entire data set ▪ Cannot provide a unique value

DATA PROFILING TECHNIQUES FOR MEASURES OF VARIATION

While the measures of centrality give one single value to explain the distribution of data, often that one single value cannot provide much insight on the data set. While central tendency tells you where most of the data points lie, variability summarizes how far apart your points are from each other. A low dispersion or variation indicates that the data points tend to be clustered tightly around the center, while a high dispersion signifies that data points tend to fall further away. In the context of data quality, variability refers to the inconsistencies in the data.

According to quality guru Edwards Deming, understanding variation is the key to success in quality and business. Data sets can have the same central tendency but different levels of variability or vice versa. Together, the measures of centrality and variation give you a complete picture of the data. As an example, let us look at the processing times of claims handled by two different insurance claims agents in Figure 6.2. On both data sets, the arithmetic mean, median, and mode values are the same. So, who is a better claims agent just based on the centrality value of processing times? This is where the measures of variation come into the picture.

Claims Agent 1	
#	Processing Time
1	7
2	8
3	12
4	9
5	10
6	8
Mean	9
Mode	8
Median	8.5

Claims Agent 2	
#	Processing Time
1	8
2	8
3	16
4	3
5	9
6	10
Mean	9
Mode	8
Median	8.5

FIGURE 6.2 Centrality Measures

Variability, that is, difference between the expected and an actual situation is everywhere. The auto insurance claims values aren't exactly the same each time. In a manufacturing company, the parts that come off an assembly line often have different dimensions. The wait times to get service from a bank teller generally vary. While some degree of variation is unavoidable, too much inconsistency or variation can affect the reliability of operations. Fundamentally, businesses need predictability or certainty to run the business. If a manufactured part deviates too much from specifications, it won't function as intended. If the claims amount has a large variation, processing times can also vary as more due diligence is needed on large claims amount.

Basically, variation is undesirable in business as the market is constantly evaluating the firm's services and products to determine how well they conform to the standards. Variation occurs due to two main reasons.

1. Common causes variation is inherent in a process. Addressing the common causes of variation requires improvements to the process: for example, a claims processing analyst taking a longer time to complete a regular task compared to other analysts. This shows that there is an issue in the process and the causes could be poor training, lack of skills and tools, and so on.
2. Special cause variation arises because of unusual circumstances and is not an inherent part of a process. The causes are irregular and often beyond one's influence and control, and they could be due to factors such as hurricanes, floods, and so on.

Data is a reflection of the process. A consistent process shows low variation.

INSIGHT

In this context, the common measures or KPIs of variation or spread are:

1. Standard deviation
2. Coefficient of variation

3. Standard error
4. Range
5. Interquartile range (IQR)
6. Variance
7. Kurtosis
8. Skewness
9. Outliers

Standard Deviation

The standard deviation (SD or σ) measures the dispersion of a data set relative to its arithmetic mean. If the data points are further from the mean, there is a higher standard deviation within the data set. Standard deviation is a measure of accuracy. The formula for standard deviation for sample data is

$$\sigma = \sqrt{\frac{\sum_{i}^{n}(x_i - \bar{x})^2}{n-1}}$$

- ▪ Σ = sum of the value in the data set
- ▪ $\bar{x}$ = mean of the sample data set and
- ▪ n is the number of data points in the population. If sample data is selected, the denominator is $n-1$.

Based on this, the insurance claims table to calculate standard deviation is as follows.

Sales Order Identifier	Sales Order Amount in '000s (x)	x-Mean	(x-Mean)²
1	2	−4	16
2	4	−2	4
3	3	−3	9
4	3	−3	9
5	1	−5	25
6	6	0	0
7	4	−2	4
8	24	18	324
9	7	1	1
Mean	6	Sum	392

$$SD = Sqrt\left(392/(9-1)\right) = Sqrt\left(392/8\right) = Sqrt\left(49\right) = 7.0$$

Coefficient of Variation (CV)

Technically the standard deviation (SD) value of 7 doesn't give much information unless it is compared against the standard deviation of another data set. However, when an individual data set needs to be analyzed for variation, the coefficient of variation (CV) comes into the picture. CV measures the relative dispersion of data points in a data set around the mean. In the above example, CV = Standard Deviation/Mean = 7/6 = 1.17. Again, what does this value of 1.17 say?

■ Data sets with a CV close to 0 show a very consistent and stable process.
■ CV values close to 1 are considered to have some amount of variation.
■ CV values of over 10 are considered to have extreme variation and depict an unstable process.

This is the case when we have a sales order data set that is high in variation as the value is 1.17. In the insurance and banking industry, CV is important in investment selection as it represents the risk-to-reward ratio. CV allows investors to determine how much volatility, or risk, is assumed in comparison to the amount of return expected from investments. The lower the CV value, the better risk-return trade-off.

Standard Error

Closely associated with SD is the standard error (SE). SE indicates how much the sample mean would vary if one were to repeat a study using new sample data sets from within a single population. The SE is important because it helps to estimate how well the sample data represents the whole population. So what is the difference between SD and SE? Basically, the SD describes variability within a single sample, while SE estimates the variability across multiple samples within a population (see Figure 6.3). Basically, standard deviation is a measure of accuracy, whereas standard error is a measure of variation.

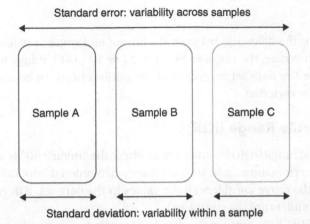

FIGURE 6.3 SD versus SE

But how does one calculate SE? For a given sample size, the standard error equals the standard deviation divided by the square root of the sample size. A high standard error shows that sample means are widely spread around the population mean, while a low standard error shows that sample means are closely distributed around the population mean; that is, the sample is representative of the population.

$$SE = \frac{\sigma}{\sqrt{n}}$$

As an example, in a random sample of 200 retail customers, the mean sales order amount is $550 and the standard deviation is $180. In this case, the sample is the 200 customers, while the population is all customers in the region. The standard error reflects on average how much each sales order amount differs from the mean sample sales order value of $550. The SE is 180/Sqrt (200) = 180/14.1 = 12.8. This value shows that the mean sales order of the entire population from a random sample of 200 customers is 550 ± 12.8.

Another way of looking at standard error and standard deviation is that standard error is a measure of the precision in the sample data, while the standard deviation is the measure of the accuracy in the data. Overall, if the data set has a low standard deviation and a low standard error, then the data set is considered to be of good quality, as the variation is low.

Range

The range is the difference between the largest and smallest values in a set of values. In this case, the range is 24 – 1 = 23 or $23,000. Range is considered when the entire data set regardless of the outliers needs to be considered for assessing the variation.

Interquartile Range (IQR)

Interquartile range (IQR) is a measure of where the "middle 50" is in a data set. The IQR describes the middle 50% of values when ordered from lowest to highest. While the range considers all the values in the data set, IQR is a measure where the outliers are not considered.

To find the IQR, arrange the data in ascending or descending order. Then find the median (middle value) of the lower and upper half of the data. These values are quartile 1 (Q1) and quartile 3 (Q3). The IQR is the difference between Q3 and Q1. In our example, the sales order data when arranged from smallest to largest will be 1, 2, 3, 3, 4, 5, 6,7, 24. The median or Q2 is 4. Q1, the middle value of the lower half of the data, is (2+3)/2 = 2.5. Q3, the middle value of the upper half of the data is (6+7)/2 = 6.5. Hence, IQR = Q3 – Q1 = 6.5 –2.5 = 5.

Note that the range for the same data set was 23 and the IQR value is 5. Usage of the range or IQR depends on the assumptions and constraints. If the business considers that 1 and 24 are outliers and should not be considered as regular business process, then IQR should be used. If not, range can be considered when the assumption is that each data point is independent in nature and valid.

Variance

The variance is a numerical measure of how the data values is dispersed around the mean. Variance is the square of standard deviation. The formula for sample variance is:

$$\sigma^2 = \frac{\sum(x - \bar{x})^2}{n - 1}$$

In the above sales order example of a transportation company, variance is square (7) = 49. Again, variance tells the degree of spread in the data set. The more spread in the data, the larger the variance is in relation to the mean.

Kurtosis and Skewness

Normal distribution is the most frequently used data distribution in business. Statistically, it shows that data near the mean are more frequent in occurrence than data far from the mean. Normal distribution data is important and relevant in business for three main reasons.

■ Business phenomena and the pertinent data are often distributed normally.
■ Many kinds of statistical tests assume that the data distribution is normal.
■ Finally, if the mean and standard deviation of a sample data set are known, it is easy to understand the data distribution of the entire population. This means that, for all normal distributions,

1. 68.2% of the observations will appear within plus or minus one standard deviation of the mean;
2. 95.4% of the observations will fall within +/− two standard deviations;
3. 99.7% within +/− three standard deviations.

So, in a given a data set, how can one determine if the data set is normally distributed? Two measures or KPIs, that is, kurtosis and skewness, can help to determine if the data set is normally distributed.

Kurtosis is used to find the presence of outliers in the data. Data sets with high kurtosis tend to have heavy tails, or outliers. Data sets with low kurtosis tend to have light tails and a few outliers. Basically, a large kurtosis is associated with a high level of variation. In this regard, if the kurtosis value of the data set is between +3 and −3, the data set is normally distributed.

The second measure of checking if a data set is normally distributed is skewness. Skewness measures the degree of symmetry of a distribution. When data is symmetrically distributed, the left-hand side, and right-hand side, contain the same number of observations. For example, if the data set has 100 values, then the left-hand side has 50 observations, and the right-hand side has 50 data points. In this regard, if the skewness value is between +0.8 and −0,8, the data set is normally distributed from a normal distribution perspective.

Overall, for an acceptable level of normal distribution, the kurtosis value should be between +3 and −3, and the skewness value should be between +0.8 and −0.8. Manual calculation of kurtosis and skewness value is complex and usually programs such as Analytics Toolpak in Excel, the moments package in R, and SciPy Library in Python are used to calculate these values.

Outliers

Outliers are data points that are far from other data points. In simple terms, they are unusual values in a data set. Even though outliers represent abnormal values, finding the outliers in a data set will help to better understand the data and the business process. Outliers are of three main types:

1. Global Outliers. A data point is considered a global outlier if its value is far outside the entirety of the data set in which it is found.
2. Contextual Outliers. Contextual outliers are data points whose value significantly deviates from other data within the same context.
3. Collective Outliers. A subset of data points within a data set is considered anomalous if those values as a collection deviate significantly from the entire data set, but the values of the individual data points are not themselves anomalous in either a contextual or global sense.

INSIGHT

Outliers are not always bad or undesirable. While they could represent measurement errors, data entry errors, poor sampling, and more, some outliers represent natural variations and carry significant information on the business processes.

For example, if the ecommerce shipment within a certain product type is no more than $1,000 and suddenly there are two shipments of $50,000 each in the span of three days, it is a **global anomaly** because this event has never before occurred in this product's history. A sudden surge in shipments could be a **contextual outlier** if this high volume occurs outside of a known promotional discount or high-volume period like the Christmas season. The credit rating of a company is never a static thing. But if the credit ratings of all companies in the portfolio remained the same for an extended period of time, then that would be a **collective outlier**.

How to find the outliers in the data set? There are two main ways to find outliers – the IQR rule and Z-score rule. The IQR rule states that an observation is an outlier if it has a value 1.5 times greater than the IQR or 1.5 times less than the IQR (see Figure 6.4).

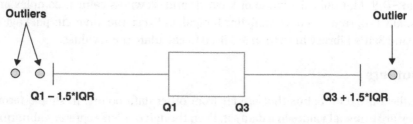

FIGURE 6.4   IQR Rule

For the sales order data example, the IQR is Q3 − Q1 = 6.5 − 2.5 = 4. Now if you multiply IQR by 1.5, you get 1.5 × 4 = 6. Six less than the Q1 is 2.5 − 6 = −4. No data point is less than this value. Also, six greater than the Q3 is 6 + 6.5 = 12.5. However, there is one data value − 24 −that is greater than this. Hence the IQR rule says that this data point 24 is an outlier.

The second method of finding the outlier is the Z-score rule. The Z-score or standard score is the number of standard deviations by which the observed value or data point is above or below the mean. This is the formula:

$$Z = \frac{x - \bar{x}}{\sigma}$$

As per the Z-score rule, any Z-score value greater than 2 or less than −2 is considered to be an outlier. In the claim data table, the mean is 6, and the standard deviation is 7. The Z-score values for each of the sales order data is as shown below.

Sales Order Identifier	Order Amount in '000s	Z = (x-Mean)/SD
1	2	−0.57
2	4	−0.29
3	3	−0.43
4	3	−0.43
5	1	−0.71
6	6	0.00
7	4	−0.29
8	24	2.57
9	7	0.14

Except for the order amount value of 24, whose Z-score is 2.57, none of the other sales order values have a Z-score value that is greater than 2 or less than −2. So, from these two outlier tests, that is, IQR rule and Z-Score rule, the sales order value of 24 is an outlier in the data set.

 ## INTEGRATING CENTRALITY AND VARIATION KPIs

Profiling data typically includes the measures of both centrality and variation measures on the relevant attribute of the transactional data, given that measuring the transactional data offers the most business impact. Here is an example of profiling data using both measures of centrality and variation on a purchase order where the transactional data attribute is the purchase order value (see Figure 6.5).

#	Basic Data KPI	Profile Score
1	Count (rows)	265
2	# Attributes (columns)	6
3	File Size	12 KB
#	Reference Data KPI	Profile Score
1	# of NULL Values	13 (4%)
2	# of Factors/Classes	19
#	Master Data KPI	Profile Score
1	# of Unique Elements	259 (4%)
2	Duplicates on Primary Key	6 (98%)
3	Inconsistent Naming	189 (71%)
4	Blank Values	453 (27%)
#	Transactional Data KPI on PO Value	Profile Score
1	Mean	626.8
2	Median	640
3	Mode	540
4	Standard Deviation	121.06
5	Coefficient of Variation (CV)	1.17
6	Standard Error	24.21
7	Variance	14656
8	Kurtosis	−1.56
9	Skewness	0.39
10	Minimum	380
11	Maximum	860
12	Range	480
13	IQR	327
14	Number of Outliers	18

FIGURE 6.5 Data Profile Sample

What does this report tell? This report has many good data quality attributes such as consistent process (CoV is 1.17), a normally distributed data set to conduct statistical tests (kurtosis is –1.56 and skewness is 0.39), and a low number of outliers (18 out of 265 data records). But the real utility of this data profiling report is in benchmarking and comparing it to the performance standards. The data profiling reports are useful only if you know what you are trying to accomplish. One of the core reasons to use data in business is to measure and improve business performance. If the objective statement or the performance goals – including targets, tolerances, thresholds, and control limits – are missing, these data profiling metrics are of little practical utility or business value. In this backdrop, Dr. Donald Wheeler, an expert in statistical process control (SPC), divided process into four states: the ideal state, the threshold state, the brink of chaos, or the state of chaos. These four states, which are based on control charts, are as shown in Figure 6.6.

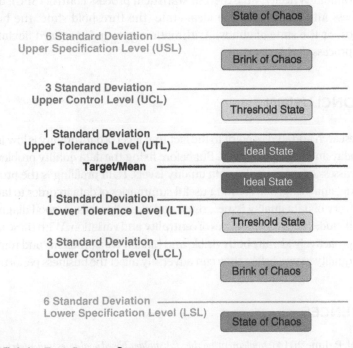

FIGURE 6.6 Four Process States

KEY TAKEAWAYS

Following are the key takeaways of this chapter.

- Before you fix the data quality problem, you need to assess or measure the level of the data quality.
- Fundamentally, data profiling has two main benefits. Firstly, assessment is a key component of learning and understanding. Assessment helps in evaluation, making judgments about performance, and improving upon it. Secondly, data profiling helps to save money by implementing an important 1-10-100 quality rule. If it costs $1 to govern data, it will cost $10 to verify data, and $100 to fix it.
- Holistic data profiling, which is done on the transactional data, has two main measurement aspects – centrality measures and variation measures.
- Centrality KPIs represent the center point or location of the given data set. Variability KPIs describe how far apart your data points from each other.
- Dr. Donald Wheeler, an expert in statistical process control (SPC), divided process into four states: the ideal state, the threshold state, the brink of chaos, or the state of chaos. Arithmetic mean and standard deviation of the process decide the states.

CONCLUSION

All the research and studies point to the fact that level of data quality is low in businesses today and needs to be fixed. But before fixing the data quality problem, one needs to assess or measure the data quality levels. Data profiling is the process of examining, analyzing, and creating useful summaries of data in order to facilitate the discovery of data quality issues, risks, and overall trends. A good diagnosis of the data includes both the measures of centrality and variation. With these metrics one can proactively identify both visible and hidden data problems and remediate the data quality issues, before they can adversely affect the business performance.

REFERENCES

Southekal, P. (June 2014). *Implementing the stakeholder based goal-question-metric (GQM) measurement model for software projects*. Trafford Publishing.
Southekal, P. (April 2020). *Analytics best practices*. Technics Publications.

PART THREE

Realize Phase

## CHAPTER SEVEN

Reference Architecture for Data Quality

 INTRODUCTION

The previous three chapters looked at the analyze phase of the DARS model. Specifically, we analyzed the cases of poor data quality, impact of data quality in its lifecycle, and profiling of data. The next three chapters will be on the **realize phase** of the DARS model. In this chapter we look at the architectural and design patterns that enterprises can adopt to improve data quality. Categorically, this chapter discusses the following topics.

1. Four key frameworks to manage data quality in the DLC
2. Mechanisms to deliver quality data for business results
3. Architectural frameworks to access and manage data in today's distributed and heterogenous system IT landscape

Today, enterprises have different types of data to be managed. These may be structured data, such as relational tables in databases, semi-structured data such as XML documents, and unstructured data such as images, videos, audios,

115

and documents. Architecting for data quality is basically identifying reusable design patterns. This chapter looks at the important architectural frameworks and design patterns or best practices for managing data quality.

 ## OPTIONS TO REMEDIATE DATA QUALITY

Achieving and maintaining data quality needs to be addressed holistically, that is, technically and functionally. Overall, while the technical aspects, which are closely associated with the metadata, are relatively easy to define, the business or functional or the semantic aspects are challenging. From a system architecture perspective, there are four main architectural frameworks associated with data quality management, especially on data definitions.

1. Master data management (MDM)
2. Data integration methods
3. Data wrangling
4. Semantic layer

These four architectural frameworks, which are relevant in the different stages of the data lifecycle (DLC), are technical in nature, and have to be supported with data governance, leadership support, data literacy, and other process, system, and people aspects. Let us discuss these four solution options to remediate data quality.

Master Data Management (MDM)

MDM is a technology-enabled discipline in which business and IT work together to ensure the uniformity, accuracy, stewardship, consistency, and accountability of the enterprise's critical data assets (Gartner 2022). These critical data assets or CDEs are often the master data and reference data: they could be customers, products, vendors, currencies, general ledgers, plants, product categories, and more. The goal of MDM is to provide a trusted, single version of the truth (SVOT) so that organizations do not use multiple and inconsistent versions and definitions of the same data in different systems. The MDM initiative typically starts early in the data lifecycle (DLC) and includes defining the data, formulating the business and data rules, setting up the data standards and workflows, mapping roles to positions, formulating the governance policies, processes, procedures, standards, nomenclature, taxonomies, and so on.

Data Integration

The second possible solution to fix the inconsistency of data in different IT systems is with data integration tools. The data integration process (such as EAI, ESB, Message Queue, and so on) happens in the middle of the DLC. The selection of these data integration tools and practices to address data inconsistencies is based on three key factors.

1. Capabilities of APIs (REST, SOAP, RPC, GraphQL, and more) and their request-response dependencies
2. Number of transactional systems in scope that have inconsistent data definitions that need to be integrated
3. Sequence of Transfer, Transpose, and Orchestration (TTO) in the data integration process
4. Data integration best practices will be covered in detail in Chapter 9.

Data Wrangling

Data wrangling often refers to cleansing the data in the canonical system such as the data warehouse or data mart. Data wrangling – also called data cleaning or data munging – is the process of cleaning and unifying data sets for easy access and analysis. In technical terms, data wrangling is the process of formatting, de-duping, renaming, correcting, improving accuracy, populating empty data attributes, aggregating, blending, and any other data remediation activities that help to improve data quality. The majority of the data cleaning work is manual and contextual, even though stored procedures (set of SQL statements that are reused and shared) and automated routines are often used to support this manual labor.

Semantic Layer

The fourth option to manage data quality issues is using the semantic layer. The semantic layer is a good option if the purpose is deriving insights from analytics. A semantic layer is a business representation of data that helps users access data using common business terms. While the semantic layer per se does not have any data (and hence cannot fix the data quality issue), it maps business data into familiar business terms to offer a unified, consolidated view of data across the organization. The implementation of the semantic layer process happens at the end of the DLC and is generally considered part of "last mile analytics" – the key piece that connects insights to business results. In simple terms, the semantic layer creates the context for actionable analytics.

The semantic layer is a layer of abstraction built on the source data where all the metadata is defined. This hides the complexity of the data, enriches the data model, and becomes simple enough for the business user to understand.

Fundamentally, all these four solutions (MDM, data integration, data wrangling, and semantic layer) are dependent on data mapping to bring consistency. This is the process of creating data element linkages between data attributes. Each of these four methods are dependent on specific use-cases, and the control that one needs to have on data quality in the data lifecycle (DLC). Overall, the MDM is more suitable for compliance and operations. But if the use-case is on deriving insights from analytics, then the semantic layer can be an option to manage the relationships between the various data attributes for a unified business view.

DataOps

DataOps is not a technology, but rather an approach to building, deploying, and consuming data efficiently for improved operations, compliance, and analytics.

Data operations or DataOps, which stands for data operations, is a collaborative data management framework focused on improving the communication, integration, and automation of data flows between data creators and data consumers in the organization. The goal of DataOps is to deliver value faster by creating predictable delivery of quality data, data models, and related artifacts. DataOps uses technology to automate the design, deployment, and management of data delivery with appropriate levels of governance, and it uses metadata to improve the usability and value of data in a dynamic environment. Overall, the goal of

DataOps is to improve quality, speed, and collaboration and promote a culture of continuous improvement in the area of data analytics in the entire data life-cycle from data capture to data consumption.

DataOps exerts control of the workflow and processes, eliminating the numerous obstacles that prevent the data teams from achieving high levels of productivity and quality. DataOps further brings three key methodologies – that is, Agile development, DevOps, and Lean manufacturing – to improve quality data availability for the business.

1. Agile is an application of the Theory of Constraints (ToC) to software development. The Theory of Constraints is a methodology for identifying the most important limiting factor – that is, constraint – that stands in the way of achieving a goal and then systematically improving that constraint until it is no longer the limiting factor. The core idea in ToC is that every system has a limiting factor or constraint. Focusing improvement efforts on the constraint is normally the fastest and most effective way to improve profitability (ToC 2022).
2. DevOps is a result of applying lean principles (e.g., eliminate waste, continuous improvement, broad focus) to application development and delivery to shorten the systems development lifecycle and provide continuous delivery with high software quality.
3. Lean manufacturing also contributes a relentless focus on quality, using tools such as statistical process control, data analytics, and more. The goal is to maximize productivity while minimizing waste within an operation (see Figure 7.1).

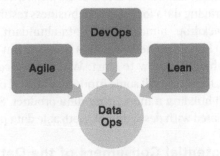

The Content is the Intellectual Property of DBP-Institute

FIGURE 7.1 DataOps

The core technical or tangible component of DataOps is the **data pipeline**, which is a series of data-processing steps starting with data extraction from various data sources and ending with consumption. A data pipeline – whether batch-based or streaming-based – moves data from one place (the source) to a destination (such as a data warehouse) and along the way, data is transformed and optimized for business consumption including improved operations, compliance, and analytics. The key characteristics of a data pipeline are:

- Real-time data processing for access to the most accurate and recent data
- Elasticity and agility of the multi-cloud environments
- Dedicated compute resources for data processing
- Self-service management
- Fault-tolerant architecture where the backup plan turns on another node or server in case the original one fails.

 DATA PRODUCT

Today many companies deal with data to solve pressing business problems using data products. Typical examples of data products include Google search, Bloomberg terminal, Netflix recommendations, and more. But what exactly is a data product? Fundamentally, a data product is an outcome of the data and analytics activity to generate new revenue sources, enhance customer service, improve business efficiency, and offer new solutions to problems that span the industry. According to McKinsey, creating reusable data products and patterns for piecing together data technologies enables companies to derive value from data (Veeral, Fountaine, and Rowshnkish 2022). Gartner says data products hold the key to leveraging data for improved business results (Gartner 2019).

Against this backdrop, almost every data-abundant company today is exploring options to build a monetizable data product. But most of them have challenges about where and how to start. While every company is different with varying needs, there are still some fundamental and common design factors associated with building a monetizing data product. Specifically, two key questions are associated with designing monetizable data products.

Who Are the Potential Consumers of the Data Product?

At the highest level, a data product relies on raw data, aggregated data, and insights. So building the data product involves the level of information, that is, raw data, aggregated data, and insights, that need to be shared with the target customers in the data product. Technically, the data in the data product can be zero-party data, second-party data, and third-party data. The target market for data can be the firm's internal employees or even external stakeholders, which includes customers, vendors, regulators, partners, and competitors.

What Are the Compliance Requirements Associated with Data?

The second design factor in the design of data products pertains to data compliance. An average company requires large amounts of time and effort to harness data. Can the firm afford to easily give away that data as a data product? Data is increasingly seen as the moat, that is, the competitive advantage the company can hold against other businesses. In this context, data compliance ensures that the critical data of the company is protected so as to maintain the firm's competitive advantage including satisfying regulatory compliance. For example, if the product profit margin data is shared with the vendors as a data product, it might jeopardize the competitive advantage of the firm. Data compliance also includes adherence to the regulations that the organization must follow on how to manage their entire data lifecycle. For example, sharing privacy data to outside stakeholders may adversely affect the legal compliance requirements defined in HIPAA, GDPR, CCPA, and more.

Once these two design-related questions are addressed, building data products rest on five key elements: Collection, Consumption, Channels, Compliance, and commercialization. The following sections look at the salient capabilities organizations need in order to successfully build a data product.

Collection

In a typical enterprise, data is captured and stored in various formats, types, systems, and so on. As discussed earlier, over 80% of the data in business is in unstructured formats like text, images, audio, and video. Unstructured data comes without a standard data model and data type, thereby affecting the capabilities to query and process it efficiently. Hence, data in data products should be transformed to have a standard data model and data type (nominal, ordinal, or continuous) to enhance the utility of data. In simple terms, data in the data products have to be collected or reformatted consistently so that it is of high quality and so that the data can be easily queried and processed for deriving the insights. The insights could come from descriptive, predictive, and prescriptive analytics algorithms where the output is presented in reports, visuals, and dashboards.

Consumption

Data products are valuable only when they are consumed to enhance business performance (i.e., data products should facilitate the creation of transactional documents, which are considered to be first-party data by the enterprise). Transactional data is important as it holds the key to improved business performance in operations, regulations, and decision making. While this transactional data is often considered as zero-party, second-party, or third-party data in data products, it should be in the most granular form to create optimal value in a data product. Overall, the more granular or detailed the data, the more precise and accurate analytics can be performed.

Compliance

If data has to be monetized in a data product, striking a balance between revenue generation opportunities and the organization's data compliance mandates is essential.

INSIGHT

Given that data is a valuable business asset, the sharing of data in a data product needs to comply with the organization's data protection and data ethics rules, especially on privacy, security, and so on. In other words, building a data product should not adversely affect the competitive advantage of the firm. The data compliance issues in a data product can be addressed using data-manipulating techniques such as encryption, anonymization, scrambling, tokenizing, and masking,. Chapter 11 will look at strategies to protect data.

Channels

Middleware or channels deliver data and insights to the consumers – either synchronously or asynchronously. If the data and insights need to be delivered synchronously, then APIs (application programming interface) can be leveraged. However, if the need is to deliver data asynchronously, other data integration mechanisms such as ETL (extract, transfer, and load), EAI (enterprise application integration) and more could be considered. As discussed in a the previous chapter, the selection of the data integration method in a channel rests on:

1. Pull vs. push; that is, whether it is the sender (data provider/data product) or receiver (data consumer) who takes the initiative for data consumption.
2. The volume and velocity of data to be integrated.
3. The number of systems involved in the integration.
4. The sequence of data transfer, transpose, and orchestration.

Commercialization

The data product is monetizable only if it can be taken to market to improve the business performance of the target companies. This involves building the eco-system with the right pricing. The ecosystem is important if data products have to collaborate with other products in the value chain to offer solutions holistically. This encompasses creating a strong value proposition by looking at the entire value chain holistically and identifying value leakages. Value leakages typically happen when there is a hand-over or transition from one value stream element. The value created is determined by the market's willingness to pay (i.e., the highest point the market goes to buy the data product).

DATA FABRIC AND DATA MESH

A data fabric is a single environment consisting of a unified architecture – that is, services or technologies running on that architecture – that helps organizations manage their data. Conceptually, a data fabric is essentially a metadata-driven way of connecting a disparate collection of data tools that address data quality issues in a cohesive and self-service manner. Specifically, data fabric solutions deliver capabilities in the areas of data access, discovery, transformation, integration, security, governance, lineage, and orchestration. The four important features of data fabric solutions are:

1. Semantic layer of data definitions that enable users to discover and access relevant data
2. Centralized data governance and security process that is consistent across all environments
3. Improved data integration in distributed data environments
4. Data lifecycle management including development, operations self-service orchestration, integration, testing, and production release of data-driven applications (see Figure 7.2)

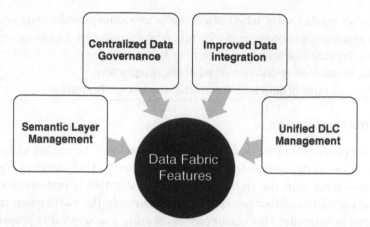

The Content is the Intellectual Property of DBP-Institute

FIGURE 7.2 Data Fabric Features

Data mesh emphasizes enterprise agility by empowering data owners, data producers, and data consumers to access and manage data without the trouble of delegating to the data lake or data warehouse team.

INSIGHT

Closely related to data fabric is data mesh. Data mesh is a data management approach that is designed for data analytics. It is a concept and practice for managing large amounts of data across a distributed environment. The use cases for data mesh are for data democratization so that data can be more quickly and effectively accessed by the users. The salient feature of data mesh is enabling easy data access where it lives without transferring the data to a canonical database such as the data lake or data warehouse. This decentralized strategy of data mesh distributes the data ownership to domain-specific teams for them to manage data as a product. The four important features of data mesh solutions are:

1. Domain-oriented decentralized data ownership and architecture
2. Data as a product
3. Self-serve data infrastructure as a platform
4. Federated computational governance (see Figure 7.3)

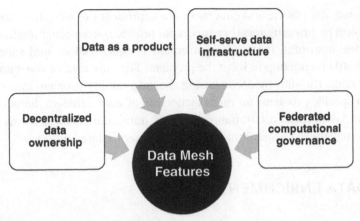

The Content is the Intellectual Property of DBP-Institute

FIGURE 7.3 Data Mesh Features

Both data fabric and data mesh architectures focus on data products. Data fabric is technology-agnostic architecture that delivers data products as one of the many outputs. Data mesh is an architecture that only produces data products specific to business domains.

INSIGHT

So, what is the difference between data fabric and data mesh? Data fabric and data mesh are similar in that they are frameworks for laying the foundation for how organizations deal with large amounts of data. While a data mesh aims to solve many of the same problems as a data fabric – especially on the difficulty of managing data in a heterogenous and distributed data environment – it tackles the problem in a fundamentally different manner. In short, while the data fabric seeks to build a single, virtual management layer atop the distributed data sources, data mesh promotes teams to manage data as they see fit, albeit with some common governance provisions. According to Forrester's Yuhanna, the key difference between the data mesh and the data fabric approaches are in how APIs are accessed. A data mesh is basically an API-driven solution for developers, unlike data fabric. Data fabric is the opposite of data mesh. It is a low-code, no-code, which means that the API integration is happening inside of the fabric without actually leveraging it directly, as opposed to data mesh (Woodie 2021).

Overall, data fabric and data mesh are approaches to solve the data quality problem by bringing together successful practices from other domains and industries, assuming that the organization is decentralized and siloed and there is little ownership to solve the problem. The core idea of the data mesh is to leverage the silos by decomposing the data quality problem into smaller domain-specific problems for more ownership of each problem domain. Data fabric and data mesh are frameworks for IT, data, and business teams to collaborate together in a distributed and heterogeneous data landscape.

DATA ENRICHMENT

 Data quality is a profound issue in analytics compared to operations and compliance, as the analytics models are based on hypothesis, and the hypothesis typically have an element of ambiguity and uncertainty.

Often business enterprises need more data to improve the accuracy and the reliability of the existing data, especially during analytics. This is because analytics is primarily hypothesis-driven where the insights are derived based on continuous inquiry. To implement analytics, the existing data set needs to be continuously enriched. *Data enrichment* refers to the process of appending, that is, enhancing the available first-party data with relevant data obtained from additional sources. At the same time, data enrichment is also about handling missing data. Basically, data enrichment is the process of enriching the existing data with new data or augmenting the existing data with missing data. Data enrichment is important because it helps to increase the data footprint without increasing user friction and the cost involved in data collection.

Data enrichment is not a one-time activity in the data quality journey of a business. For example, income levels of customers are constantly changing. People move from one place to another, and addresses change. New businesses get acquired, and systems need to be integrated. New regulations force new data to be acquired. As the businesses continuously evolve and change, it is essential that organizations enrich data continuously. So, how can a company enrich its existing data first-party data? There are four main data enrichment strategies.

1. Feature engineering
2. Third-party data integration
3. Synthetic data
4. Data imputation

Feature Engineering

Feature engineering is the process of creating new data attributes or data fields with values from the existing data using domain knowledge and a bit of creativity. This could include transforming unstructured/text data to structured data, decomposing reference data to more granular levels, splitting the date-time, reframing the measurement units, and so on. In Figure 7.4, the original data has just three attributes. But after applying some basic domain knowledge elements, four additional attributes or feature were created or engineered. The time-stamp attribute "Created On" was used to create additional features such as "Weekday," "Hour," and "Shift Period." The master data attribute "Product Id" was mapped to the "Product category" attribute.

Feature Engineering Example

Original Data				Transformed Data				
Quantity	Created on	Product Id		Quantity	Weekday	Hour	Category	Period
52	2019-05-04 13:00	80818579		52	4	1	Life	Day
56	2019-05-04 14:00	86858562		56	4	2	Auto	Day
54	2019-05-04 15:00	80878581		54	4	3	Home	Day
20	2019-05-04 16:00	80818569		20	4	4	Life	Break
55	2019-05-04 17:00	80818566		55	4	5	Life	Night
54	2019-05-04 18:00	80818579		54	4	6	Life	Night
57	2019-05-04 19:00	86858562		57	4	7	Auto	Night
52	2019-05-05 13:00	80878581		52	5	1	Home	Day
56	2019-05-05 14:00	80818569		56	5	2	Life	Day
54	2019-05-05 15:00	80818566		54	5	3	Life	Day
21	2019-05-05 16:00	80818566		20	5	4	Life	Break
54	2019-05-05 17:00	80818579		55	5	5	Life	Night
54	2019-05-05 18:00	86858562		54	5	6	Auto	Night
56	2019-05-05 19:00	80878581		57	5	7	Coupling	Night

FIGURE 7.4 Feature Engineering

Basically, one can create new features or attributes using the domain knowledge and a bit of creativity. For example, the industry sector (reference data) attribute can be created from the company name (master data) like P&G is associated with the CPG (consumer packaged goods) industry sector. You can also leverage the Unit of Measures (UoM) attribute and create new UoM attributes. For example, if the crude oil volumes are captured in cubic meters, that is, M3, it can be easily converted into barrels by multiplying the M3 values by 6.28.

Third-Party Data Integration

The first-party data or existing data can be further enriched by acquiring the second-party and third-party data – basically external data. For example, many property-and-casualty (P&C) insurers today are using address data from third-party data providers to decide where they should provide coverage for a specific property. Sales in retail stores depend on the weather as rain and snow have a large effect on store traffic. Hence retail companies also use third-party weather data to determine the pricing and promotions for increased store sales. Another example in the retail sector is using a data enrichment API service call to data providers such as Nielsen, Axciom, or Experian to receive more information on the customer's past buying habits, demographic preferences, total income, and more. Overall, while some external data can be purchased from data providers such as Statista, Neilson, Bloomberg, and Environics, or some data could also be accessed for free from open data platforms such as GitHub and Kaggle.

However, once the external data is acquired, this data needs to be integrated or blended to the existing data. The process of taking data from multiple data sources and integrating it into one unified view is typically done using the two key SQL operations or commands – JOIN and UNION. SQL commands are the instructions used to communicate with the database.

1. The JOIN SQL operator combines columns from one or more tables in a relational database using values/keys common to each.
2. The UNION SQL operator combines the results of two or more queries into a distinct single result set after removing the duplicates.

Figure 7.5 shows the difference between Union and Join SQL operations.

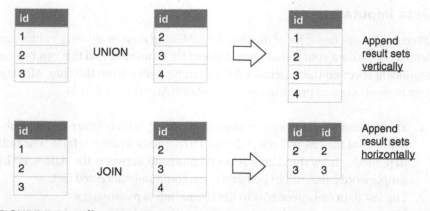

FIGURE 7.5 Difference between Union and Join

Synthetic Data

The third option to enrich existing data is to use synthetic data. Synthetic data is algorithmically or programmatically created by mimicking the real data. Basically, synthetic data is the data that is artificially manufactured rather than generated by real-world business events. The key characteristics of synthetic data are:

- Synthetic data mirrors the statistical or numerical properties of the original data.
- It aligns the original data structure and format.
- Synthetic data does not have mappings or traceability or linkage.
- Synthetic data does not adhere to data protection rules or other regulations including data privacy, as the data is not considered real or production data.

The business value of synthetic data is that organizations are free to use, share and train, and validate analytics models without being restricted by poor data quality or data availability or data compliance issues. In the financial services sector, many banks and insurance companies extensively use synthetic data techniques to optimize product selection, underwriting, pricing, claims management, and more. Amazon uses synthetic data to train Alexa, and Google's Waymo uses synthetic data to train its self-driving cars.

Data Imputation

Often businesses find a lot of missing data. Missing data or missing values are defined as the data values that are not stored for a variable, and this can have a significant effect on the conclusions that can be drawn from the data. Missing data presents various problems to the business (Anesthesiol 2013).

1. The absence of data reduces statistical power, which refers to the probability that the test will reject the null hypothesis when it is false. The null hypothesis states that there is no relationship between the data sets. In simple words, the null hypothesis is the commonly accepted fact.
2. The lost data can cause bias in the estimation of parameters.
3. Missing values can reduce the representativeness of the samples.
4. It may complicate the analysis of the study.

Missing data can fall into three main categories.

1. Missing at Random (MAR). Missing at Random means the data is missing relative to the observed data. The data is missing only within sub-samples of the data.
2. Missing Completely at Random (MCAR). In the MCAR situation, the data is missing across all observations regardless of the expected value or other variables.
3. Missing Not at Random (MNAR). The MNAR category applies when the missing data has a structure or noticeable trend to it. In other words, there appear to be reasons the data is missing. For example, a specific group of people – say women – did not answer a question.

When data is missing, data imputation is a viable data-enriching solution. Data imputation is replacing missing values with an estimate and then analyzing the full data set as if the imputed values were the actual observed values. Some of the common imputation techniques are:

1. Hot deck imputation. This is imputing a value randomly from a similar case.
2. Cold deck imputation. This is imputing a value from a similar case , but there is no randomness.
3. Regression imputation. Regression imputation uses the prediction model to substitute the missing values in the dependent variable or output variable.

4. Interpolation and extrapolation imputation. Interpolation and extrapolation imputation techniques are both used to estimate hypothetical values for a variable based on other observations.

    a. Interpolation is used to predict the value of the dependent variable for an independent variable that is in between data. Newton's formula is a good technique for data interpolation.

    b. Extrapolation is used to predict the value of the dependent variable for an independent variable that is outside the range of the data. Trend line is a good technique for data extrapolation.

Delivering high-quality complete data is often a challenge for many businesses. In those circumstances, the four data enrichment techniques discussed here augment the existing data thereby making the existing data more useful.

 KEY TAKEAWAYS

Following are the key takeaways of this chapter.

- Architecting for data quality is based on proven data governance and data management architectural frameworks and design patterns, that is, industry best practices.
- Data definition problems can be technically addressed with master data management (MDM), data integration, data wrangling, and the semantic layer solutions.
- DataOps is a set of practices, processes, and technologies to deliver high quality data as rapidly as possible for business.
- A data fabric is an architecture for accessing data across heterogeneous environments.
- Data mesh focuses on organizational change – enabling business teams to own the delivery of quality data.
- A data mesh is a data architecture framework that organizes data by a specific business domain to provide more data ownership to the business users.
- Both data fabric and data mesh are data architectures that enable organizations to access data in a distributed data landscape.

■ Data enrichment is enhancing the quality of available data using techniques such as:

- ■ Feature engineering
- ■ Third-party data integration
- ■ Synthetic data
- ■ Data imputation

 CONCLUSION

Data architecture is a key enabler for an enterprise to acquire quality data and become data driven. It is the practice of designing, building, and optimizing data-driven systems by incorporating the company's vision, strategies, business rules, standards, and capabilities to manage the data. At the highest level, data architecture offers solid strategies for companies to manage their data in the entire data lifecycle. In today's data-centric business world, the data quality journey for the business should start with a solid foundation – the data architecture. The foundation itself has little value to the business; but the foundation helps to build scalable and robust data-driven systems for business productivity and sustainable competitive advantage.

REFERENCES

Anesthesiol, K. (May 2013). The prevention and handling of the missing data. https://.www.ncbi.nlm.nih.gov/pmc/articles/PMC3668100/.

Gartner. (July 2019). Gartner Research Board identifies the Chief Data Officer 4.0. https://www.gartner.com/en/newsroom/press-releases/2019-07-30-gartner-research-board-identifies-the-chief-data-officer-4point0.

Gartner. (September 2022). Master data management. Gartner Glossary. https://www.gartner.com/en/information-technology/glossary/master-data-management-mdm.

Veeral, D., Fountaine, and Rowshankish, K. (June 2022). How to unlock the full value of data? Manage it like a product. https://www.mckinsey.com/business-functions/quantumblack/our-insights/how-to-unlock-the-full-value-of-data-manage-it-like-a-product.

Woodie, A. (October 2021). Data mesh vs. data fabric: understanding the differences. https://www.datanami.com/2021/10/25/data-mesh-vs-data-fabric-understanding-the-differences/.

## CHAPTER EIGHT

Best Practices to Realize Data Quality

 INTRODUCTION

The previous chapter looked at the architectural aspects of data quality. Based on the architectural elements discussed in the previous chapter, this chapter looks at the key principles and patterns, that is, the best practices required to improve data quality in the organization. As mentioned in Chapter 4, databases in business enterprises rarely begin their lives empty. Often, data origination and data capture activities start from data conversion or migration from some legacy database, spread sheets, and paper documents that often have their origins in mergers, acquisitions, and divestures. Hence the primary focus of this chapter is to look the key principles and patterns required to improve the quality of existing data. Principles provide high-level guidelines. They are abstract and not concrete. Patterns on the other hand are concrete and proven solutions to real-world problems. They are instantiation of the principles. Principles and patterns together form the best practices.

OVERVIEW OF BEST PRACTICES

> **Data is a reflection of the process. A quality process both in business management and data management leads to quality data.**
>
> **INSIGHT**

Organizations today are now looking for best practices or proven processes on improving data quality in a reliable and efficient manner. In simple terms, a best practice is a guideline or idea that has been generally accepted as superior based on proven principles and patterns because it produces efficient results that are prescriptive, superior, and reusable. Overall, best practices serve as a roadmap for an organization on how to conduct business efficiently and provide the best way to deal with issues that arise. A best practice tends to be accepted throughout the industry after repeated evidences of success has been demonstrated and has served as a general framework in a variety of business situations across numerous industry sectors. For instance, in financial accounting, the generally accepted accounting principles (GAAP) represent best practices on financial statements. The health care industry relies on best practices on areas such as Health Technology Assessment (HTA), Evidence-Based Medicine (EBM), and Clinical Practice Guidelines (CPGs) to offer quality care to patients. Novarica research offers technology trends and other best practices for insurance companies. However, best practices serve only as a general framework. It is ultimately the responsibility of each company to define, implement, and audit the best practices depending on their specific needs.

In this backdrop, this chapter and the next chapter looks at 10 key data quality best practices (BP). It has often been said that an average strategy well executed will always outperform a superior business strategy that is poorly executed. While strategy elements such as culture, governance, senior management support, incentive structures, and education are all important, execution aspects such as monitoring the progress of the plan, formulating the right roles and responsibilities, providing continued support, and other tactical factors bring the strategy to life.

These ten data quality best practices are compiled from literature study, validation with data and analytics experts, and deployment experience on numerous digital and data quality initiatives – both successful and failed. These 10 data quality best practices are:

1. Identify the business KPIs, the ownership of these KPIs, and the pertinent data
2. Build and improve the data culture and literacy in the organization
3. Define the current and desired state of data quality.
4. Follow the minimalistic approach to data capture
5. Select and define the data attributes for data quality
6. Capture and manage critical data elements (reference data and master data) in the MDM systems
7. Rationalize and automate the integration of the reference and master data elements
8. Define the SoR (system of record) and securely capture the transactional data in the SoR OLTP systems.
9. Build and manage robust data integration capabilities
10. Distribute data sourcing and insight consumption

There is an overlap of these 10 best data quality practices with data management, and data governance processes. Also, the implementation of these 10 best practices varies from one organization to another company, and hence these best practices should be used as a guideline and not as mandates. Also, these 10 best practices are recommended to be implemented sequentially as there is a strong dependency on each of the preceding best practice (s) on data quality. Overall, the data quality is enhanced when efforts are made in the initial stages of the data lifecycle, that is, during the data capture and data integration steps as shown in Figure 8.1.

Simplified Data Flow

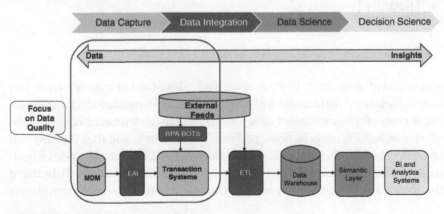

FIGURE 8.1 Data Quality in DLC

Again, improving the data quality early in the DLC matters. We all know the adage that "Prevention is better than cure." This applies in medical sciences, business, manufacturing and even in digital and data management. In Chapter 3, we looked the 1-10-100 data quality rule. The National Institute of Standard Technology (NIST) found that the average time to fix an error in the production stage is 15 hours compared to five hours of effort if the same error were found in the build stage. IBM has reported that the cost to fix an error found after product release was four to five times as much as one uncovered during design, and up to 100 times more than one identified in the maintenance phase (Burns 2017). Overall, an early detection allows for quicker action, saves precious time, and prevents complications and rapid worsening of the problem.

Coming back to the list of best practices, the first six best practices (BP) are related to data capture and will be covered in this chapter. The next four best practices are on data integration and data consumption and will be discussed in the next chapter, that is, in Chapter 9.

BP 1: IDENTIFY THE BUSINESS KPIs AND THE OWNERSHIP OF THESE KPIs AND THE PERTINENT DATA

Performance frameworks such as balanced scorecard (BSC) and goal-question-metric (GQM) can be leveraged to formulate the KPI framework.

INSIGHT

Management guru Peter Drucker once said, "You cannot manage what you cannot measure." In this regard, a KPI is a quantifiable measure used to evaluate the success of a measurement entity in meeting its performance objectives. In other words, KPIs offers business performance visibility, and that visibility can provide details to derive the business value. Apart from this, KPIs drive business behavior, results, and the organization culture (Southekal 2020). Building the KPIs framework that is specific to the organization starts by formulating powerful questions based on business strategy and objectives. Given that KPIs are a combination of formula and data, once the KPIs are identified, the critical data objects can also be determined. To get meaningful business improvements, these KPIs have to be mapped to the targets or goals, tolerances, control limits, and specification limits.

Once the KPIs framework is developed, the next step is to identify the ownership for the KPIs. While designing and implementing the KPI model is complex, more challenging than that is integrating the insights from the KPIs into a business's operating model and bring performance improvement in operations, compliance, and decision making. Successful change initiatives are often associated to accountability or ownership. This means having an accountable leader who is close to the KPI being tracked for performance. For example, if the KPI is on "Data Completeness on the Customer Master," it is advisable to have the Sales Manager track and improve the quality of the customer master records. Once we have the KPIs selected and ownership for these KPIs, the relevant data objects in the KPIs need to be identified.

But often the business leader has to manage business deliverables instead of focusing on data quality. In Chapter 1, we looked at the incentives and drivers for the business leader to be held accountable for data ownership. This also begs the question on the incentive, commitment, and the skills required in the business leader to take data ownership.

1. Firstly, what is the incentive for business leaders to take data ownership? While data offers improved business opportunities and growth, not managing data well results in increased complexity and business risk. Delegating the data ownership to IT can only be on storage, processing, and security. Consumption of data would be the responsibility of the business. For example, in 2017, when hackers accessed millions of customer records from the credit reporting agency, Equifax. and the company spent US$1.4 billion to transform the technology infrastructure. The Facebook–Cambridge Analytica data scandal resulted in Facebook losing US$35 billion in market value following reports that Cambridge Analytica had unauthorized access to over 50 million Facebook user accounts. These are some examples on how inappropriate data consumption will jeopardize the business.

2. Secondly, today every company is a data company and hence every person today is a data professional. So, everyone in the firm, including the

business leader, needs to be data literate to understand and manage data. Data literacy will be a fundamental skill going forward due to the rapid rate of digitization. Today over 93% of all high-value work is digital, and the output of these digital processes is data (Hurst 2018). Data literacy is one the 10 best practices and will be covered next.

3. Thirdly, if the business leader doesn't have the bandwidth to take this additional role of data ownership, he or she can delegate the ownership to a different data owner. The role of the data owner will be covered in detail in the data governance chapter in the sustain phase of the DARS methodology.

BP 2: BUILD AND IMPROVE THE DATA CULTURE AND LITERACY IN THE ORGANIZATION

In the first best practice, we discussed identifying the critical data object that matter for business performance and identifying the owner to improve the data quality based on the business KPIs. In the context of data quality, data ownership holds the key. One effective way to realize data ownership is with good education or data literacy. Data literacy is the ability to understand and communicate data and insights. MIT professor Catherine D'Ignazio and research scientist Rahul Bhargava define data literacy as the ability to (Brown 2021):

▪ **Read data**, which means understanding what data is and the aspects of the world it represents.
▪ **Work with data**, including creating, acquiring, cleaning, and managing it.
▪ **Analyze data**, which involves filtering, sorting, aggregating, comparing, and performing other analytic operations on it.
▪ **Argue with data**, which means using data to support a larger narrative that is intended to communicate some message or story to a particular audience.

It is often said, data literacy is to the twenty-first century what literacy was in the last century. In fact, a data literacy survey by Accenture of more than 9,000 employees in a variety of roles found that only 21% were confident in their data literacy skills (Accenture 2020). According to Gartner, data literacy is the second key reason that is preventing companies from becoming data-driven (Gartner 2017). So, how can data literacy be inculcated in the business enterprise?

A strong data and analytics culture rests on improving business performance with measurement. If the organization doesn't believe in measurement and performance improvement, the value of realizing business results from data and analytics will be challenging.

Successful implementation of data literacy depends on a strong data culture. But what exactly is a data culture? Technically, data culture is the collective beliefs and behavior of the people in the organization for leveraging data for improved business performance. Fundamentally, a data-centric culture enables organizations to be more effective and efficient. According to Forrester, organizations that use data to derive insights for decision making are almost three times more likely to achieve double-digit growth (Evelson 2020). A report from MIT found that a data-driven culture results in increased revenue, improved profitability, and enhanced operating efficiencies (Brown 2020). Research from IDC shows that organizations realize the full value of their data when they have a data culture (IDC May 2021).

So, how can an organization build a data culture to enhance data literacy and data quality? While there are many methods, below are three key enablers for enterprises to build a data culture in the enterprise (Southekal 2022).

1. Inculcate the service culture. Service culture is an outlook that focuses on consistently creating value and trust with stakeholders. This is because to provide consistent service, there has to be a reliable frame of reference on the service levels, and this reliable frame of reference comes from quality data.
2. Focus on continuous performance improvement. A consistent service depends on quality data to measure and improve its performance. At the core, measurement creates visibility, and visibility drives performance. In other words, performance management enhances the level of data quality.

3. Emphasize consensus culture over hierarchical culture. A consensus-based culture relies on insights driven by data, unlike the hierarchical culture where the decision making is based primarily on title, position, and seniority.

With a string data culture as the foundation, there are two key best practices to achieve data literacy:

1. Implementing the training program
2. Leveraging descriptive data analytics

Implementing the Training Program

Managing data is a multi-disciplinary field that needs expertise in business, mathematics, social science, computer science, and more. Hence a data literacy training curriculum should include relevant topics from these domains for assessing employees' current skill levels, and laying out appropriate learning paths. Specifically, the data literacy training program should cover:

1. Technical needs. This should address the management of data across the entire lifecycle including data security and data storage.
2. Organizational needs. In most companies, data is managed by the IT or data team, forcing them to take on the responsibility of "keepers of data." This can lead to data silos. However, often the root cause of data silos is organizational silios. Hence the organizational aspects of the data literacy should focus on elements that foster team collaboration and data sharing.
3. Personal need. For many business users' new tools, techniques, and processes to manage data can be overwhelming. The data literacy program should address individual needs and clarify any misconceptions about the capabilities and limitations of data for people to engage effectively.

In this regard, Figure 8.2 shows the 10 data literacy technical competencies, that is, the knowledge and skills one needs to effectively work with data. Appendix 3 discusses these 10 competencies in detail along with the relevant soft skills.

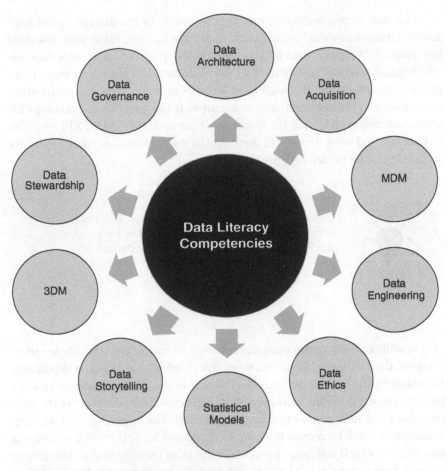

FIGURE 8.2 Data Literacy Competencies

Leverage Descriptive Analytics

While training is an important aspect to improve data literacy, data teams typically learn by doing. Basically, everyone learns differently. This includes using data and insights in operations, compliance, and decision making. Training together with hands-on skills will create a common way of talking about data and insights throughout the enterprise. Getting hands-on and practical exposure will give one confidence as one will learn the concepts, their implementation, troubleshooting skills, and more. One key approach to this learning-by-doing concept is to leverage descriptive analytics with reports and dashboards. But what exactly is descriptive analytics in the context of data literacy? Descriptive analytics is interpreting historical data to better understand the past business performance.

In simple terms, descriptive analytics answers the question of "what happened?" using historical business data. Examples include, What were our sales last quarter? Which product had the most sales? Who are the top five customers based on revenue? Questions like these enhance data literacy as these types of basic questions and the associated KPIs form a common communication terminology in the organization. For example, if the project is to optimize CCC (cash conversion cycle), but the teams don't understand the CCC KPI and how it is derived and what it means to them and to the organization, they might not end up using the related insights.

Getting business results from data and analytics is primarily managing change and the key enabler for change in business is education or understanding.

INSIGHT

In addition, descriptive analytics relies on historical data, which are more accurate than data used for predictive analytics, which are based on hypothesis. For example, the accuracy of the sales revenue in the previous quarter (descriptive analytics) is generally more accurate than the predicted accuracy of the sales revenue in the next quarter (predictive analytics). The sales revenue in the previous quarter will be derived from the ERP systems for GAPP/IFRS accounting compliance, which will foster trust, while the sales revenue in the next quarter will not be accurate as it is hypothesis based. Basically, insights from historical data are more accurate and reliable than the insights derived from predictive analytics because predictive analytics is about the future, which is inherently probabilistic. Overall, descriptive analytics improves the manner in which data is used to deliver business performance with improved communication as the data and insights are more reliable and accurate than other types of analytics.

BP 3: DEFINE THE CURRENT AND DESIRED STATE OF DATA QUALITY

As discussed in Chapter 6, data quality assessment or data profiling holds the key in improving data quality. In data quality, you need to know where you stand in order to improve the data quality, that is, the desired state of data quality, and this is done with data profiling. Data profiling is the process of examining, analyzing, reviewing, and summarizing data to gain insight into the quality of data. Specifically, data profiling is analyzing data sets to summarize their "3D" characteristics.

1. Discover underlying data structure including important variables, relationships, etc.
2. Determine the data distribution
3. Detect anomalies

As discussed in Chapter 6, profiling data on critical numerical attributes should cover the measures of both centrality and variation on the measurement entity along with the relevant data quality dimensions such as accuracy, completeness, integrity, and so on. This assessment process will serve as the baseline on where the enterprise currently stands in data quality. After the assessment on the current state of data quality is done, one can set up goals on the KPIs on the desired state based on larger organizational objectives and the resources available. These target on the KPIs should be supported with tolerances, control limits, and thresholds or specifications.

■ The **target value** is the desired state that is preferred for the measurement entity. The target value is the goal or the mean value.
■ **Tolerance limits** are the limiting values for the measurement entity to be acceptable. Typically, the upper tolerance limit (UTL) and the lower tolerance limit (LTL) are usually ±1 standard deviation from the mean or the target if the standard deviation is known.
■ Control charts are used to determine if the measurement entity is in the state of control. These are known as **control limits,** and they serve as warning indicators. The control chart contains a center line that represents the mean value, that is, the target along with two other horizontal lines: upper control limit (UCL) and the lower control limit (LCL). UCL and LCL are usually ±3 standard deviations from the mean or the target.
■ Control limits are surrounded by the upper and lower **specification limits** or thresholds. These limits cannot be crossed, and suitable corrective action should be taken immediately if the measurement entity crosses the specification limits. The upper specification limit (USL) and the lower specification limit (LSL) are usually ±6 standard deviation from the mean or the target

The relationship between the targets, control limits, and thresholds is as shown in Figure 8.3.

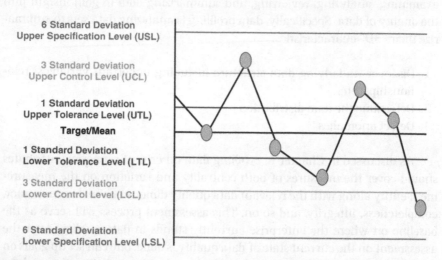

6 Standard Deviation Upper Specification Level (USL)	
3 Standard Deviation Upper Control Level (UCL)	
1 Standard Deviation Upper Tolerance Level (UTL)	
Target/Mean	
1 Standard Deviation Lower Tolerance Level (LTL)	
3 Standard Deviation Lower Control Level (LCL)	
6 Standard Deviation Lower Specification Level (LSL)	

FIGURE 8.3 Targets, Tolerances, Control Limits, and Specifications

The following is an example on the current state of data quality on product master data mapped to the desired state of data quality based on six data quality dimensions.

#	Product Master Data Quality KPI	Current Level	Target	LTL	UTL	LCL	UCL	LSL	USL
1	Conformance to standards	53%	80%	78%	82%	75%	85%	70%	90%
2	Completeness	70%	80%	78%	82%	75%	85%	70%	90%
3	Cardinality/uniqueness	58%	80%	78%	82%	75%	85%	70%	90%
4	Currency/recency	20%	70%	68%	72%	65%	75%	60%	80%
5	Coverage	40%	75%	72%	77%	70%	80%	65%	85%
6	Accuracy	55%	80%	78%	82%	75%	85%	70%	90%
	Data Quality Index (DQI)	49%							

Once the data quality KPIs start to show improvement, the benefits of improved data quality should be regularly communicated to the business stakeholders to further bolster the changes needed to reach the desired state. Data leaders need to measure the impact of the data quality improvement programs, and communicate the results periodically in terms of business impact such as revenue improvement, cost reduction, risk mitigation, and more to the right stakeholders. Overall, every performance improvement initiative, including the data quality improvement initiative, should be contextual and this context to the KPI can come from targets, tolerance limits, control limits, and specification limits.

 ## BP 4: FOLLOW THE MINIMALISTIC APPROACH TO DATA CAPTURE

 More isn't always better, especially in data management. In fact, having too much data can be just as bad as having too little data.

INSIGHT

Today companies collect large amounts of data. This is often based on the idea that the more data you have the better it is. But this idea is overlooking the fact that the more data you collect the more noise, redundant, and obsolete data there will be, and the more difficult it will be to manage and analyze. While that is a lot of data, how much of it is actually useful? Not much. Research by IBM and Carnegie Mellon University found that 90% of the data in a typical business enterprise is dark data (Southekal 2020). Dark data is basically unused data in business. First and foremost, why do enterprises carry dark data?

1. First, many organizations say they keep dark data in an effort to maintain adherence to regulatory compliance. For example, according to the Office of the Privacy Commissioner of Canada (OPC), insurance providers should keep insurance records for a minimum of three years. as a three-year retention period was rationally linked to fraud detection and prevention in the insurance industry. The U.S. Food and Drug Administration's Code of Federal Regulations, Title 21, mandates that pharmaceutical companies in the United States retain the data pertaining to drug production, control, or distribution for at least one year. During this period, the consumption is practically minimal and after the retention period, most companies ignore and forget to archive or purge the data.

2. Second, dark data exists due to organization silos and lack of collaboration between teams. This results in poor management of the unused data stored in legacy and retired applications, dormant content servers, log files, customer complaints, geolocation data, data integration payloads, departed employees' mailboxes, shared network drives, and many other repositories.

3. Third, many companies have a mindset wherein they retain everything from production reports and contracts to invoices and maintenance records, due to risk aversion. Enterprises often steer clear of potential risk, even when the potential benefits of an action equal or exceed the loss.

 The goal of data management and data governance is not to manage more data, but to manage the right data.

INSIGHT

Overall, when the majority of the data that is captured by business is not used, improving data quality becomes challenging as lots of effort go wasted on improving the quality of data that is never used or wanted. Just as an unused machine or inventory is a liability, likewise, any unused data asset is both a liability and risk. While too little data impairs data-driven business performance, a lot of data – especially dark data – can also hamper the enterprise. Thus, a good data strategy involves finding the right balance between enough data and dark data. A "less data, more efficiency" approach makes it easier to save time and reduce costs, while improving data quality. So, what are the best practices of data minimalism or minimum viable data (MVD) during data capture? Basically, three principles.

1. Capture data based on purpose.
2. Reuse data for standardized business process.
3. Structure data.

 Business agility comes with letting go of the unwanted and only keeping what is used regularly.

INSIGHT

Let us discuss each of the three data minimization practices in more detail. Now that the KPIs are selected and the data elements are identified in BP 1, we are focusing our efforts on capturing and improving the data quality of only the relevant data. Or at the most, organizations should focus on data that is closely related to the critical data elements (CDE). While it might be challenging to come up with a comprehensive catalog of the all-critical data elements, capture only those data elements that are applicable for the three main purposes of data: operations, compliance, and decision making. Basically, the data capture should be purpose driven and not driven because the data storage, in on-premise servers or cloud servers, is cheap and easily available.

Also, during data capture, plan to reuse data with master data management for operations and compliance, semantic layer for analytics, and so on. MDM and semantic layer was discussed in Chapter 7, and it will be discussed again as a best practice in the following section. Data reuse saves time, reduces the cost of storage, and accelerates the pace of discovery. In addition, data reuse helps to exploit the existing data and may find new opportunities for the business. So, what is the best practice for data reuse? Data reuse can be enabled on standardized business process. Value stream maps (VSM) can be used as a supporting tool as they help build a reduced number of digital systems, efficient data models, and consistent data definitions. Figure 8.4 is a simple VSM example of essential or critical data in an insurance company.

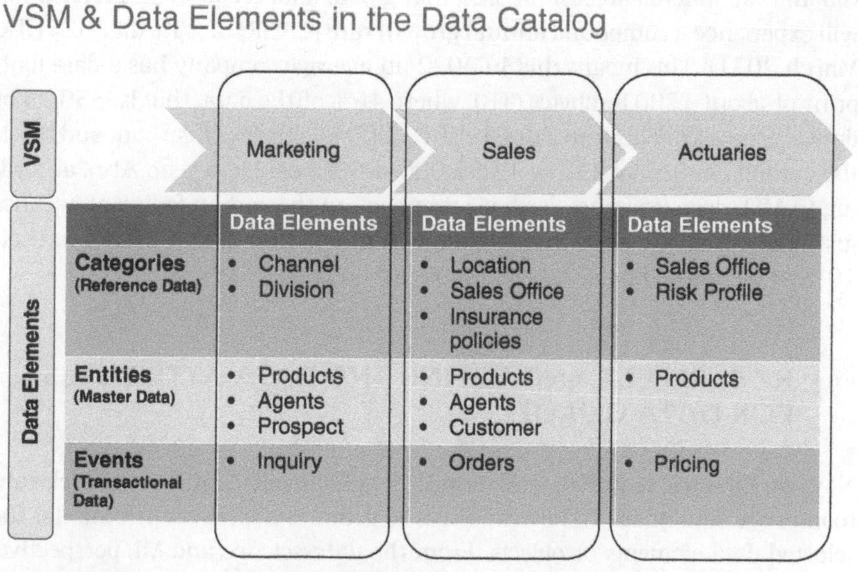

VSM & Data Elements in the Data Catalog

VSM	Marketing	Sales	Actuaries
Data Elements	Data Elements	Data Elements	Data Elements
Categories (Reference Data)	• Channel • Division	• Location • Sales Office • Insurance policies	• Sales Office • Risk Profile
Entities (Master Data)	• Products • Agents • Prospect	• Products • Agents • Customer	• Products
Events (Transactional Data)	• Inquiry	• Orders	• Pricing

FIGURE 8.4 Value Stream Mapping to Data Elements

The third data minimalism practice is structuring data. Structuring data leverages predefined data models. Today, over 80% of business data is documents, audio, video, images, and more (Davis 2019). While the unstructured data allows for easy and rapid data capture in the native format, the unstructured data does not have a predefined data model and a right data structure when captured. Due to the lack of a predefined data model and a right data structure, enablement of efficient data access, querying, and processing becomes an issue for business consumption, especially in analytics compared to structured data that allows for easy manipulation and querying of data.

On a related note, dark data, that is, unused data also had an impact on the environment. Specifically, today ESG (environment, social, and governance) is an important initiative in many companies. Today digital technologies are responsible for 4% of greenhouse gas emissions (GHG), and the energy consumption from digital technologies is increasing by 9% a year. For instance, according to Stanford University storing 100 gigabytes of data in the cloud per year would result in a carbon footprint of about 0.2 tons or 200 kilograms of carbon dioxide (Rona 2020). Where does this data consumption stand when compared to transportation?

An average car which burns 2,000 liters of gasoline every year, releases about 4,600 kilograms of CO_2 into the atmosphere. Also, in 2016 an average company had a data footprint of 350 terabytes (TB), where 46% of the data, that is, 163 TB of data was processed every year (IDG 2016). Also, IDC's recent Global DataSphere Forecast predicts that global data creation and replication will experience a compound annual growth rate (CAGR) of 23% till 2025 (IDC March 2021). This means that in 2022 an average company has a data footprint of about 1200 terabytes (TB), where 46% of the data, that is, 550 TB of data is processed. This translates to 1,092,000 kilograms of carbon, and this is the carbon emitted by 237 (= 1,092,000/4,600) cars in a year. Also, according to MIT, deep learning also has an impact on the carbon footprint because just training an AI algorithm can emit as much carbon as five cars in their 10-year lifetimes, that is, 2,300 tons of carbon (Hao 2019).

 BP 5: SELECT AND DEFINE THE DATA ATTRIBUTES FOR DATA QUALITY

Now we have the required or the critical set of data elements that are relevant to improve data quality. The next step is to define the specific attributes for the selected data elements or objects. From the data science and ML perspective, these data attributes are also the called features or labels. For example, if the product master data is a critical data element (that is identified as part of the BP 4), then attributes such as identifier, description, UoM, size, weight, category, and so on are the relevant attributes or features for data quality management.

Once the data attributes are selected, these data attributes should be defined. Defining the data attributes for the selected data element should comprehensively cover both technical and functional aspects. The technical data definition includes format, type, length, and so on. This is basically the metadata characteristics that were discussed in Chapter 3. However, often the problem is defining the data attributes from a semantic or functional view. This is because context plays a big role in the way business users' access, communicate, interpret, and consume data. Basically, defining the data functionally in a comprehensive and consistent manner is very challenging.

But what is the business impact of poor data definitions? Why does semantically defining the data matter? Semantically defining the data is based on the context in which the business users consume the data. The context in business is severely magnified due to the volume, velocity, and variety of data that is getting ingested into the IT systems, and its variation can come in three main flavors – diverse stakeholder views, value chain idiosyncrasies, and business process differences. Let us take a look at the impact of the semantic or functional definition of data based on the above three main aspects using some common and simple business examples.

1. **Diverse stakeholder views.** Stakeholders have different relationships to the organization in terms of their roles and responsibilities. For example, finance and procurement often have diverse views on managing vendor and agents' relationships. While the vendor or agent is looked at as a service provider by procurement, finance often looks at the same vendor from the costing and budgeting perspective. A low payment term is desirable for procurement as it improves the service levels from the vendor. However, this low payment term affects the cash flow, which is often not supported by the finance department. So are vendor payment terms a service element or a cost element?

2. **Value chain idiosyncrasies.** Inconsistent data definitions also arise due to unusual characteristics of the value chain. Is the customer a prospect or an account (who pays for the invoice)? Do customer, lead, prospect, and account refer to the same entity? If a vendor is an entity who gets paid for providing goods and services, can an employee be defined as a vendor, given that the employee also provides services and gets paid for the work?

So, unless one defines the customer or the vendor semantically based on their impact in the value chain, there will be misunderstandings on the use of data.

3. **Business process differences**. Differences in data definitions can also come in the form of the variation in business processes. Let us take an example of claims processing in the insurance industry. Does the start time for processing the claims application begin when the adjudicator receives the file from the claimant, or is it when the processing of the previous claims application is completed by the adjudicator? Unless the start time is clearly defined, there could be multiple interpretations of these start time in calculating the SLAs (service-level agreements). Another common example, which was discussed earlier, is using the telephone numbers to derive the jurisdiction and tax rates in the invoices.

To address the above kinds of contextual issues, we need to clearly define the data from a functional or consumption perspective. There are three main ways to handle this data definition problem: master data management (MDM), data integration methods, and semantic layer. Fundamentally these solutions, which were discussed in Chapter 7 are dependent on specific use-cases and the control one has on data quality in the data lifecycle (DLC).

It is strongly recommended that all data elements and its attributes (technical and functional) be maintained within the central store, as a data catalog and links to that store should be used in all dashboards, reports, and interfaces. The data catalog is an inventory of available data in the enterprise. Data catalogs not only provide context to users on finding and understanding data, they also automate metadata management . Simply put, a data catalog is an organized inventory of data assets in the organization to give a single, overarching view and deeper visibility into all of the data in the enterprise to support data discovery and governance. Data catalogs are an integral part of data discovery and data governance, where data owners, stewards, custodians, and business users use the data catalog to know the data assets are located in the enterprise.

The semantic layer and the data catalog are just a representation of the data. Fundamentally they are the same thing – a metadata layer, and they do not contain any data. The semantic layer is specific to analytics, as it contains information about the objects in the data source, which it uses to generate queries to derive insights from data.

So how is the data catalog different from a semantic layer? Both the data catalog and the semantic layer are just representations of the data. They do not hold any data, but they point to the data source using the metadata. The main difference between the two is in the stage of the DLC and the purpose for which they are used. The semantic layer sits on top of a canonical data store like the data warehouse or data mart and makes it easier for a business to serve analytics needs with reports, dashboards, or for running ad hoc queries. The data catalog, on the other hand, is an organized inventory of all the data assets in the organization in its native state for data discovery and data governance. Overall, the data catalog and the semantic layer are complementary in that they should share metadata with each other bi-directionally. For example, semantic layer tools such as AtScale have integration with data catalog tools like Alation and Collibra so that the analytics models can be discovered by end users, and IT can use data lineage programs in the semantic layer to run impact analysis on database changes from the data catalogs. Figure 8.5 shows how the data catalog and the semantic layer complement each other.

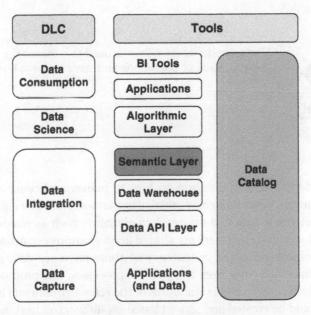

FIGURE 8.5 Data Catalog and Semantic Layer in DLC

BP 6: CAPTURE AND MANAGE CRITICAL DATA WITH DATA STANDARDS IN MDM SYSTEMS

Now we have the critical data elements and their pertinent attributes. But where do we actually store and manage these CDEs? As discussed before, there are three main types of business data from an integration perspective – reference data for business categories, master data for business entities, and transactional data for business events. The reference and master data elements are the foundational elements, as they are shared throughout the enterprise by various business functions as critical and sensitive data. Sensitive data is mostly associated with privacy aspects and other confidential transactional data attributes such as profit margin, customer discounts, and salary details. Sensitive data in business encompasses both privacy data and confidential data. But how can an enterprise provide data consistency on critical data elements at scale? Specifically, the two key questions are (1) how to manage reference and master data that are used consistently enterprise wide for managing the business processes (2) where to manage the reference and master data, that is, in which system in the data lifecycle.

Data standards are primarily used to enhance the effectiveness of operations and compliance in business.

Let's address the first question on how to manage reference and master data consistently. What is the best practice to manage reference data and master data? Reference data and master data elements such as plants, payment terms, products, and customers are shared across various organizational divisions or business units. The consistency of these reference data and master data elements could come from the policies, processes, and procedures of the company, that is, internal data standards or the reference data and master data elements could be created and shared based on industry data standards, that is, external data standards such as UNSPSC (United Nations Standard Products and Services Code), HL7 (Health Level Seven International), PIES (Product Information Exchange Standard), and more. Data standards ensure that all parties use the same language and approach to sharing, storing, exchanging, and interpreting data thereby enhancing reusability, improving reliability, and reducing the cost of data management.

Basically, data consistency from data standards comes in the form of format, definition, structuring, tagging, and more. For example, ISO 15926 is a data standard on the lifecycle of industrial plants, which includes the engineering, construction, and maintenance phases in oil and gas production. The PIES is the aftermarket industry data standard on product data in the automotive industry. UNSPSC is a global, multi-sector taxonomy standard for classifying goods and services. HL7 is a data standard for developing and exchanging electronic health records (EHRs). In all, managing reference and master data consistently should be based on data standards – internal or external.

Now, let us look at the second question on where to manage the data, that is, in which system should the reference data and master data elements be managed? The best practice for managing reference data and the master data is by using master data management (MDM) systems. MDM systems offer policies, processes, procedures, data standards, and tools to help organizations define and provide a standardized and consistent single point of reference for critical reference and master data objects such as plants, account groups, vendors, items, and more. Basically, MDM helps in creating a single master record for reference data and master data elements. In addition, with MDM, the reference and master data elements can be de-duplicated, classified, reconciled, and enriched for a consistent and reliable source of critical business data across the enterprise. Once created, the reference and master data can serve as a trusted view of business-critical data that can be managed and shared across the business to promote improved operations and compliance.

But typically, there are hundreds of reference data and master data elements that need to be managed. So, what specific reference data and the master data objects should be mastered? Given the complexity, risk, and size involved in identifying and managing the reference and master data elements, how should the organization prioritize the selection of specific reference and master data elements in MDM deployment? Is it customers, assets, vendors, projects, or any other reference or master data element? While every company is different, given the industry dynamics, competitive landscape, internal challenges, and more, there are three important rules or best practices that enterprises can adopt in selecting the data elements for MDM implementation.

Rule 1: Business Strategy Drives Data Strategy

If the business strategy is on front-end processes like customer relationships, revenue management, and so on (as in the retail and CPG), MDM can start with master data elements such as customers and products. On the other hand, if the business strategy is focused more on back-end processes such as operations and regulations (as in the oil/gas, mining, and pharma sectors), the focus can be vendors, items, and asset master data elements. Basically, front-end-centric industries focus on customers and products, while back-end-centric industries focus on markets and commodities. While front-end processes drive revenue and free cash flow (FCF) for the business, the back-end processes typically focus on minimizing risk and costs. Therefore, since every company needs both front-end and back-end processes to succeed, getting the balance right can sometimes be tricky, and this is when the second rule comes into play.

Rule 2: Cash Is King – Always and for Every Business

The value of standardized and consistent data should be associated with the business impact and measured using the free cash flow (FCF) metric. But, why is FCF important? Quality data is all about business transactions, and FCF is a metric used to measure a company's financial health based on business transactions. FCF is the amount of cash a business has after paying for operating expenses (OPEX) and capital expenditures (CAPEX). FCF reports how much cash a business has available, and this is an indicator of a company's profitability and valuation. In this regard, how can standardized and consistent data drive the FCF in the company?

Cash is vital to every business because it is the most liquid asset an enterprise can have. Every business must generate enough cash to cover its expenses and have enough left over to repay investors and grow the business. The cash conversion cycle (CCC) KPI shows how long it takes for a company to convert its resources into cash, and is closely tied to the FCF. FCF is a measure of the money while CCC is the measure of time to achieve that money in the FCF. The CCC KPI has three components: inventory, accounts receivable or sales, and accounts payables. If the vendor and items master data quality is bad, then the accounts payable KPIs will also bad. For example, incorrect vendor payment terms might result in an incorrect account payable KPI. If product master data quality is poor, the inventory metrics will also be poor, thereby affecting the CCC and FCF. If the quality of customer master data attributes, say address data, is incorrect, the company will take a lot of time to collect the money from the customer, and accounts receivable KPIs will also be bad. However, the dependencies between the three components in the CCC will often result in implementation complexity, and to manage this complexity, the next rule can help.

Rule 3: Every Management Is Change Management

While MDM is a simple concept, it is very hard to implement in business enterprises. While all business units want a Single Version of Truth (SVOT) of the business data, not many business units are willing to give up their control over master data. Organizational silos play a significant role in determining the success of the MDM project. So, selecting the master data focus on those business units that have an executive-level champion who not only understands the value of master data (and reference data) but also can devote sufficient time and resources for the management of reference and master data for improving the business performance is critical.

Once the appropriate MDM solution is implemented, and reference and master data elements are maintained in the MDM system as the SVOT, communicate to the relevant stakeholders on the right system to source the reference and master data. The MDM governance process should include the business rules, changing the workflows, roles mapping, archiving of integration messages, and so on, along with the right technical support, documentation, and leadership support.

 KEY TAKEAWAYS

Following are the key takeaways of this chapter.

- Data quality best practices (BPs) are key principles and patterns on data governance and data management to implement a solution and deal with problems. Principles provide high-level guidelines. They are abstract and not concrete. Patterns, on the other hand, are concrete and proven solutions to real-world problems. They are instantiations of the principles. Principles and patterns together form the best practices.
- Best practices produce efficient results that are prescriptive, superior, and reusable.
- While there are 10 key best practices to improve data quality, this chapter looked at six key data quality best practices related to data capture.
- The following table summarizes the first six data quality best practices (BPs).

#	BP Name	Rationale	Key Activities
1	Identify the business KPIs and the ownership of these KPIs	Every meaningful initiative starts with a purpose that needs to be objectively measured with KPIs. As KPIs involve data (and formula) identifying the KPI owner will result in the data owner.	1. Identify the business KPIs and their owner. 2. Identify the data associated with the KPIs. 3. Assign/delegate the data ownership to the KPI owner.
2	Build and improve the data literacy in the organization	Data ownership holds the key to leveraging data for business performance, and one effective way to inculcate data ownership is by building data literacy.	1. Implement the data literacy training program. 2. Leverage descriptive analytics (reports and dashboards) for better communication. 3. Build communication strategy with the artifacts, common terminology, right channels, and feedback loops.
3	Define the current and desired state of data quality	Assessment is the starting point in any performance improvement initiative. You need to know where you stand in order to improve the data quality.	1. Profile the current state of data with measures of centrality and variation on the relevant data quality dimensions. 2. Define the target state objectively with target tolerance limits, control limits, and specification limits. 3. Communicate the benefits of improved data quality regularly to business stakeholders.

#	BP Name	Rationale	Key Activities
4	Follow the minimalistic approach to data capture	Today, the majority of the data captured is not used. So improving data quality becomes challenging as many efforts are wasted on improving the quality of data that is never used.	1. Capture data based on business purpose, that is, operations, compliance, and decision making. 2. Reuse data with standardized business process. 3. Structure data as per predefined data models.
5	Select and define the data attributes	Every data element is composed of multiple attributes or fields. Once the relevant data element is selected, focus on the pertinent data attributes associated with the data object.	1. Define the metadata or technical attributes. 2. Define the semantic or functional attributes. 3. Maintain data attributes (technical and functional) in a central store as a data catalog.
6	Capture critical data elements (reference and master data) with data standards in MDM systems	Reference data and master data elements are shared throughout the enterprise and hence should be standardized and consistent. The effective way to make reference and master data standard and consistent is with data standards and master data management (MDM).	1. Leverage data standards for reference and master data elements in the MDM system. 2. Select the reference and master data objects based on business strategy – front-end processes or back-end processes. 3. Link the value of MDM to business impact, especially the free cash flow (FCF) and cash conversion cycle (CCC) KPIs. 4. Have an executive-level champion for MDM.

CONCLUSION

As data is becoming a core part of every business activity, the quality of the data that is captured, stored, exchanged, and consumed will determine business success. Given that the first step is data capture, capturing the data in the right manner creates efficiencies, reduces errors, and improves outputs. The six best practices discussed here are focused on business performance, especially in the data capture phase of the data lifecycle. Implementing these practices involves a combination of tactical and strategic elements such as culture, governance, senior management support, and incentive structures, to successfully implement these best practices.

REFERENCES

Accenture. (2020). The human impact of data literacy. https://www.accenture.com/_acnmedia/PDF-115/Accenture-Human-Impact-Data-Literacy-Latest.pdf.

Brown, S. (September 2020). How to build a data-driven company. https://mitsloan.mit.edu/ideas-made-to-matter/how-to-build-a-data-driven-company.

Brown, S. (February 2021). How to build data literacy in your company. https://mitsloan.mit.edu/ideas-made-to-matter/how-to-build-data-literacy-your-company.

Burns, E. (March 2017). The cost of fixing bugs throughout the SDLC. https://techmonitor.ai/technology/software/cost-fixing-bugs-sdlc#:~:text=The%20Systems%20Sciences%20Institute%20at,uncovered%20during%20design%2C%20and%20up.

Davis, D. (July 2019). AI unleashes the power of unstructured data. https://bit.ly/3bD9QkC.

Evelson, B. (May 2020). Insights investments produce tangible benefits – yes, they do. https://www.forrester.com/blogs/data-analytics-and-insights-investments-produce-tangible-benefits-yes-they-do/.

Gartner. (November 2017). Survey analysis: Third Gartner CDO Survey – how chief data officers are driving business impact. https://www.gartner.com/en/documents/3834265.

Hao, K. (June 2019). Training a single AI model can emit as much carbon as five cars in their lifetimes. https://www.technologyreview.com/2019/06/06/239031/training-a-single-ai-model-can-emit-as-much-carbon-as-five-cars-in-their-lifetimes/.

Hurst, H. (November 2018). 5 systems of record every modern enterprise needs. https://www.workfront.com/blog/systems-of-record.

IDC. (March 2021). Data creation and replication will grow at a faster rate than installed storage capacity. https://www.idc.com/getdoc.jsp?containerId=prUS47560321.

IDC. (May 2021). How data culture fuels business value in data-driven organizations. IDC Thought Leadership white paper.

IDG. (2016). Data & analytics survey. https://cdn2.hubspot.net/hubfs/1624046/
    IDGE_Data_Analysis_2016_final.pdf.
Rona, E. (December 2020). Cloud footprint. https://kurious.ku.edu.tr/en/cloud-
    footprint/.
Southekal, P. (2020). *Analytics best practices.* Technics Publications.
Southekal, P. (September 2020). Illuminating dark data in enterprises. https://www
    .forbes.com/sites/forbestechcouncil/2020/09/25/illuminating-dark-data-
    in-enterprises/?sh=37e4fd6bc36a.
Southekal, P. (June 2022). Data culture: What it is and how to make it work. https://
    www.forbes.com/sites/forbestechcouncil/2022/06/27/data-culture-what-it-is-
    and-how-to-make-it-work/?sh=733c63120965.

CHAPTER NINE

Best Practices to Realize Data Quality

 INTRODUCTION

Chapter 8 discussed the fact that the first six best data quality practices are related to data capture. This chapter will discuss the next four data quality best practices on data integration. Today, business data is rarely in one system in one format. It is often in many systems in varied formats. For example, if a telecom company needs a complete customer view, the data must be combined from many systems such as ERP, CRM, web traffic, marketing software, websites, IoT sensors data, and even data from agents and partners. If an oil company needs a complete vendor view, the data must be combined from many systems such as ERP, procurement, websites, credit rating data, bank account data, and even product catalog data from vendors. Data integration brings together data gathered from different systems into one common format that can be accessed from one unified source. From the analytics perspective, the pool of data integrated in the integration process is often collected in the common unified system called the data warehouse. But data can also be integrated from different transactional systems into one common transactional system to further improve operations and compliance processes.

The primary objective of data integration is to quickly and consistently achieve a complete view of enterprise-wide data. However, data integration is extremely time consuming and expensive and organizations report that poor data integrations take a toll on the business every year in the form of lost sales orders, missed SLAs, lost revenue opportunities, and increased costs. In fact, 80% of the work in analytics pertains to data integration (Southekal 2020). While there is no one standard approach to data integration, there are always some recommended best practices, and those best practices will be covered in the following sections.

In this context, data integration is commonly associated with the data pipeline. A data pipeline is a set of tools and processes used to automate the movement and transformation of data between the source systems and the target repository, which could be a transactional system or a unified data store like the data warehouse or data lake or a data lakehouse.

 BP 7: RATIONALIZE AND AUTOMATE THE INTEGRATION OF CRITICAL DATA ELEMENTS

Often, the reference and master data elements and their respective data attributes that are used enterprise-wide are managed in different systems by different lines of business resulting in multiple versions of data. Even though many organizations have implemented MDM, there are multiple MDM systems in many firms. These data elements need to be rationalized so that the right data is shared as a single version. For instance, a business unit in Europe might have a vendor who is paid in EUR, while a business unit in the United States might have the same vendor in their system paid in USD. So, from the enterprise there are two vendor records, but physically they are one entity. So how can a single version of truth for the vendor master be created? There are different integration patterns that can be adopted by an organization when to create a single version of truth or golden record for reference and master data elements. Based on the work of the leading MDM solution provider Stibo (Lonnon 2018), there are four key MDM integration styles or architectures for creating the single version of truth for reference and master data elements.

MDM Implementation 1: The Registry Style

Registry style is mainly used to spot duplicates by running cleansing and matching algorithms from various source systems. It assigns unique global identifiers to matched records to help identify a single version of the truth. However, this style does not send data back to the source systems. So any changes to master and reference data in the source systems should be manually managed. The registry architecture or solution cleans and matches the identifying cross-referenced information and assumes that the source system can manage the quality of its own data. Information needed to match and provide the link between corresponding records is stored, and a view of this data can be accessed as required. When a single, comprehensive view of a customer is needed, it uses each reference system to build a 360-degree view. However, central governance of the data is required to ensure that the golden reference and master data record is reliable (see Figure 9.1).

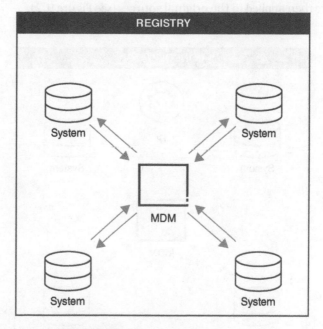

FIGURE 9.1 The Registry Style

So, what are the benefits of a registry-style implementation? If there is a large number of systems with redundant and duplicate reference and master data, it can be difficult to establish an authoritative source. A registry-style approach can quickly analyze the data while avoiding the risk of overwriting information in the source systems. This will help avoid potential compliance failure or other regulatory repercussions that could occur if source data is changed. Fundamentally, registry style provides a read-only view of data without modifying the reference and master data elements and is a useful way to remove data duplications and gain consistent access to the reference and master data. It offers low-cost, rapid data integration with the benefit of minimal intrusion into the source systems.

MDM Implementation 2: The Consolidation Style

With a consolidation style, the reference and master data elements are generally consolidated from multiple sources in the hub to create a single version of truth, known as the golden record. This golden record is stored in the central hub and used for business operations. However, any updates made to the master data are then applied to the original sources (see Figure 9.2).

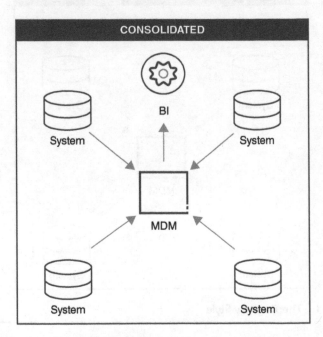

FIGURE 9.2 The Consolidation Style

The key benefit of a consolidation style implementation is that you can pull reference and master data elements from a number of existing systems and channel them into a single integrated MDM hub. This data can then be cleansed, matched, and integrated to offer a complete single record for one or more master data domains. Consolidated or integrated MDM hubs are inexpensive and quick to set up, providing a fast and efficient way for enabling a single version of truth.

MDM Implementation 3: The Coexistence Style

A coexistence style allows you to construct a golden record in the same way as the consolidation style. But the reference and master data are stored in the central MDM system and also updated in its source systems. The coexistence style can be more expensive to deploy than the consolidation style as the reference and master data changes can happen in the MDM system as well as in the source systems. All attributes of the reference and master data attributes must be consistent and cleansed before uploading them into the MDM system (see Figure 9.3).

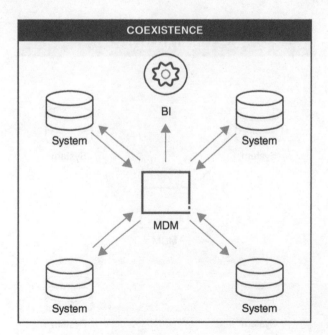

FIGURE 9.3 The Coexistence Style

The main benefit of coexistence style implementation is that data is mastered in source systems and then synchronized with the centralized MDM hub. In this way the data can coexist harmoniously and still offer a single version of the truth. Another benefit of this approach is that the quality of reference and master data is improved, and data access is faster as the reference and master data attributes are physically in a single repository.

MDM Implementation 4: Transaction/Centralized Style

The transaction or centralized style stores and maintains reference and master data attributes using linking, cleansing, matching, and enriching algorithms to enhance the data. The enhanced data can then be published back to its respective source system. The hub supports the merging of reference and master records, and source systems can subscribe to updates published by the central system to give complete consistency. However, this style does require intrusion into the source systems for the two-way interactions. This is the pinnacle of MDM implementation styles where the hub becomes the single provider of master data for a single version of truth for the entire organization (Figure 9.4).

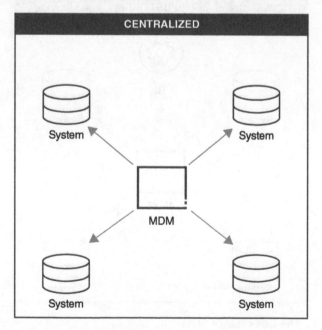

FIGURE 9.4 The Centralized Style

The benefits of a transaction/centralized style implementation is that the reference and master data is accurate and complete at all times while security and visibility policies at a data attribute level can be supported by the transaction-style hub. You gain a centralized set of reference and master data for one or more domains. Large global companies like Shell and P&G have this style of architecture to manage their reference data and master data (Southekal 2017).

The above four MDM implementation styles should help the organization manage and maintain its most critical data elements (CDE), that is, reference data and master data. Each MDM implementation style can evolve from one style to another depending on their needs. So, the selection of MDM platform should consider these implementation styles. However, implementation of these integration styles varies widely between organizations, as the deployment style depends on the role of data in achieving the company's objectives, business process, and the culture of data sharing and collaboration, and more. Overall selecting the right MDM architecture style depends on two key factors (see Figure 9.5):

- Volume of data
- Culture of data sharing

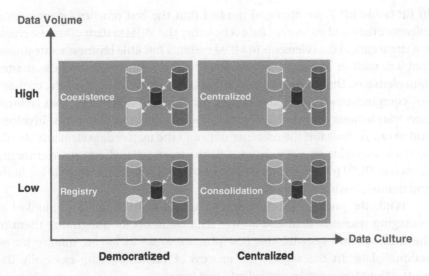

FIGURE 9.5   Key Factors in the Selection of MDM Architectures

In addition, selection of any of the four MDM architectures for implementation is basically balancing the level of reference and master data quality required and the effort required to achieve the SVoT, that is, the golden record (see Figure 9.6). While the registry MDM architecture is quick to implement, the data quality will not be high; the centralized MDM architecture takes lot of effort and time, but the data quality levels are high.

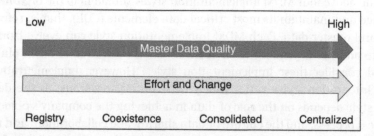

FIGURE 9.6　Master Data Architecture Style Maturity Continuum

BP 8: DEFINE THE SoR AND SECURELY CAPTURE TRANSACTIONAL DATA IN THE SoR/OLTP SYSTEM

In BP 6 and BP 7, we discussed the fact that the best practice for managing reference data and the master data is by using the MDM systems. But just creating these critical data elements in MDM systems has little business value unless they are used in business transactions. These reference data and the master data elements, that is, the CDEs such as plants, currencies, products, customers, equipments, and more should be used in business activities, that is, business transactions like purchase orders, claims, contracts, shipments, invoices, and so on. Technically, the reference data and the master data elements should be made available on a timely basis in the transactional systems commonly known as OLTP (online transaction processing) systems that typically facilitate and manage business transactions.

While the previous two best practices, that is, BP 6 and BP 7, looked at managing reference data and master data elements for integrating them to the transactional systems, this best practice looks at having quality transactional data. In this regard, the process of capturing data especially the transactional data can be divided into two types.

▪ **Manual Data Capture (MDC)**

In MDC, the data is entered manually by a person. MDC works when the data and the data capture process is one-off or discrete, unique, and specific. Despite the fact that this method of collecting data is time consuming and labor intensive, the manual method will continue to exist as many business processes such as inquiries, orders, returns, and claims are inherently discrete. While one of the reasons for poor data quality is the manual method of data entry, the issues can be resolved with proper training based on their roles, applying quality control methods, and so on.

▪ **Automated Data Capture (ADC)**

This method involves the use of computerized technology to capture data. ADC works when the data and the data capture process is defined, standardized, and predictable. Automated data capture has a high initial cost in terms of the initial investment required for the purchase of technology. However, over time the operating costs would reduce significantly as it requires low manpower. Some of the common technologies on ADC are Optical Character Recognition (OCR), Intelligent Character Recognition (ICR), Optical Mark Reading (OMR), Magnetic Ink Character Recognition (MICR), Magnetic Stripe Cards, Smart Cards, Web Data Capture, Voice Recognition technologies, and more that can offer improved data quality.

ADC should the preferred method for data capture wherever applicable. However, the success of ADC depends on formulating rules pertaining to business, workflow, and data. Studies have shown that when data is automatically captured, the average mistake rate was 0.38 errors for 30 data sheets, as against 10.23 errors when processed manually on the same 30 data sheets (Barchard 2009). Technically the selection of the appropriate ADC method, requires a clear understanding of format, source, integration APIs, and quantum of data. Given the speed and the volume at which data is captured these days, one effective strategy to minimize errors is to automate the data capture in the systems of record (SoR) with robotic process automation (RPA), or RPA Bots. RPAs work by emulating human actions by interacting with IT systems at a much faster pace and with better accuracy.

But what exactly is a SoR (system of record)? A SoR is a transactional OLTP (online transactional processing system) IT system used to run core business processes or transactions such as procurement, HR, finance, and so on to create an authoritative data source for business transactions. According to Bain Capital's Ajay Agarwal, "A system of record (SOR) is software that serves as the backbone for a particular business process" (Agarwal 2016). But how does a SoR enable data quality? While not all OLTPs are SoRs, at the core a SoR enables data quality in the enterprise because:

- They are typically positioned close to the point of data origination, and this enables timely capture of data.
- They provide consistent data definitions and ensure data integrity with many tables to create a third normal form (3NF) centric data model. In simple terms, a 3NF data model removes the redundancy effectively so the data become consistent as well as maintains the data integrity.
- They engage a large user community where many users are trying to access the same data at the same time. In other words, users rely on the same data models with the common definitions. This in turn improves data literacy and data quality.
- SoRs are typically relational databases that are designed to process one record at a time by complying with the ACID model (atomicity, consistency, isolation, and durability). The ACID model results in a consistent database – it will either complete, producing correct results, or terminate, with no adverse consequence.
- SoRs provide a short system response time for users to remain productive. So, when users are productive, there is a good chance that data quality goes up.

So, what does it mean to create a SoR? How can one enable an OLTP to be an authoritative source of truth, that is, the SoR? For example, sales and marketing tools like Salesforce and HubSpot are used by many companies for managing clients and prospects respectively. ERP applications like SAP and procurement applications like Coupa are used by many companies for accounting and procurement functions. So, which of these OLTP systems would be the SoR? Will it be Salesforce or HubSpot for sales and marketing? Will it be SAP or Coupa for procurement? Here are three rules or criteria to define a OLTP as a SoR.

1. Firstly, an OLTP that serves more business users has more features, prebuilt API connectors, a large ecosystem (of developers, system integrators, and so on) and could be the potential SoR. For example, any accounting software or service that works with SAP bears the responsibility of coordinating their integration with SAP, not the other way around. The same is true with integrating with large transactional applications such as Apple, Oracle, Salesforce, and so on.
2. Secondly, an OLTP system that is used for regulatory compliance, such as GAPP, IFRS, SoX, HIPAA, and GDPR, financial statements, stakeholder relations, and more could be a potential SoR. Regulatory compliance, which

is the organization's adherence to laws, regulations, guidelines and specifications, needs high data quality. The data quality in these systems should be of high quality because violations of regulatory compliance, that is, poor data quality often result in legal punishment, including federal fines. As mentioned in Chapter 1, when Nexen, an oil company based in Alberta, Canada, spilt over 31,500 barrels of crude oil in Alberta, Canada, the Alberta Energy Regulator (AER) ordered immediate suspension of 15 pipeline licenses issued to Nexen due to lack of maintenance records (AER 2015).

3. Third, a system that has a long life span with a low rate of system change could be a potential SoR. In other words, stability is key in a SoR. This is because standardized business processes such as procurement, accounting, HR, and so on run in these SoR systems resulting in having well-defined data models and well-established work flows.

Hence data quality improves when data is captured and managed in these SoRs, which is the transactional data as often they are closer to the business processes. According to data quality expert, Tom Redman, "To improve data quality, start at the source" (Redman 2020) and that source should be the SoR. In addition, as the data collected in the SoR, it is often the first-party data. This not only avoids the loss of data, but also improves data governance practices resulting in high confidence and trust in business data.

While the data that is captured in the SoR is usually the structured data, the management of unstructured data is to keep digital files digital in the enterprise content management (ECM) systems. ECM systems support unstructured information – such as documents, emails, and scanned images in a secure manner that is accessible only to authorized users. According to the Association for Intelligent Information Management (AIIM), a typical ECM solution performs five key functions (Mixon 2022). They are capture, manage, store, preserve, and deliver:

- The **capture** component involves creating content by converting unstructured content such as invoices, contracts, and research reports into an electronic format.
- The **manage** component connects, modifies, and employs content through means such as document management, collaborative software, web content management, and records management.
- The **store** component temporarily backs up frequently, changing content in the short term within flexible folder structures to allow users to view or edit content.

- The **preserve** component backs up infrequently, changing content in the medium and long term, and is usually accomplished through records management. It is commonly used to help organizations comply with government and other regulations.
- The **deliver** component provides clients and end users with requested content.

Additionally, the SoR transactional system, including the ECM system, needs to be managed securely. Security of the SoR transactional systems is the process of protecting both the software and data against threats such as unauthorized access and modification. Measures such as authentication, authorization, logging, and security testing can significantly enhance the level of software security in the SoR transactional system.

- Authentication: Authentication is recognizing a user's or system's/API identity. It is the process of determining whether someone or something is, in fact, who or what it says it is. This can be accomplished by requiring the user to provide a user name and password when logging in to the application. Authentication can be further bolstered with multi-factor authentication, which requires something you know (user name and a password), something you have (a mobile device), and something you are (a thumbprint or facial recognition). In this context, SOR should also be governed with the right levels of authentication with single sign-on solutions through Active Directory, LDAP, OAuth, or any other authentication platforms.
- Authorization: After a user or system/API has been authenticated, the user is authorized to access the application based on roles. Role-based access control (RBAC) is commonly used to assign permission to users based on their role within an organization. This should cover the ability to protect sensitive data attributes, limit data access according to the user's business roles, and, more.
- The confidentiality mechanisms protect sensitive information from unauthorized disclosure.
- Logging: Logging can help identify who got access to the data. If there is a security breach in the application, logging can provide a time-stamped record of which aspects of the application were accessed and by whom. Non-repudiation further ensures that the log file has not been tampered with, so that the original raw log file can be used for analysis without questioning the authenticity.

■ Application security testing: This is a necessary process to verify and validate that all of these security controls work properly.

Data security is covered in detail in Chapter 11.

 BP 9: BUILD AND MANAGE ROBUST DATA INTEGRATION CAPABILITIES

Even if there is an accepted SoR in the enterprise, in many organizations the data, especially the transactional data, is still distributed in different formats in various transactional systems. Additionally, organizations today hate monolithic, one-size-fits-all IT systems, and instead are opting for specialized and fit-to-purpose transactional systems, including data warehouses, data lakes, and analytics engines to increase business agility, scalability, and reliability. The data elements coming from these various IT systems need to be integrated for a unified view, and the data that is integrated is technically known as the payload. But often data quality issues arise when integrating data and given the scale, volume, and automation associated with data integration these days, even the smallest of the data quality problem gets amplified and affects business performance. To prevent this from happening, the data integration process in a company should be carefully designed leveraging data integration best practices.

The selection of best practices to integrate data is based on four key factors. This data could be reference data or master data or even the transactional data.

1. Pull vs. push based whether it is the sender (server) or receiver (client) who takes the initiative in the integration process
2. Number of systems in scope for integration
3. The volume of data to be integrated
4. Sequence of data transfer, transpose, and orchestration (TTO)

Overall, when business data is integrated and unified, it becomes exponentially powerful, especially for analytics as businesses can adopt analytics holistically and meet specific use cases. Let us look at these four key data integration factors in detail.

Pull vs. Push

The pull and push integration method is based on which system takes the initiative in the data integration process – the sending system or the receiving system. When data is pulled by the client from the server, that means the client is retrieving data. When the data is pushed from the server, it means the server is putting or pushing the data into the client. Basically, if you are taking data out of a database, that is pulling. If you are putting information into the database, that is pushing.

Let us take the example of the pull and push integrations in the context of an OTA (online travel agency) like Expedia. In pull integration the user via Expedia wants a certain hotel room category on specific dates. Expedia (on behalf of the user) sends the information request (dates, room type, price, and so on) to the provider (i.e., the hotel) and pulls the availability in real time. In the push integration, it is the provider (server) – that is, the hotel – who takes the initiative to send relevant data to the OTA on the changes to their database. One example is to indicate that a certain room category is no longer available on specific dates. This data from the hotel goes not only to Expedia, but also to other OTA platforms such as Booking.com, VRBO, Airbnb, and more. To summarize, push integration is suitable for large data loads, while pull integration is more accessible for specific low volume data records (see Figure 9.7).

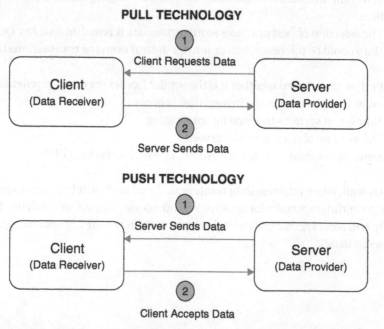

FIGURE 9.7   Pull and Pull Data Integration

The Volume of Data to Be Integrated

Today, enterprises have a need to integrate large volumes of data that is captured from many heterogeneous devices and platforms, including mobile devices, blockchain systems, IoT sensors, and so on. This data, which is in diverse formats, needs to be unified or integrated to get a better understanding of the business. Unifying data from disparate sources into a single view not only offers improved operations and compliance, but also creates a platform to offer more complete, timely, and accurate insights from analytics to the business.

Number of Systems to Be Integrated

System integration is the process of linking various IT systems physically or functionally to act as a coordinated whole. Some challenges in system or data integration include the number of systems to be integrated, lack of willingness to share data with other parties, lack of clear communication guidelines, disagreement on where functionality should reside, high cost of integration, API standards, and more.

TTO Capabilities

As discussed earlier, data integration involves three main "TTO" capabilities:

- Transfer of data from one system to another
- Transpose of data from one type or format into another
- Orchestration of data such as bringing data together from multiple systems, combining it, sequencing the data flow, provisioning resources, scheduling the data flow and more

In today's digital landscape, the actual or payload data including the pertinent metadata involved in the TTO operations is captured mainly in XML (Extensible Markup Language) and JSON (JavaScript Object Notation) formats. JSON is faster because it is designed specifically for data interchange because JSON encoding is terse as it requires less bytes for transit. JSON parsers are less complex, which requires less processing time and memory overhead. XML on the other hand, is slower, because it is designed for a lot more functionalities than just data interchange. Overall, JSON is said to be slowly replacing XML because of several benefits like ease of data modeling or mapping directly to domain objects, more predictability, and easy to understand data structure.

From these four criteria, the following are the eight main data integration best practices. The implementation of these best practices depends on the business purpose or use-cases. Also, all these integration practices are usually managed using middleware systems such as SAP PO, Talend, IBM WebSphere, MuleSoft, Apace MQ, and more. Middleware is software that bridges gaps between other applications, tools, and databases in order to provide unified services to users. It is commonly characterized as the glue that connects different IT platforms together. However, not all IT systems are compatible with middleware, and organizations need a skilled developer to manage the middleware, which can increase operational costs. While middleware is an optional system, it can be a valuable system to further enhance TTO capabilities, offer many trouble-shooting features, and reduce the complexity in data integration.

Application Programming Interface (API)

With API the client pulls the data from the server using appropriate API functions or routines. The request-response feature in the API calls is based on synchronous communication. This means that the data-sending and the data-receiving systems involved in data integration must be available at the time the API call is made. APIs are suitable for data integration processes in which data, especially the transactional data, is immediately required for consumption when pulled from the server by the client.

Additionally, APIs are treated more like products than software code. They are designed for consumption for specific audiences, and they are documented and versioned for security, performance, and scale. Though there are many API architectures or formats, the three common types are:

- REST API Architecture. REST (representational state transfer) is a collection of guidelines for lightweight, scalable APIs to exchange structured and unstructured data such as images and documents. Today, the majority of web application APIs are built on REST, as they enable quick, easy, and secure data transfers using web URLs. Also REST APIs are "stateless," which means the API stores no data or status between requests and responses.
- SOAP API architecture. SOAP (Simple Object Access Protocol) is a stricter protocol with defined metadata formats and is considered more secure than REST API architecture. It is recommended for integration with internal IT systems: that is, systems within the firewall.

■ RPC Architecture. This is a data-integration API protocol that is written with XML or JSON. While RPC APIs are simple and easy to implement, they are not secure compared to REST or SOAP APIs. Basically, RPC-based APIs are a poor choice for enterprise-level APIs because of their limited data type support and limited security.

Practically, there are two main API choices for business enterprises: REST and SOAP. The table lists the salient features of these two API formats.

REST	SOAP
Works with XML, JSON, HTTP, and plain text. Parsing with JSON is faster than parsing in XML.	SOAP works with XML by relying on XML schema and other rules to enforce the structure of its data payloads.
Loose and flexible guidelines with modest security. Suitable for external and partner application integration.	Strict, clearly defined guidelines with advanced security. Suitable for internal application integration (within the firewall).
Works well with data – structured and unstructured.	Works well with processes (actions).
REST is fast as it uses low bandwidth and is highly scalable. Works for real-time application like ecommerce sites.	Slow as it uses more bandwidth with limited scalability. Works for discrete process applications like ERP.

Overall, the selection of the API format – REST or SOAP, is based on the complexity of the information that must be exchanged, the level of data security needed, and the speed of data exchanges. Also, when it comes to data minimalization, APIs help to acquire data based on need. However, to function well APIs need good network connectivity and system availability. But with advances in fiber optics and 5G enabling terabytes of data at very close to the speed of light at low cost, APIs are an attractive option today for data integration to achieve quality data.

Data Virtualization (DV)

Data virtualization (DV) creates a logical data layer that integrates data across the disparate OLTP systems for a unified view. It is commonly called virtual data warehousing. It is also based on APIs and allows an application to retrieve data without requiring technical details about the data, such as how it is formatted at source, or where it is physically located and so on. Basically, DV is a good option for reporting when there are no canonical databases like the data warehouse (DWH) in the company because in DV there is no need to move data or replicate it from the source OLTP systems.

Extract Transform and Load (ETL)

ETL processes enable bulk or batch data movement by consolidating data from various source systems into the organizational data warehouse or any other unified data repository. ETL data is regularly pushed as batch jobs. Basically, ETL is extracting data from different source systems, transforming the data into a format that can be queried, and loading that data into the systems so that the data can be accessed to derive insights. While ETL solutions improve data quality by performing data cleansing prior to loading the data to a different repository for deriving insights, it is very time-consuming. Hence ETL is recommended for integrating data sets that require less frequent data updates in the canonical target system. The ETL process is shown in Figure 9.8.

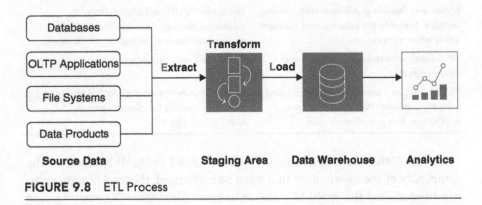

FIGURE 9.8   ETL Process

A simple ETL example could be extracting a consolidated or a complete list of sales orders for a given customer account group over a six-month time period from various sales applications in the United States, Canada, and the UK, transforming the currencies to USD and the UoM to meters, and loading the transformed data sets to the data warehouse for further analysis with appropriate data science tools.

Enterprise Application Integration (EAI)

EAI is data replication or synchronization. It is the frequent copying, that is, pushing of data from one database to another to allow all users to share the same level of data in all the systems, especially the transactional systems. Usually, data integration between the transactional systems is done with EAI integration and data integration between the transactional system and the data warehouse using ETL integration. In other words, the volume of data involved in EAI is much smaller than the data involved in ETL process; EAI is process- or application-oriented, while ETL is data oriented to support decision making. For example, you call the insurance provider to inform them that your address has changed. The customer service person may update your address on a CRM system, but the address also gets updated across all of the company's other IT systems.

Message-Based Integration

Message-based data movement, aka message queues, groups relevant data into messages from the source systems and pushes the data at regular time intervals into other systems. These messages are based on EDIFACT (Electronic Data Interchange for Administration, Commerce and Transport) and ANSI (American National Standards Institute) X12 standards. The message-based data movement works like a phone call – if you ring someone and if they are not there, you leave a message for them. Similarly, in message-based integration one system sends data to another system, and, even if the receiving system does not receive the data immediately, the data is not lost. The payload data will continue to persist in the system – either in the source, middleware, or target system.

Enterprise Service Bus (ESB)

ESB distributes data to different connected transactional systems that need the same data at the same time. ESB acts as a sort of telephone switchboard between IT systems. The core concept of the ESB architecture is integrating different applications with a communication bus that enables each application to talk to the bus. This decouples systems from each other, allowing them to communicate without dependency on, or knowledge of, other systems on the bus. The bus concept that decouples applications from each other is usually achieved using a messaging server and the data that travels on the bus is a canonical format and is often in XML format. This canonical message format is like the contract for the system to collaborate as there is one consistent message format traveling on the bus. This enables every application on the bus to communicate with each other as long as they adhere to this data format. Figure 9.9 illustrates the ESB.

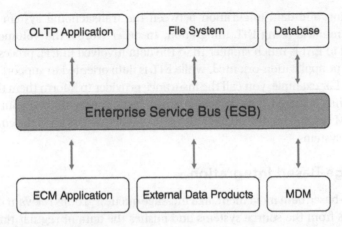

FIGURE 9.9   ESB Process

For example, say a retail enterprise has two different billing systems that need to be connected to get the latest customer master data. The ESB-based integration can enable the two billing systems to communicate through the ESB layer.

Stream Data Integration (SDI)

Streaming is used to describe continuous data streams that can be utilized or acted upon without needing to be downloaded. This integration pattern is especially considered for time-series or telemetry data. While batch data processing methods require data to be downloaded before it can be processed or analyzed, streaming data, allows data to be processed simultaneously. In this regard, SDI refers to integrating data with data pipelines to analyze information in near real-time. Data pipelines are typically associated with real-time data flows of time-series or continuous data. The need for stream data integration has emerged in recent years due to the increase in big-data-centric data sources such as mobile devices, IoT devices, social media, and more, that did not exist a decade ago.

Robotic Process Automation (RPA)

RPA is a form of business process automation that allows anyone to define a set of instructions for a robot or bot to perform. RPA tools such as Blue Prism, Nintex, and UiPath, are governed by business logic and structured data inputs, aimed at automating business processes. RPA is used in most industries, particularly those that include repetitive tasks such as to approve claims, reconcile accounts, process invoices and payments, and more. RPA involves a combination of both push and pull data integration techniques. While RPA can streamline business operations and reduce costs by automating monotonous rules-based business processes, it can be also viewed as part of a roadmap to ML and AI by performing tasks that typically require human intelligence.

Technically the data integration can be done completely by the APIs. But that doesn't mean you have optimized your options. So, each of the eight integration options are based on best-for-fit use cases. While the technical issues such as payload processing failures, network unavailability, and so on are relatively easy to fix, significant issues remain on data integrity. Despite having a good integration method, there could be situations where there is a need to troubleshoot issues associated during the integration process. This is where data lineage traceability has to be built into the data integration methods, and data lineage was covered in detail in Chapter 5.

On a related note, once the reference data and master data are created in the MDM systems using one of the four MDM architecture styles discussed in BP7, the reference and master data need to be integrated for use in business transactions or activities. What is the point in creating a quality customer master record or product master record, if they are not used in sales orders, shipments, and invoices? Hence the reference data and master data elements need to be interfaced to the transactional systems like ERP, CRM, PLM, and more. The eight integration patterns discussed here are applicable even for integrating the reference data and master data to the transactional systems.

 ## BP 10: DISTRIBUTE DATA SOURCING AND INSIGHT CONSUMPTION

This best practice looks at two main areas: data sourcing and data consumption. Let us first start with data sourcing.

As mentioned, several times in this book, data has three main purposes in business: operations, compliance, and decision making. Operations and compliance activities are defined and deterministic, while data for analytics is based on hypothesis, where the data needs are ambiguous. So, if the business purpose is to have quality data for operations and compliance, then the focus should be on managing reference data and master data with MDM systems and integrate the reference data and master data in the MDM systems to the transactional systems that can serve as SoR to run core business processes. However, if the purpose is to have quality data for analytics and decision making, then the focus should be on managing the transactional data using the data warehouses (or any unified data repository) together with the semantic layer. In other words, systems should be leveraged appropriately, based on business need.

INSIGHT

A hammer can also be used to cut an apple. But the hammer works best to drive a nail, and a knife is a better tool to cut an apple. Similarly, MDM works best for operations and compliance on reference and master data managed in ERP and CRM systems, and the semantic layer works best on transactional data to derive insights from the data warehouses.

Basically, MDM can be the system of record (SoR) on the CDEs for operations and compliance, and the semantic layer can be the SoR for analytics. Overall, the selection of the system, that is, MDM or the semantic layer, depends on the fit for purpose or use cases. A hammer can also be used to cut an apple. But the hammer works best to drive the nail, and a knife is a better tool to cut an apple. MDM works best for operations managed in ERP and CRM systems that need consistent data, and the semantic layer works best to derive insights from the data warehouses.

But how does the semantic layer help in achieving quality data for analytics? As mentioned earlier, a semantic layer is a business representation of data that helps users access data using common business terms. A semantic layer maps business data into familiar business terms to offer a unified, consolidated view of data across the organization. Say, marketing calls a business a prospect, sales might call this business a client, and finance calls the same business entity a counterparty. So, you need one definition for this business entity, and you can use both MDM and semantic layer to fix it. But using MDM to fix this data quality issue would take a lot of time and effort as the operations and compliance requirements, which are long-term, need to be satisfied. Also changing past data records would create a lot of confusion in the business as the needs or views of the stakeholders are different. However, with the semantic layer, the different data definitions from all the different sources can be quickly mapped for a unified and single view of data to be used only for analytics. In addition, the insight utilization is often a short-term need where speed and flexibility are needed. Basically, the semantic layer manages the relationships between the various data attributes to create a simple and unified business view that can be used for querying and deriving insights quickly and cost effectively. The relationship is shown in Figure 9.10.

Simplified Data Flow

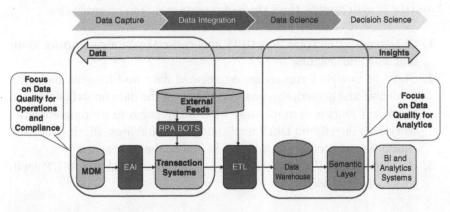

FIGURE 9.10 Data Quality Management in the DLC

Technically, the semantic layer platform links the analytics consumption platform with the data platforms, that is, the data warehouse using the facts (data values), dimensions (data attributes), and hierarchies (i.e., taxonomies) in the data warehouse or any other canonical data platforms such as the data lakes or data marts or lakehouses. The consumption or analytics tools can be Power BI, Tableau, Python, Business Objects, Looker, Jupyter Notebook, and even Microsoft Excel. The queries from the business users could be in SQL (SQL is a query language to store, query, and manipulate data in databases), DAX (DAX, or Data Analysis Expression, is a language to build formulas and expressions), MDX (MDX, or Multidimensional Expressions, is a query language for multidimensional data in OLAP cubes), and so on using the tool-specific native protocols such as XMLA, JDBC, ODBC, SOAP, and REST interfaces. By abstracting the physical form and location of data, the semantic layer platform makes data stored in the data warehouse and data lakes accessible with the one consistent and secure interface for the business users. Overall, the semantic layer is just a metadata layer – it does not contain any data. The semantic layer contains information about the objects in the data source and uses the mapping in the queries.

While the last few lines discussed the data sourcing for operations, compliance, and analytics, what about the effective consumption of data especially the analytics reports or insights? Basically, not all insights from analytics need to be derived from the data warehouses, OLAP cubes (a data structure that stores data in a multidimensional format), and the semantic layer. As businesses have limited amounts of time and resources to manage data quality, consumption insights can be distributed to three types of reports or sources. From the IT systems side, three kinds of reports matter in an enterprise:

1. OLTP reports that come from OLTP applications or databases are for granular data and insights.
2. OLAP or analytics reports for aggregated data and insights including predictive and prescriptive analytics. Though the data analytics trend in the recent years is to move away from OLAP cubes to running analytics workloads directly on OLTP applications or databases, OLAP cubes still continue to be used in many legacy BI and analytics systems.
3. Dashboards for KPIs where the data is typically sourced from OLTP applications or databases.

This strategy, where the consumption insights are distributed to three types of reports, is based on the MAD Framework. The Data Warehousing Institute (TDWI) came out with the MAD Framework as the optimal way to deliver insights. The MAD Framework consists of three layers of consumption insights where each layer has a target audience, insight type, and the desired outcome (Southekal 2020).

1. Monitor. The monitor type of insights is presented to address the information needs of the C-suite. A business dashboard is not much different from the dashboard in a car. It visually conveys a quick snapshot of the required information or KPIs.
2. Analysis. The analysis level provides the ability to dig a little deeper to understand the issue and to serve the insight needs of the middle management. For example, when using the sales reports, one can analyze the details on sales managers, products, stores, customers, and so on. The data and insights in this category will typically have charts and KPIs at an aggregated and multidimensional level. In other words, it is mostly the BI reports.
3. Detail. Often analysts needs the most granular data – that is, the details. For example, one sales area's margin might be much lower on average than other regions and a sales analyst might want to view all the details of pertinent transactions. The insights here are often the reports coming directly from the transactional systems.

Overall, within the MAD framework, the monitor function is for the senior management, the analysis function is mainly for the managers, and the detail function is for the analysts. Finally, distributing the management of data and consumption insights in the three reports also helps in data personalization. According to global consulting firm McKinsey, personalization, specifically, data-driven personalization, will be the prime driver of business success by 2024 (McKinsey 2019). In OLTPs, the data and the reports are created specific to the user and their roles in the most granular fashion. In BI, highly formatted reports are created and distributed to the department or organization to address KPIs. The MAD framework is shown in Figure 9.11.

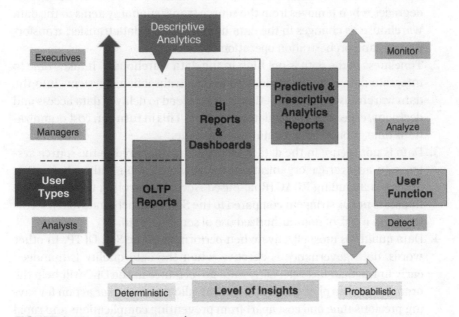

FIGURE 9.11 MAD Framework

The following table contains the mapping of the MAD framework to the user type and the types of analytics or insight reports.

Insight Types	Monitor	Analyze	Details
Descriptive Analytics – OLTP Reports		Managers	Analyst
Descriptive Analytics – BI Reports		Managers	Analyst
Predictive Analytics	Executives and managers	Managers	
Prescriptive Analytics	Executives and managers	Managers	
Dashboards	Executives and managers	Managers	

Today many companies consume reports for regulatory purposes from the data warehouses. It is always prudent to address regular compliance when the data was initially captured, and that system is typically the SoR OLTP. Getting regulatory reports from the data warehouse is a bad and risky practice because:

1. The data integrity in the data warehouse is not comparable to the source systems. Regulators need the most authoritative source of data, and this data is available in the source systems, that is, the SoR. Data often degrades when it moves from the source transactional systems to the data warehouse as changes in the data happen during data transfer, transformation, and orchestration operations.

2. Timeliness of the data is not high in the data warehouses. It takes time to integrate data from the various source or transactional systems into the data warehouse. If data isn't timely, it can lead to delayed data access and decisions, especially on regulatory matters. This in turn can cost organizations time, money, and reputational damage.

3. Data is not secure in the data warehouse as compared to the source systems. In an average organization, the authentication and authorization processes including RBAC (Role-Based Access Control) in the data warehouses is not as stringent compared to the SoR transactional systems. This results in a risk of non-authorized use of sensitive data.

4. Data quality is most effective when performed in the SoR OLTP. In other words, data governance is effective when the data quality is managed early in the data lifecycle. Early data governance in the DLC will help the organizations to plan ahead and thereby allows for quicker action for saving precious time and cost apart from preventing complications and rapid worsening of the data quality issues.

 KEY TAKEAWAYS

Following are the key takeaways of this chapter.

■ Data quality often degrades when (1) data moves from the source transactional systems to the data warehouse, (2) one transactional system to another transactional system, as changes in the data happen during data integration processes such as transfer, transformation, and orchestration.

■ Integrating data involves transfer, transformation, and orchestration of reference data, master data, and transactional data.

▪ Considering the risk, volume, and the changes associated with integrating master data to transactional systems, there are four key architectural patterns – registry, coexistence, consolidated, and centralized. The selection of the right MDM architecture style depends on (1) the volume of data and (2) the culture of data sharing in the company.

▪ Transactional data should be managed in the OLTP system that serves as the authoritative source of truth, that is, the SoR.

▪ The selection of best practices to integrate reference data and master data to the SoR and transactional data with the data warehouses and other transactional systems is based on four key factors.
  1. Pull vs. push, based on whether it is the sender (server) or receiver (client) who takes the initiative in the data integration process
  2. The number of systems in scope for data integration
  3. The volume of data to be integrated
  4. Sequence of transfer, transpose, and orchestration (TTO)

▪ As businesses have limited amounts of time and resources to manage data quality, insights consumption can be distributed to three types of reports based on the MAD framework:
  1. OLTP reports for granular data and insights
  2. OLAP or analytics reports for aggregated data and insights including predictive and prescriptive analytics
  3. Dashboards for KPIs

     In the MAD framework, the monitor insights are for the senior management, the analysis insights are mainly for the managers, and the detailed insights are for the analysts.

▪ The following table summaries the last four data quality best practices (BPs).

#	BP Name	Rationale	Key activities
7	Rationalize and automate the integration of critical data elements (CDE)	Reference and master data elements and their respective data attributes, which are used enterprise-wide, need to be shared so that enterprises are referencing a single version.	Select the appropriate MDM implementation styles to integrate the critical data elements (CDE) based on: ▪ Volume of data ▪ Culture of data sharing in the enterprise ▪ Level of data quality required ▪ Effort required to achieve the SVoT, that is, the golden record

#	BP Name	Rationale	Key activities
8	Define the SoR and securely capture transactional data in SoR/ OLTP system	Just creating CDEs in MDM systems has little business value unless they are used in business transactions. Hence CDEs should be made available on a timely basis in the OLTP systems to manage business transactions.	1. Deploy ADC (automatic data capture) techniques for data capture wherever applicable 2. Define the SoR (System of Record) OLTP as the authoritative data source especially for core business processes transactions 3. Secure the SoR transactional system with authentication, authorization, confidentiality mechanisms
9	Build and manage robust data integration capabilities	Enterprise data is distributed in different formats in various MDM and OLTP systems. The data elements coming from these various systems need to be integrated for a unified view based on robust data integration best practices.	Select one of the eight data integration methods or techniques based on four key factors: 1. Pull vs. push of data 2. Number of systems in scope for data integration 3. The volume of data to be integrated 4. Sequence of data transfer, transpose and orchestration (TTO)
10	Distribute data sourcing and insight consumption	Business data has three main purposes: operations, compliance, and decision making, and data sourcing and consumption should be based on the purpose of data.	1. For operations and compliance, manage the CDEs in MDM and for analytics manage data in the data warehouses and the semantic layer. 2. For effective consumption of data especially the analytics reports or insights, the consumption based on the MAD framework can come from the three types of sources: 1. OLTP reports for granular data and insights 2. OLAP or analytics reports for aggregated data and insights including predictive and prescriptive analytics 3. Dashboards for KPIs

CONCLUSION

Data integration is combining data from various systems and other sources to provide a unified view of data for business. Today, an average enterprise has 464 custom applications deployed and will deploy 37 new applications every year (MacAfee 2017). The tremendous size of the application landscape has resulted in data silos, thereby hampering business performance. An effective data integration solution based on proven best practices can support AI and analytics solutions, thereby helping businesses create new revenue sources, lower expenses, and mitigate risk. Overall, the data integration best practices discussed here are not a product you can buy off the shelf. The implementation of these data integration best practices involves management of technology, data, processes, and change. It is an ongoing and evolving process that brings together disparate data sources for enhanced business results.

REFERENCES

AER. (September 2015). News release. https://static.aer.ca/prd/documents/news-releases/AERNR2015-15.pdf.

Agarwal, A. (March 2016). How to create a billion-dollar SaaS company: build a "system of record." https://venturebeat.com/2016/03/19/how-to-create-a-billion-dollar-saas-company-build-a-system-of-record/.

Barchard, K. (2009). Double entry: accurate results from accurate data. http://barchard.faculty.unlv.edu/doubleentry/Double%20Entry%20APS%202009%20handout.pdf?origin=publication_detail.

Lonnon, M. (March 2018). 4 common master data management implementation styles. https://www.stibosystems.com/blog/4-common-master-data-management-implementation-styles

MacAfee. (April 2017). Every company is a software company. https://www.mcafee.com/blogs/enterprise/cloud-security/every-company-is-a-software-company-today/.

McKinsey. (January 2019). The future of personalization – and how to get ready for it. https://www.mckinsey.com/business-functions/marketing-and-sales/our-insights/the-future-of-personalization-and-how-to-get-ready-for-it.

Mixon, E. (April 2022). What is enterprise content management? Guide to ECM. https://www.techtarget.com/searchcontentmanagement/definition/enterprise-content-management-ECM.

Redman, T. (February 2020). To improve data quality, start at the source. *Harvard Business Review.*

Southekal, P. (April 2017). *Data for business performance.* Technics Publications.

Southekal, P. (April 2020). *Analytics best practices.* Technics Publications.

PART FOUR

Sustain Phase

## CHAPTER TEN

Data Governance

 INTRODUCTION

In the previous chapters pertaining to the first three phases of the **DARS framework** – Define, Analyze, and Realize – we discussed the importance of data to improved business performance. We also analyzed the poor state of data quality and suggested measures including key best practices to improve or realize the data quality. But once these data quality practices are implemented or realized, these measures need to be controlled or managed to ensure that data quality levels are sustained. The fourth phase of the DARS model is the **sustain phase** that looks at measures so that the data quality efforts are supported and maintained to ensure optimal performance. While there are many practices to sustain data quality, one solution to improve and sustain the data quality in business is with effective data governance. In Chapter 1, we discussed that data management and data governance work together to improve data quality in the business. While the previous chapters were primarily on data management, this chapter will go deeper into the role of data governance in data quality.

What exactly is data governance? According to Gartner, "Data governance is the specification of decision rights and an accountability framework to ensure the appropriate behavior in the valuation, creation, consumption and control of data and analytics" (Gartner 2022a). But, why is data governance needed? What is the value of data governance? The main purpose of data governance is to securely manage the quality of data in the entire data lifecycle (DLC) – from capture to consumption so that the right people are managing the right data in the right manner. Overall, the goal of data governance is to establish the methods, set of responsibilities, and processes to standardize, integrate, protect, store, and retire business data.

An effective data governance when applied across all data sources and its movement in the DLC provides the following benefits to an organization, including:

1. Improved data literacy. Data governance provides a consistent and common terminology for data. This will enable clear processes thereby enabling the organization to become more agile and scalable

2. Improved quality of data. Data governance ensures that the 12 key dimension of data quality such as accuracy, completeness, consistency, and more which were discussed in Chapter 3 are properly addressed.

3. Better regulatory compliance. Data governance enables the protection of data by adhering to regulations, such as the General Data Protection Regulation (GDPR), Sarbanes-Oxley Act (SOX), the U.S. HIPAA (Health Insurance Portability and Accountability Act), and industry standards such as PCI DSS (Payment Card Industry Data Security Standards).

4. Improved data management. Data governance brings the human dimension in an increasingly highly automated, model driven, and data-centric world where data is treated as a source of business value. Data governance enforces the best practices in data management, making certain that the concerns and needs of businesses are addressed to achieve quality business data.

Ultimately, all these benefits coming from data governance result in improved operations, compliance, and decision making. This in turn leads to increased revenue, reduced costs, and lowered risks for the business. But implementing the data governance solutions comes with lot of challenges. Figure 10.1, from Gartner, lists some of the important barriers to achieve data governance (Gartner 2022b).

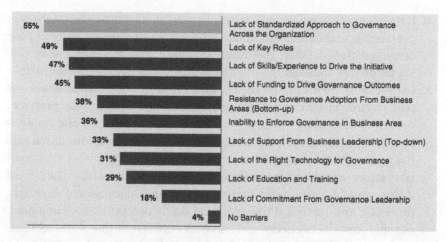

FIGURE 10.1 Barriers to Achieving Data Governance Objectives

In this regard, despite the fact that successful AI models are a combination of (a) well-designed models or algorithms and high-quality data, too much time is spent on improving the model or algorithm – often overlooking the data. This is not a best practice. Studies have shown that just 1% of AI research deals with data. Andrew Ng, a globally recognized leader in AI argues that a data-centric approach leads to better-performing AI solutions. Table 10.1 shows the improvement in accuracy with a model-centric approach vs. a data-centric approach (Ng 2022).

TABLE 10.1 The Impact of Improving the Algorithm versus the Data on Model Performance

	Steel defect detection	Solar panel	Surface inspection
Baseline	76.2%	75.68%	85.05%
Model-centric	+0% (76.2%)	+0.04% (75.72%)	+0.00% (85.05%)
Data-centric	+16.9% (93.1%)	+3.06% (78.74%)	+0.4% (85.45%)

 DATA GOVERNANCE PRINCIPLES

To realize the benefits listed above, an effective data governance program needs to be well designed. The following are seven key principles of data governance:

1. Data governance rests on trust and transparency. All stakeholders in the data governance and data management processes must have integrity in their dealings with each other. They must be truthful and forthcoming in discussing the drivers, constraints, options, and impacts for data-related decisions.

2. Data-related decisions, processes, and controls must be auditable as part of data governance. Data governance and stewardship processes require transparency. It must be clear to all participants and auditors how and when data-related decisions and controls were introduced into the processes. They must be accompanied by documentation to support compliance-based and operational auditing requirements. They must define who is accountable for cross-functional data-related decisions, processes, and controls. Programs must define accountabilities in a manner that introduces checks and balances between business and technology teams, and between those who create/collect/collate data, those who manage it, those who use it, and those who introduce standards and compliance requirements.

3. Data governance programs must introduce and support standardization of enterprise data, especially the CDEs. It is ensuring that business users have access to quality data, and that they follow data standards for storing data in a secure and governed place. In addition, data governance solutions must support proactive and reactive change management activities for reference data values and the structure/use of master data and metadata.

4. Data governance (DG) must be performed throughout the data lifecycle (DLC) regularly, especially in early stages of the DLC, that is, the data management and data integration stages. Data governance in the early stages of the DLC provides improved "1-10-100" business value (i.e., $1 spent on prevention will save $10 on appraisal and $100 on failure costs). This rule was discussed in detail in Chapter 6.

5. Data governance is about data utilization, that is, using data to improve the productivity of the business. It is about striking a balance between data protection and data democratization with clear use-cases. Data democratization is enabling everyone in the organization, irrespective of their technical know-how, to work with data. Data democratization works to ensure that everyone in the organization has access to data when required. Data protection will be covered in Chapter 11.

6. Governing data is not a one-size-fits-all approach. The one-size-fits-all data governance approach is flawed because fundamentally every business and its needs are different and varied. Hence data governance should be adapted to suit the needs of individual needs of the organization based on proven best practices.

7. Root cause analysis (RCA) holds the key to long-lasting and sustainable data quality solutions. RCA works on the principle that problems can be effectively solved by eliminating the causes rather than addressing the symptoms. RCA was discussed in detail in Chapter 4.

 DATA GOVERNANCE DESIGN COMPONENTS

Based on the seven data governance principles discussed in the preceding section, the design of the data governance program should address three key questions or elements. The combination of these three design elements or questions is fundamentally the data governance framework.

1. What data to govern?
2. How to govern data?
3. What organization mechanisms are required to govern data?

The Data Objects to Govern

Let us start with the first design element in data governance – what data objects to govern? Given that there are various types of data in a business enterprise with varying degrees of importance, the selection of data objects should be based on business value. In Chapter 3, we discussed that there are three types of data assets in a business enterprise:

1. Reference data on business categories like plants, customer account groups, payment terms, locations, and so on.
2. Master data for business entities like customers, vendors, products, agents, GL accounts, and more.
3. Transactional data on business events like orders, prices, invoices, claims, and so on.

While the specific data type to govern in a company depends on prevailing business needs, data governance works effectively:

1. When the data objects are managed early in the DLC especially during data capture and data integration.
2. On reference data and master data objects that are shared and reused enterprise-wide in creating business transactions such as purchase orders, sales orders, and invoices.

Data governance is not a one-time endeavor. If quality data is needed in business, data governance needs to be performed throughout the data lifecycle especially on the critical data elements (CDE).

Fundamentally, if high data quality is desired, then the data governance practices should focus on reference data and master data, that is, the critical data elements (CDE) in the initial stages of the data lifecycle (DLC). A simplified example of a data flow diagram in a business enterprise with focus on data governance is as shown in Figure 10.2. Overall, managing data quality as early in the DLC as possible is an effective solution. But often times the data analytics teams try to fix the data quality in the data warehouse first without engaging the source data teams. Fixing just in the EDW (enterprise data warehouse), means other preceding business processes don't have the advantage of the improved data quality. So, it is better to govern data in the early stages of the DLC, that is, in the source system where all the functions, that is, operations, compliance, and decision making are benefited.

Mechanism to Govern Data

The second aspect in the data governance framework is how to govern data. This is mainly about setting up the 3Ps – Policy, Process, and Procedures.

■ A **policy** is a rule that helps an organization govern the data and manage risks based on data standards. A data standard – internal or external – makes the policy more meaningful and effective. A typical data standard includes:
  ■ Naming standards, that is, a set of rules for naming data objects in a logical and standardized way.
  ■ Taxonomy, that is, classification of data into categories and subcategories.
  ■ Ontologies, that is, the relationship of the data object with other data objects.
  ■ Data modeling standards and guidelines for describing conceptual, logical and physical data models. The data modeling standards and guidelines emphasize what data is needed and how it should be organized instead of what operations will be performed on data.

- A business **process** is a series of related, structured activities performed by the data governance team to accomplish a specific objective. These processes could be on data quality surveillance, data exchange, data lineage tracking, data profiling, validation of compliance to regulations, data archiving, and more,
- A **procedure** is a sequence of steps or work instructions to complete an activity within a process. For example, the data archiving procedures could include what data must be archived, assigning a retention schedule for each data object, and so on (see Figure 10.2).

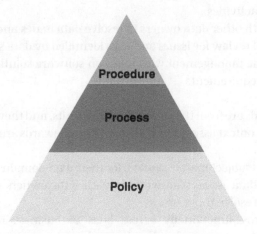

FIGURE 10.2 Policy, Process, and Procedure Hierarchy

Organizational Mechanisms to Govern Data

Data governance is not just about setting policies, processes, and procedures for data. At the core, data governance is a cross-functional and a collaborative endeavour. Hence the third element of data governance is setting up organizational mechanisms to govern data. Based on the work of Gregory Vial (Vial 2020), the three organizational mechanisms to govern business data are structural, procedural, and relational.

Structural Mechanisms

Structural mechanisms are about the creation of data governance roles to enable the creation of policies, process, and procedures. A good data governance program typically includes the steering committee with three main groups – data owners, data stewards, and data custodians. The three positions all work together to create the policies, processes, and procedures for governing data especially the reference data and master data elements.

The data owner, who is from the business is accountable for the data. The data owner makes decisions on the right to access, usage, and sharing. Data owners are responsible for:

- Approving data definitions
- Ensuring the consistent quality of data across the enterprise
- Reviewing and approving master data management approaches, outcomes, and activities
- Working with other data owners to resolve data issues and risks
- Second-level review for issues and risks identified by data stewards
- Providing the management with input on software solutions, policies, or regulatory requirements

Data stewards are from the various business units, and they are responsible for content and context associated with data. Data stewards are responsible for:

- Being SMEs (subject matter experts) for their data domain
- Identifying data issues and working with data owners and other data stewards to resolve these issues
- Working cross-functionally across lines of business to ensure their domain's data is managed and understood

Data custodians are from IT, and they are responsible for the safe and secure capture, integration, and storage of data. Specifically, the data custodians are responsible for

- Maintaining physical and system security with appropriate classification levels of the data in their custody.
- Complying and enforcing with the applicable security standards of the organization. Maintaining backup, disaster recovery plans, and other data safety practices in the event systems or facilities are impaired, inaccessible, or destroyed.
- Managing access of data as prescribed and authorized by appropriate data stewards and data owner.
- Following data handling and protection policies and procedures established by appropriate data stewards and data owner.
- Complying with all regulations and policies applicable to the data in their custody.

Figure 10.3 shows how the three data governance roles come together in the governance of the customer master data.

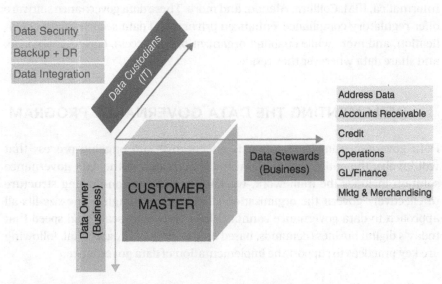

FIGURE 10.3 Data Governance on Customer Master

Procedural Mechanisms

Procedural mechanisms are used by the organization to ensure compliance to the structural mechanisms. This is where the data owner, the data stewards, and the data custodians come together to monitor data quality with appropriate data profiling KPIs. The data profiling KPIs were discussed in Chapter 6. Specifically, data quality monitoring includes setting targets, tolerance limits, control limits, and specification limits. The goal is to ensure conformance to the set values, and effectively communicating the KPIs to stakeholders for taking corrective measures.

Relational Mechanisms

Relational mechanisms include key activities to support collaboration between different data governance teams. Effective data governance requires data owners, data stewards, and data custodians to collaborate for improving the quality of the data in the enterprise. The data stewards and data custodians are responsible for data quality work under the strategic direction of the data owner who is accountable for the quality of the data element or object.

The three design components or elements, that is, data objects, 3Ps (polices, processes, and procedures), and organizational mechanisms, can be implemented with data governance tools from leading companies such as SAP, Informatica, IBM, Collibra, Alation, and more. These data governance software offer regulatory compliance, enhanced privacy and data security, data classi-fication, and more while enabling organizations to access, curate, categorize, and share data wherever they reside.

 ## IMPLEMENTING THE DATA GOVERNANCE PROGRAM

Data governance implementation is an iterative and ongoing process that will involve the entire organization. Implementation of the data governance solution includes the framework, workflows, and decision-making structure to effectively govern the organization's data. Even though a one-size-fits-all approach to data governance cannot deliver the value, scale, and speed that today's digital business demands, based on the work of Gregory Vial, following are key practices to support the implementation of data governance.

1. **Start at the top**

    Data governance should have buy-in from the top leadership, that is, to govern data. Leaders need to acknowledge the strategic relevance of quality data for improved business performance. This could be done by looking at the business KPIs and identifying the pertinent data elements especially the critical master and reference data.

2. **Link data governance to business results**

    A strong data governance strategy ensures that data is consistent, trustworthy, and that the business users have secure access to the right information at the right time. While governing data is often perceived as a way to control data access within the organization as part of regu-lations and other compliance mandates, data governance, also ensures data supports innovation and collaboration.

3. **Design the data governance framework**

    The design of the data governance framework includes:

    ■ Identifying the critical reference data and master data that are in the initial stages of the data lifecycle (DLC)

    ■ 3Ps – policy, process, and procedures – for data access and sharing

    ■ Structural, procedural, and relational mechanisms for collaboration between data owners, data stewards, and data custodian

4. **Leverage the data catalog**

As discussed in Chapter 8, data catalogs are an integral part of data governance, where data owners, stewards, custodians, and business users use the data catalog to know where the data assets are located in the enterprise for effective data governance. An effective data catalog rests on strong metadata management throughout the data lifecycle.

5. **Execute governance practices**

Even though there is not a one-size-fits-all approach to data governance, execution of the practices can be centralized or decentralized. Although a centralized approach to data governance program is a more traditional approach, it requires strict rules and procedures. A more democratized or decentralized approach, on the other hand, opens the data to more users and can lead to faster decision making. Selection of centralized or decentralized approaches requires striking the best balance between control and flexibility or speed.

For example, insurance and financial services companies typically operate in heavily regulated environments, which argues for an emphasis on a centralized approach. Retail and technology firms operating in a less-regulated environment, where intense competition requires robust customer analytics, might emphasize a decentralized approach. Regardless, both approaches include engaging with key stakeholders such as data owners, data stewards, and data custodians to deploy the policies, processes, and procedures leveraging the technology infrastructure, workflows, compliance, decision-making structure, and reporting mechanisms.

6. **Monitor performance of the governance initiatives**

Regularly, evaluate the impact of data governance policies on business outcomes. This will help to identify relevant areas for improvement based on maturity, culture, and risk appetite of the organization. A key tool that is often considered the backbone of data governance solutions is the data catalog. The data catalog, as discussed before is the organized inventory of all data assets to help to identify data assets, assess the usage, improve data quality, check for regulatory compliance, and more.

 DATA OBSERVABILITY

Often traditional data quality processes and tools focus on improving data quality assuming that data is static, that is, data is at rest. In the process they often miss out on the journey of the data across the enterprise. Data observability offers the capability to diagnose the end-to-end data lifecycle by helping organizations get full visibility into the data pipelines by understanding the data flows, identifying data bottlenecks, preventing data downtimes, addressing data quality issues, and more. Fundamentally, data observability helps to minimize the cost of data downtime by predicting, identifying, prioritizing, and helping resolve data quality issues before they impact the business. In other words, data observability is one of the key enablers to realize the 1-10-100 data quality rule.

But why is reducing the data downtime in data pipelines important? Today, data pipelines ingest data from various transactional systems (including external data sources) that may or may not have an API, all with different data models. This means one needs to transform, enrich, and aggregate all that data, in all the various formats, to make it all usable for operations, compliance, and analytics. This is an extremely complex and critical activity, which deals with managing diverse data formats, multiple processing stages, complex routines and business rules, and so on. This demands continuous visibility into the dependencies of data assets and their impact on data quality thereby demanding early identification and remediation to prevent data downtime. Gartner estimates that data downtime, that is, data that is not available or data that is of poor quality, can cost about $140,000 to $540,000 per hour to an average business enterprise (Lerner 2014).

According to Barr Moses, data observability expert and the co-founder and CEO of Monte Carlo Data, "Data Observability, a DataOps process, refers to an organization's ability to fully understand the health of the data in their system, eliminating periods of data downtime with automated monitoring, alerting, and triaging" (Moses 2020). The objective of data observability is to identify and evaluate data quality and discoverability issues, leading to healthier pipelines, more productive teams, and happier customers. In this regard, the five pillars of data observability are:

- ■ Freshness: Is the data up to date? Are there gaps in time where the data has not been updated?
- ■ Distribution: How healthy is the data at the field or attribute level? Is the data within expected ranges?
- ■ Volume: Is the data intake meeting expected thresholds?
- ■ Schema: Has the formal structure of my data management system changed?
- ■ Lineage: If some of the data is down, what is affected upstream and downstream? How do the data sources depend on one another?

Data observability is typically automated and tools, such as Monte Carlo Data, Cisco Appdynamics, Amazon CloudWatch, Acceldata, Collibra, and more, provide end-to-end visibility into the systems and proactively identify potential data quality issues in the data pipelines. Given that majority of issues in data quality come from data integration, data observability enables enterprises to understand the state of its data and especially to get visibility into their data pipelines. In addition, data observability empowers data teams to understand data flows, identify and remove data bottlenecks, and eventually prevent data downtimes.

DATA COMPLIANCE – ISO 27001, SOC1, AND SOC2

While working with business partners, especially external business, compliance to external data standards is very important. Fundamentally, data standards promote interoperability and help in exchanging data between disparate systems, thereby ensuring improved data quality. For example, the EDIFACT data standard is the international EDI standard to help ensure EDI is structured to work for multi-industry and multi-country exchange. In the domain of data compliance, there are a few important industry data standards such as ISO 27001, SOC1, and SOC2. Given that almost every company today is managing a tremendous amount of data, companies including the cloud providers like AWS (Amazon Web Services), Microsoft Azure, GCP (Google Cloud Platform) and more are adhering to these top three data compliance standards.

ISO 27001 provides a framework to help organizations of any size or any industry to protect their data by offering policies, procedures and other controls associated with people, processes, and technology. ISO 27001 provides organizations with the necessary know-how for protecting their data, thereby showing its customers, partners, and other stakeholders that it safeguards the data in line with proven data management practices defined in ISMS (information security management system). Basically, the focus of the ISO 27001 standard is to protect the confidentiality, integrity, and availability of the data by identifying what could happen to the data (i.e., risk assessment), and then defining what needs to be done to prevent such problems from happening (i.e., risk mitigation or risk treatment) by implementing 10 management system clauses and 114 information security controls (Kosutic 2022).

Often discussed with the ISO 27001 standard are two other data compliance standards used by the auditors, that is, SOC 1 and SOC 2. A SOC 1 (Service Organization Control 1) report is a documentation of the internal controls relevant to audit the organization's financial statements. SOC 1 is divided into Type 1 and Type 2 reports. Type 1 reports are on the organization's suitability of the controls on a specific date, while Type 2 reports are on the effectiveness of the controls over a time period. If the company is publicly traded in the United States, SOC 1 is important as Sarbanes-Oxley Act (SOX) compliance is part of SOC 1. SOC 1 also covers the requirements of another data compliance standard, that is, SSAE 16. SSAE 16 (Statement on Standards for Attestation Engagements 16), is a regulation created by the American Institute of Certified Public Accountants (AICPA) for redefining and updating how companies report on compliance controls.

SOC 2 reports on various organizational controls related to security, availability, processing integrity, confidentiality, or privacy of data. Similar to SOC 1, SOC 2 also offers a Type 1 and Type 2 report. The Type 1 report is a point-in-time snapshot of the organization's controls, validated by tests to determine if the data compliance controls are designed and implemented appropriately. The Type 2 report looks at the effectiveness of the controls over an extended period – usually 12 months.

Basically SOC 2 and ISO 27001 data compliance standards both provide companies with strategic frameworks and standards to measure the effectiveness of security controls and systems while managing data. ISO 27001 is mainly about developing and maintaining an ISMS, while SOC 2 audits essential data security controls. As a result, ISO 27001 requires more extensive compliance measures in order to achieve the certification. Basically ISO 27001 is a good choice if the organization is looking to create an ISMS or have international clients. ISO 27001 is a universal data compliance standard around the globe and is recognized by all industries and regions. SOC 2, on the other hand, is useful for organizations that want a data security audit and conduct business primarily in the United States.

 KEY TAKEAWAYS

So, what did we learn in this chapter? The following are the key takeaways.

- Data governance is the specification of decision rights and an accountability framework to ensure the appropriate behavior in the valuation, creation, consumption, and control of data for business purposes.
- Research by McKinsey found that data governance is one of the top three differences between firms that capture this value and firms that don't.

In addition, firms that have underinvested in governance have exposed their organizations to real regulatory risk, which can be costly (McKinsey 2020).

- Data governance is applicable throughout the data lifecycle. But data governance works best when it is implemented early in the data lifecycle.
- The value of data governance is to securely manage the quality of data in the entire data lifecycle – from capture to consumption, so that the right people are managing the right data in the right manner.
- An effective data governance program has seven key principles, namely:
  1. Data governance rests on trust and transparency.
  2. Data-related decisions, processes, and controls must be auditable as part of data governance.
  3. Data governance programs must introduce and support standardization of enterprise data, especially the CDEs.
  4. Data governance (DG) must be performed throughout the data lifecycle (DLC) regularly; especially in early stages of the DLC, that is, the data management and data integration stages.
  5. Data governance is about data utilization, that is, using data to improve the productivity of the business.
  6. Governing data is not a one-size-fits-all approach. Data governance should be adapted to suit the needs of individual needs of the organization based on proven best practices.
  7. Root cause analysis (RCA) holds the key to long-lasting and sustainable data quality solutions.
- Designing a strong data governance framework rest on three key components.
  1. What data to govern
  2. How to govern data
  3. What organization mechanisms are required to govern data
- Executing the data governance framework requires striking a balance between guidelines and control, and access and empowerment. This in turn is dependent on the:
  1. Role of regulations in the industry
  2. Resources available
  3. Culture of data sharing and collaboration
- While working with business partners, especially external business, data compliance to external data standards is very important as external data compliance standards are generally accepted by the industry, such as ISO 27001, SOC 1, and SOC 2.

- ISO 27001 is a universal data compliance standard around the globe and is recognized by all industries and regions. SOC 2is useful for organizations that want a data security audit and conduct business primarily in North America. If the company is publicly traded in the United States, the organization needs to pursue SOC 1 as part of the Sarbanes-Oxley Act (SOX).

CONCLUSION

They say that data governance is like the brakes on a car; brakes aren't there so you can drive slowly. Brakes actually protect you when you drive fast.

INSIGHT

Today data governance is not an option; it is a required capability to help businesses make the most of their data. Governing data helps an organization safeguard its strategic business assets, as it helps in risk mitigation given that businesses today hold incredible amounts of data about customers, suppliers, prices, products, employees, and more that need to comply with laws, regulations, industry standards, internal business processes, and ethics. At the same time, data governance is also required to support operations, decision making, and innovation. Overall, data governance helps businesses to properly and proactively manage data. This means good quality data, better models, better insights, better business decisions, and ultimately superior business performance and results.

However, data will never be of 100% quality, and a certain level of poor data quality has to be tolerated in the enterprise. This is primarily because every business is an evolving entity that is constantly changing, and data, which is a recording of past events, will never will be able to match the level of concurrency of the business. Also, a company does not always need 100% perfect data quality; sometimes they can do with the level that is "good enough." When it comes to insights and decision making, research has shown that 75% data quality is good enough for decision making (Schleckser 2022). Even if the data quality is not very high, the key is to have control so as to mitigate the data quality issues and manage the consequences if they arise. The 10 data quality best practices discussed in Chapters 8 and 9 should serve as a guideline for leveraging and governing data for better business performance.

REFERENCES

Gartner. (2022a). Data governance. https://www.gartner.com/en/information-technology/glossary/data-governance.

Gartner. (April 2022b). Enhance your roadmap for data and analytics governance. https://www.gartner.com/en/publications/enhance-your-roadmap-for-data-and-analytics-governance.

Kosutic, D. (2022). What is the meaning of ISO 27001? https://advisera.com/27001academy/what-is-iso-27001/.

Lerner, A. (July 2014). The cost of downtime. https://blogs.gartner.com/andrew-lerner/2014/07/16/the-cost-of-downtime/.

McKinsey. (June 2020). Designing data governance that delivers value. McKinsey Digital. https://www.mckinsey.com/capabilities/mckinsey-digital/our-insights/designing-data-governance-that-delivers-value.

Moses, B. (December 2020). Introducing the 5 pillars of data observability. https://towardsdatascience.com/introducing-the-five-pillars-of-data-observability-e73734b263d5.

Ng, A. (2022). MLOps: from model-centric to data-centric AI. https://www.deeplearning.ai/wp-content/uploads/2021/06/MLOps-From-Model-centric-to-Data-centric-AI.pdf.

Schleckser, J. (February 2022). 75 percent of the information is all you need to make a decision. https://www.inc.com/jim-schleckser/75-of-the-information-is-all-you-need-to-make-a-decision.html.

Vial, G. (October 2020). Data governance in the 21st-century organization. *MIT Sloan Management Review.*

REFERENCES

## CHAPTER ELEVEN

Protecting Data

 INTRODUCTION

Sustaining data quality also involves protecting business data from corruption, compromise, theft, loss, and other harmful events. The importance of data protection has increased in recent times as the amount of data generated continues to grow at unprecedented rates, thereby increasing complexity and risk. Also, there is little tolerance for unavailability of data or data downtime or data loss, as almost every function in every industry is data centric. So basically data protection is centered around data security, data safety or data availability, and this chapter covers these topics. *Data security* refers specifically to measures taken to protect the integrity of the data from internal and external threats and ensures that users have the data they need to conduct business even if the data is damaged or lost.

DATA CLASSIFICATION

When it comes to data protection, classification of data is the first step. Fundamentally, data can be classified in multiple ways depending on the various criteria – business and technical. In this regard, the following material shows the five different ways data can be classified from the data protection perspective.

Origination

From the data origination view point, business data needs to be protected from two main points of view.

1. **Structured Data**

    Structured data is the data that is organized in a formatted repository (typically in a database) so that the data elements can be uniquely identified for effective processing and analysis. Research shows that just about 20% of the data managed in an enterprise is structured data (Hurwitz et al. 2013). Data protection of structured data is typically done with database controls along with authorization and authentication mechanisms.

2. **Unstructured Data**

    Data that is not stored in any predefined data structure is termed *unstructured data*. Unstructured data includes emails messages, word processing documents, videos, photos, audio files, presentations, webpages, RSS feeds, and more. The market intelligence firm IDC estimates that 60 to 80% of data created and stored today is unstructured data, and over 80% of worldwide data will be unstructured by 2025 (King 2020). Data protection of unstructured data is typically done with authentication and authorization mechanisms.

    From a data protection perspective, structured data can be protected relatively easily compared to unstructured data. While, not all unstructured data needs to be protected, there could be sensitive data in the unstructured data, such as documents preserved for legal or regulatory purposes, intellectual property data, banking details, marketing data, PII data, and more. While access to structured data can be restricted according to strict guidelines, protecting unstructured data is much harder. Though content pattern matching technology can scan servers and workstations to classify unstructured data, those solutions often result in false positives and negatives, which can have a negative impact on the business processes and workflow.

Sensitivity

Inappropriate handling of business data could result in penalties, financial loss, and invasion of privacy, among other consequences. Hence business data is assigned a level of sensitivity within the enterprise, depending on the degree of access and the consequences if it were to be compromised. As discussed in Chapter 2, from a sensitivity or compliance perspective, data can be classified into four main types.

1. Public or open data. Public data is any data that can be freely used, reused, and redistributed with no existing local, national, or international legal restrictions on access or usage. Public data has a low level of sensitivity, and examples include data for public consumption such as a company's balance sheets, details of its products and services, or its senior management profiles, among others.
2. Personal data. PII is any data that can be linked to an individual directly or indirectly and if released could result in harm to the individual.
3. Confidential data. This includes data that have medium sensitivity, including data for internal use such as employee details, product designs, non-disclosure agreements (NDAs), financial information, contracts, trade secrets, and more.
4. Restricted data. This includes regulated and personal data that have the highest level of sensitivity, including SINs, credit card numbers, bank accounts, health information, and the like.

While access to open or public data is simple and straightforward, access to the other three types of data is very contextual. Context-based classification looks at the data and its application, location, time period, roles, and other variables. Questions such as, Why is the data access needed? How is the data being used? Who is accessing it? How long is the access needed for? When are they accessing it?

Ownership

Another way to classify business data and protect it is based on who owns it. *Data ownership* refers to both the possession of and responsibility for data. The control of business data includes not just the ability to access, create, modify, package, derive benefit, sell, or purge data, but also the right to assign these access privileges to others. Data ownership within a business can exist at three levels:

■ Enterprise-owned data is shared across different departments in the company. These data elements (which are usually reference data and master data) have the highest level of process ceremony and control. For example, within the procurement department, the enterprise-owned data can be currencies, plants, payment terms, vendors, materials, and more.

■ Line of businesses (LoB)-owned data is managed by specific departments in the company. These data elements (which are usually the transactional data) have some degree of process ceremony and control. For example, within the procurement function, the LoB-owned data can be contracts and purchase orders.

■ Business function–owned business data is managed and consumed within departments, by a few users. These data elements have the least amount of process ceremony and control as they often deal with transactional data. For example, within the procurement department, the business function–owned data could include goods receiving slips.

So, how can an enterprise protect data based on ownership? Enterprise-owned data, which is shared across different departments in the company, can be owned by the data owner. LoB-specific data, which is often the transactional data can be owned by the specific data stewards from the LoB.

Lifecycle

In Chapter 5, we looked at the data lifecycle. Business data follows a lifecycle with 10 key stages or functions. Eight stages in the DLC are relevant to business: origination, capture, validation, processing, distribution, consolidation, interpretation, and consumption. Two DLC stages are relevant for IT function: storage and security. This means each stage or function has distinct data management processes based on any given stakeholder's needs; these processes address documentation, quality assurance, ownership, and more.

In the first eight stages of the DLC that are relevant to business, the ownership of data is with the business. In the two DLC stages, that is, storage and security, the data ownership is with the IT function. However, when data exceeds the required retention period or no longer serves a purpose to the organization, data should be purged. In that event, business should take the ownership of destroying the data securely. This will not only create more storage space for active data, but also reduce the carbon footprint associated with data. As discussed in Chapter 8, research by Stanford University found that storing and processing 100 gigabytes of data in the cloud per year would result in a carbon footprint of 200 kilograms.

Movement

From the data movement or data loss prevention (DLP) perspective, business data can be of two classes:

1. Data at rest. Data at rest refers to data that is stored physically in any form, including databases, data warehouses, spreadsheets, archives, tapes, off-site backups, and mobile devices.
2. Data in motion. *Data in motion*, or *transit*, refers to data being transmitted across a network. The network can be a public or untrusted network, such as the internet, or a private network, such as an enterprise local area network (LAN).

The security of data will be typically high if it stays in the same location and is subject to the same data protective measures. But data very rarely is static. Often it needs to be accessed, shared with other users, or transferred to a different application. Overall, the ownership of data when at rest and in motion will be with IT.

Figure 11.1 shows views or perspectives for classifying data to protect it.

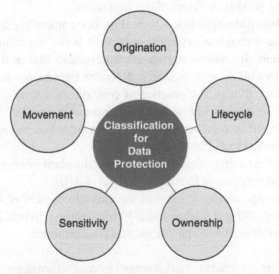

FIGURE 11.1 Classification for Data Protection

DATA SAFETY

Data safety is protecting data in four stages: storage, archival, backup, and disaster recovery (DR). The approaches under these stages, which fall under management of the data infrastructure, are closely associated with servers, software, and cloud or managed services, servers, storage, I/O, networking, and more. The following section looks at the four various ways to manage data safely. Data security is typically not discussed as part of data safety, but is handled as a separate section in this chapter.

Data Storage

Data storage is the collection and retention of data – the bits and bytes behind applications, network protocols, documents, media, address books, user preferences, and more for ongoing or future operations. Data is stored either as direct area storage (DAS) and network-based storage.

1. DAS storage is often in the immediate area and directly connected to the computing machine accessing it. DAS devices include optical discs – compact discs (CDs) and digital video discs (DVDs), hard disk drives (HDD), flash drives, solid-state drives (SSD), and so on.
2. Network-based storage allows more than one computing device to access the storage through a network, making it better for data sharing and collaboration. Its off-site storage capability also makes it better suited for backups and disaster recovery. Network-based storage is applied for data backup, that is, the practice of copying data from a primary to a secondary location, to protect data in case of a disaster. Two common network-based storage setups are network-attached storage (NAS) and storage area network (SAN).
   - NAS is often a single device made up of redundant storage containers or a redundant array of independent disks (RAID).
   - SAN storage can be a network of multiple devices of various types, including SSD and flash storage, hybrid storage, hybrid cloud storage, backup software and appliances, and cloud storage.

Further, data is stored in "hot" storage or "cold" storage repositories based on the need. The usage of temperature terms *hot* and *cold* is used to reduce data storage costs. Data storage comes with a cost that is dependent on several factors, such as the size of the storage devices, rack space, floor space, the amount of power required, the number of power supplies, redundancy and recovery capabilities, and so on. Cold storage is much cheaper than hot data storage.

- *Hot data storage* refers to stored data that's delivered quickly and is readily available for immediate use in day-to-day business activities. Hot storage holds data that needs to be available right away. Hot tier data is typically used for transactional applications
- Cold storage doesn't require fast access. It refers to data that is seldom accessed and typically has slow retrieval times. It mostly represents archived and infrequently accessed data. These are increasingly stored in low-cost object and cloud storage tiers. Cold storage is used for analytical applications.

But how is "hot" or "cold" storage of data related to data quality? As discussed in Chapter 3, one of the key data quality dimensions is availability. When data is rarely accessed, low-cost storage or cold data storage is preferred. In cold data storage, data is stored in low-cost equipment that doesn't necessarily have the performance requirements needed for high data availability. On the other hand, when there is a need for continuous on-demand data, hot data storage equipment is useful as it offers optimized low-latency data access routines to manage workloads without being held back by network and other infrastructure limitations.

Data Backup

A data backup is a copy of the data stored on the IT infrastructure and is used to restore that original data in the event of a data loss. Again, data backup ensures data availability. The optimal backup strategy is typically performed on network-based storage devices depending on each organization's needs. But there are three main types of backup methods – full, incremental, and differential.

- A full backup is when a complete copy of all files and folders is made.
- Once the one full backup is made, then afterward only the data that has changed since the last full backup will be backed up again. This is the incremental backup method.
- A differential backup is a cumulative backup of all changes made since the last full backup, that is, the differences since the last full backup.

Data Archiving

The third data safety strategy is data archiving. Data archiving is moving data that is no longer actively used to a separate storage device for long-term retention. Archive data typically consists of older data that remains important to the organization or must be retained for future reference or regulatory compliance reasons. The goal is to reduce costs on hot storage while retaining old data needed in cold storage for future reference or analysis, and information needed for regulatory compliance.

Basically, data archiving is the practice of identifying data that is no longer active. It involves moving data out of the production system into long-term storage systems in a manner that it can be brought back into service when needed. Data is usually archived that must be retained due to operational or regulatory requirements.

Disaster Recovery

The fourth data safety approach is disaster recovery (DR). DR involves processes for quickly reestablishing access to applications, data, and IT resources after an outage or disaster especially when the primary site is not available for some time to run business operations. The two key metrics in DR are Recovery Time Objective (RTO) and Recovery Point Objective (RPO).

1. RTO is the amount of time it takes to recover normal business operations after an outage.
2. RPO is the amount of data you can afford to lose in a disaster.

 DATA SECURITY

Data security or cyber security entails protecting data from destructive forces and unauthorized users or systems, in order to maintain its integrity throughout its lifecycle. Data security encompasses measures on authentication, authorization, and confidentially, with the ultimate goal of preventing unauthorized access and protect data from corruption and loss. Authentication is the ability to identify uniquely a user of a system. Authentication is the ability to prove that a user or application is genuinely who that person or what that application claims to be. Authorization limits access to only authorized users and prevents the unauthorized use of data and the applications. The confidentiality mechanisms protect sensitive information from unauthorized disclosure.

In addition, data security is applicable whether the data is in motion or at rest. Key "data in motion" protection techniques are:

- An SSL (Secure Sockets Layer) is used to establish an encrypted link between a web server and the browser.
- FTPS is FTP (File Transfer Protocol) with added SSL for security. FTPS uses a control channel and opens new connections for data transfer.
- SFTP is SSH (Secure Socket Shell) File Transfer Protocol. While SSH is a network protocol that provides a secure way to access a remote computer, SFTP was designed as an extension of SSH to provide file transfer capability. So SFTP uses only the SSH port for both data and control.

The important "data at rest" protection techniques are as follows:

- Physical control is the restriction of physical or in-person access to data center.
- Access control is achieved by the process of authentication and authorization of the data. Today, users and systems are authenticated with single sign-on solutions through Active Directory, LDAP (Lightweight Directory Access Protocol), OAuth, or any other user authentication platforms. User and system authorization is typically performed with role-based access control (RBAC) methods.
- Masking is the process of hiding original data or obfuscating original data with random characters or data with tokenization, scrambling, and other techniques. Tokenization involves substituting a sensitive data element with a non-sensitive equivalent (called a "token") that has no meaning or use. Scrambling is the process of mixing up sensitive data. This process is irreversible, so that the original data cannot be discerned from the scrambled data.
- In encryption, data is encrypted using an encryption algorithm, generating cipher text that can only be read if decrypted.
- Anonymization is the removal of sensitive information before processing.
- Database controls are building access controls in databases such as enforcing user authentication, access rights and integrity constraints. For example, record-level security and field-level security are managed using database controls. Record-level security is used to control access to specific data objects, for example, access to sales orders for a specific product category. Field-level security settings – or field permissions – control whether a user can see, edit, and delete the value for a particular field of an

object and is managed with database controls. Field-level security settings protect sensitive fields such as credit card details, SSN, and more without having to hide the candidate object.

 KEY TAKEAWAYS

The following are the key takeaways from this chapter.

- Data protection is the process of protecting data from corruption, compromise or loss. Data protection is centered around three key areas:
  - Data classification for effective management
  - Data safety or availability
  - Data security
- There are five different ways data can be classified from the data protection perspective. They are:
  - Origination
  - Lifecycle
  - Ownership
  - Sensitivity
  - Movement
- Data safety is protecting data with four key approaches: storage, archival, backup, and disaster recovery (DR) practices. Data safety is associated with data storage.
- Data security entails protecting data from destructive forces and unauthorized users or systems whether the data is in motion or at rest.

 CONCLUSION

Data protection is the process of protecting business data from corruption, compromise, or loss. Data protection ensures that data is not corrupted, is accessible for authorized purposes only, and is in compliance with applicable legal or regulatory requirements. While data protection measures might conflict with the strategy of data democratization, which strives to enable everybody in an organization to work with data, data still needs to be protected to prevent misuse. While companies want to democratize data for faster decision making, there is strong pressure on companies to maintain data security to avoid data breaches and risk regulatory noncompliance.

The three key areas of data protection, that is, data classification, data safety, and data security, ensure that the protected data is available when needed and usable for its intended purpose by the right users.

REFERENCES

Hurwitz, J., Nugent, A., Halper, F., and Kaufman, M. (March 2016). Unstructured data in a big data environment. https://www.dummies.com/article/technology/information-technology/data-science/big-data/unstructured-data-in-a-big-data-environment-167370/.

King, T. (November 24, 2020). 80 percent of your data will be unstructured in five years. *Data Management Solutions Review.*

## CHAPTER TWELVE

Data Ethics

 INTRODUCTION

Today the importance of data ethics is increasing due to the profound impact of data on business performance. Trust is an essential part of every relationship, and loss of trust can lead to loss of customer loyalty and subsequently loss of business. According to a recent Deloitte survey, 90% of global consumers said they would sever ties with an organization if the company used their data unethically (Deloitte 2017). This is important, given that many firms rely extensively on data for building trust in their products and services in the market. In addition, due to the sensitive nature of the data they collect, companies today are also subject to strict data protection regulations. While many firms are seriously taking measures to address the compliance of data to regulations concerning data, there is still a lot of grey area associated with the moral and ethical issues associated with data.

DATA ETHICS

What exactly is data ethics? Data ethics is a branch of ethics that evaluates data practices – generating, collecting, processing, consuming, and sharing data – that have the potential to adversely impact people and society. The Open Data Institute (ODI) defines data ethics as: "A branch of ethics that evaluates data practices with the potential to adversely impact on people and society – in data collection, sharing and use" (ODI 2021). It includes addressing instances of right and wrong conduct in relation to data in general and personal data in particular.

Overall, data ethics encompasses the moral obligations of managing data and how it affects individuals and society. For example, one of the most quoted examples of the unethical use of data is within the Correctional Offender Management Profiling for Alternative Sanctions (COMPAS) software. This software is used in the U.S. criminal justice system to predict the likelihood of criminals reoffending. COMPAS has come under criticism for its alleged bias against minority ethnic groups. In the insurance industry, as underwriting becomes increasingly automated with AI and ML, there is an increased risk of discriminatory outcomes being experienced by consumers. People of color seeking home loans have been overcharged by millions thanks to AI tools used by lenders. In recruitment, many employers now use AI-driven tools to screen job seekers, and many of these tools pose enormous risks for discrimination against people with disabilities and other protected groups (Akselrod 2021). An unethical approach to data has also contributed to some of the worst accounting scandals in human history. WorldCom manipulated financial data on income statements and balance sheets to make their company look much better to investors. Issues like these damage the reputation of every institution that collects and applies data (Fletcher 2022).

 IMPORTANCE OF DATA ETHICS

Fundamentally, data ethics is about responsible and sustainable use of data. As discussed, it is about doing the right thing for people and society. Getting data ethics wrong has greater consequences than ever before, as laws are much more stringent today. For example, Cambridge Analytica had to close down its business as it inappropriately accessed data of over 50 million Facebook users without their consent. But with a structured and transparent data ethics strategy, businesses can derive three important business benefits:

1. Compliance. Ensuring ethical AI helps ensure compliance to laws and regulations such as General Data Protection Regulation (GDPR), California Consumer Privacy Act (CCPA), PIPEDA (Personal Information Protection and Electronic Documents Act of Canada), and more. In this regard, the term *data subject* refers to any living individual whose personal data is collected, held, or processed by an organization.
2. Trust. Businesses that apply key ethics principles, such as ownership, privacy, transparency, and more will create more customer trust, and this in turn will build greater customer goodwill and loyalty.
3. Performance. Companies that adhere to ethical data practices make better decisions with reduced bias and ultimately achieve better business results.

The ethical use of data goes deeper than regulatory compliance. Enterprises are realizing a new reality where customers and other stakeholders want to have good understanding of what companies are doing with their personal data. According to a recent study by McKinsey, 71% of respondents said they would stop doing business with a company that gave away sensitive data without permission (Korolov 2020).

 PRINCIPLES OF DATA ETHICS

In any branch of ethics, including data ethics, intentions matter. Before collecting data, ask yourself why you need it, what you'll gain from it, and what changes you'll be able to make after analysis. If your intention is to hurt others, profit from your subjects' weaknesses, or any other malicious goal, it's not ethical to collect their data. In addition, always strive to collect the minimum viable amount of data, so you are taking as little risk as possible with your subjects. For example, in the multiple linear regression model, if the prediction of the store sales is based on the store manager's age that attribute might pose risks due to privacy aspects. Instead, a better attribute could be store manager's experience.

Following are the three key principles of data ethics; these three principles can be used to formulate appropriate strategies (OGL 2020).

Ownership

Accountability or ownership means that there are effective governance and oversight mechanisms for managing data. When it comes to personal data, the individual has ownership over their personal information. So, how can insurance companies manage individuals' data? Accountability is an integral part of all aspects of data processing, and efforts are being made to reduce the risks for the individual and to mitigate social and ethical implications. Some common ways you can obtain consent are through signed written agreements, digital privacy policies that ask users to agree to a company's terms and conditions, and pop-ups with checkboxes that permit websites to track users' online behavior with cookies.

Transparency

Transparency means that the actions and processes on data management are made open to inspection in a complete, open, understandable, easily accessible, and free format. When it comes to personal information, data subjects have a right to know how you plan to collect, store, and use data. When gathering data, exercise transparency. Data processing activities and automated decisions must be truly transparent and explainable. The purpose and interests of data processing must be clearly understood by the individual in terms of understanding risks, as well as social, ethical, and societal consequences. Withholding or lying about your company's methods or intentions is deception and both unlawful and unfair to your data subjects.

Fairness

Technically or legally, unfairness is defined as the disparate treatment of, and disparate impact on, certain unpledged groups based on protected attributes such as gender, race, religion, color, age, and more. Human beings are inherently vulnerable to biases, and there are chances for human bias to be embedded via the data in the AI systems we create. Hence it is important to eliminate any unintended discriminatory effects of data on individuals and groups. Basically, fairness is the practice of using AI and ML technologies without any favoritism or discrimination.

MODEL DRIFT IN DATA ETHICS

Ethical use of data in AI and ML is severely affected by AI model drift. Model drift is the degradation of data analytics model performance due to changes in data and relationships between the data variables. Model drift occurs when the accuracy of insights, especially from predictive analytics, are significantly different from the insights derived during the model training and deployment periods. Specifically, there are three main sources or symptoms of model drift.

1. Data drift: When the characteristics of the independent or feature or predictor variables change
2. Concept drift: When the characteristics of the dependent or label or target variables change
3. Algorithm drift: When the algorithms including the assumptions made in the algorithm selection lose relevance due to changes in business needs

What are the root causes of these three main sources or symptoms of model drift? The primary reason for model drift is change in business. Business strategies and objectives change due to mergers, acquisitions, and divestitures (MAD), new product introduction, new laws and regulations, entry to new markets, and more. Basically, a business is a constantly evolving entity. All these disruptions will change the way the original data analytics models are used by the business. But at the same time, knowing the sources of model drift will help in identifying the right remediation measures required to bring the performance of the model back to an acceptable or desired level.

What is the business impact of model drift? Today, data analytics models are increasingly becoming the major drivers of business decisions and performance. This trend will continue at a much faster pace given the rate at which data is captured and the increasing maturity of machine learning (ML) platforms. In this context, managing model drift is critical to ensure the accuracy of insights or predictions. Fundamentally, reducing or eliminating model drift will enhance trust in the models, thereby promoting the adoption of data and analytics across the organization.

At its core; model drift is not a technology management problem, it is a change management problem. This change in the context of data and analytics can be effectively managed by implementing the following three strategies.

1. The data is a reflection of reality, and often the degradation of data results in degradation of model and business performance. Hence manage data drift with effective data governance practices. We all know the fundamental principle of data processing is that garbage in, garbage out. So, identify the variables in the hypothesis, define the data quality KPIs, set targets and thresholds, and track these KPIs continually to get alerted on any drifts on data quality.
2. Continuously assess the business dynamics and constantly review the relevance of the existing data analytics models with the stakeholders. While talking to the stakeholders, use the following three questions as a reference.

1. Why do you want to have insights? How much do you want to know? What is the value of knowing and not knowing the insights?
2. Who owns the insights coming out of the models? Who is accountable to transform insights into decisions and actions?
3. What are the relevant data attributes required for the model to derive accurate and timely insights?

3. Integrate ModelOps and DataOps practices to enable quick and ethical replacement of the deployed analytics model with another if the business circumstances change. ModelOps (or AI model operationalization) is focused primarily on the governance and lifecycle management of a wide range of operationalized artificial intelligence (AI) and decision models (Gartner 2022a). DataOps as discussed in Chapter 7, is a collaborative data management practice focused on improving the communication, integration, and automation of data flows between data managers and data consumers across an organization (Gartner 2022b). Given that data is the fuel on which the models run, without data, models have practically no business utility. Basically, sound integration of ModelOps and DataOps practices helps in quickly progressing the analytics models from the lab to production.

Overall, the best way to manage model drift is by continuously governing and monitoring the model performance with the right KPIs. While deploying the data analytics models is important, what really matters are the models that are actually consumable by the business for improved business performance. As they say, change is the only constant in life, and businesses change and evolve to stay relevant as well. Involving business stakeholders early on, reviewing the change with metrics, and continuously adjusting for improvements is critical in managing model drifts.

DATA PRIVACY

A key ethical responsibility that comes with handling data these days is ensuring data privacy. Personal identifiable information (PII) is any data that can be used to identify an individual. According to NIST, PII is any information about an individual maintained by an agency, including (1) any information that can be used to distinguish or trace an individual's identity, such as name, social security number, date and place of birth, mother's maiden name, or biometric records; and (2) any other information that is linked or linkable to an individual, such as medical, educational, financial, and employment information (NIST 2022).

PII can be divided into two categories: linked and linkable information. Linked information is any personal detail that can be used to identify an individual. Examples of this kind of PII include: full name, home address, email address, SSN, Internet Protocol (IP) address, device IDs, cookies, and more. On the other hand, linkable information is indirect and on its own may not be able to identify a person, but when combined with another piece of information could identify, trace, or locate a person. Some examples of PII that can be considered linkable information are first or last name country, state, city, zip code, gender, race, and so on.

So, why is securing PII data important? Safeguarding PII data is important because, increasing numbers of organizations and their customers are at risk of identity theft where hackers create false accounts and even sell identities to individuals or companies that specialize in collecting personal data. To protect individuals' privacy and their PII data, organizations should ensure appropriate data security methods. While there are many techniques to protect sensitive PII data, data masking is the most common technique. By substituting the actual PII data with false data, organizations can disguise the identities of individuals and keep their privacy intact. In this context, the key data masking techniques are:

1. **Tokenization**

   In this type of data masking, the true or actual data values are substituted or tokenized with dummy values. For example, with a nine-digit SSN number, one might substitute the number's first six digits with a dummy value such as 0 or X, say (000)-000-972. By performing PII substitution, this data is no longer linked to a unique individual, but still preserves some relevant information (in our example, the last three digits of the SSN number).

2. **Data Scrambling**

   In data scrambling the characters of a data field are scrambled or jumbled up to obfuscate. Data scrambling can also be used to truncate data. For example, you might scramble the characters of a person's name (e.g., "Karen Smith" becomes "Krnae Stmih") to preserve the confidentiality of the data.

3. **Adding Noise**

   Adding noise to the data is also known as stochastic substitution. In this method, each field has a random amount of noise added to it. For example, if you want to disguise an individual's age, you might add or subtract a random number between 1 and 5 from the person's true age.

4. **Data Encryption**

Lastly, data encryption is a powerful method to protect PII data. To encrypt sensitive PII data is to transform it into a seemingly random string of letters and numbers. That makes it impossible for anyone without the corresponding decryption key to understand its contents.

Overall, handling PII data is risky, and it is better to be proactive than reactive when managing the PII data. Companies should follow the principle of data minimization (discussed in BP 4 in Chapter 8) and keep only the PII data they need for their business and only for as long as they need it in a single, highly secure area. If the PII data persists after the need has expired, there should follow a retention policy to determine where the PII should be kept, how to secure it, how long to keep it, and how to dispose of it securely, and more. In addition, organizations should implement the principle of least privilege when accessing PII data, that is, provide the user with only the minimum levels of access or permissions needed to perform his or her job functions.

In recent months, to manage data privacy, companies such as Google, Amazon, and Disney have used data clean rooms (DCRs) to safely share data without violating user privacy. Data clean rooms, known as the "Switzerland of data," are a secure environment that enables the connection of distributed, aggregated, and non-personal identifiable data across multiple platforms and parties. Basically, in DCR companies share aggregated data – or data that has been organized into groups or cohorts – rather than individual or granular customer data with any PII association. Examples of DCR are Google Ads Data Hub, Amazon Marketing Cloud, LiveRamp Safe Haven, Disney Data Clean Room, Snowflake, and so on.

 ## MANAGING DATA ETHICALLY

So, how can one inculcate data ethics in the organization? What practices can an organization adopt for ethically managing data. Figure 12.1 shows five domains where organizations can focus to ethically manage the data.

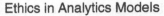

Ethics in Analytics Models

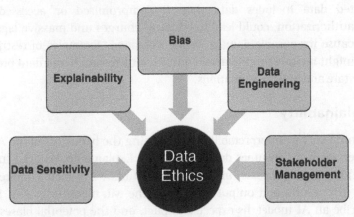

The Content is the Intellectual Property of DBP-Institute

FIGURE 12.1 Components of Data Ethics

Data Sensitivity

Data sensitivity concerns data that should be protected from unauthenticated unauthorized access due to the sensitive nature of data. Authentication is typically a technical aspect where users are authenticated with single sign-on solutions through Active Directory, LDAP (Lightweight Directory Access Protocol), OAuth, or any other user authentication platforms. Authorization is about RBAC (Role Based Access Control) including the ability to protect sensitive data attributes, limit data access as per user's business roles, and, more.

In this context, as discussed in the data classification section in Chapter 11, the four main types of sensitive data that exist in a company are: open data, personal data, confidential data, and restricted data.

1. Open data. Open data involves the idea that some data should be freely available to everyone to use and republish as they wish, without restrictions from copyright, patents, or other control mechanisms.
2. Personal data. PII is any data that can be linked to an individual directly or indirectly and if released could result in harm to the individual.
3. Confidential data. This includes any data that would cause damage to the company if accessed by an unauthorized user. This data often includes financial data, trade secrets, supplier information, and customer data, as well as other sensitive materials.

4. Restricted data. This relates to any data that has security concerns. Restricted data includes data that, if compromised or accessed without authorization, could lead to criminal charges and massive legal fines or cause irreparable damage to the company. Examples of restricted data might include proprietary information or research and data protected by state and federal regulations.

Explainability

Explainability or interpretability is explaining the behaviors of the AI and ML model when it consumes data. Specifically Explainable Artificial Intelligence (XAI) is a set of processes and methods that allows users to comprehend and trust the results and output created by the ML algorithms. XAI is used to describe an AI model, its expected impact, and the potential biases. XAI is a powerful tool for answering critical questions about AI and ML systems and can be used to address rising ethical and legal concerns. In simple terms, XAI allows human users to comprehend and trust the results and output created by ML and AI algorithms.

Why does XAI matter? When it comes to explaining decisions made by algorithms, there is no single approach that works best. There are many ways to explain the phenomena. The appropriate choice depends on the consumer persona and the requirements of the machine learning process. This lack of transparency can lead to significant losses if AI/ML models – misunderstood and improperly applied – are used to make bad business decisions. This lack of transparency can also result in user distrust and refusal to use AI applications. Overall, explainability or XAI is a powerful tool for detecting flaws in the model and biases in the data, which builds trust for all users. It can help with verifying predictions, for improving models, and for gaining new insights into the problem at hand.

Bias

As mentioned before, AI and ML models use data that often does have bias, as the data is collected based on defined business processes. In simple terms, bias is prejudice in favor of or against one thing, person, or group compared with another, usually in a way considered to be unfair. Bias in data is a type of error in which certain elements or attributes of a data set are more heavily weighted and/or represented than others. Though these are many types of bias associated with data ethics, below are some of the important types of bias. Again, biases can never be eliminated; they can only be reduced. Understanding the different types of biases can help in reducing them.

■ Selection bias: Sample bias occurs when the sample data set does not reflect the population or the environment in which the AI or ML model will run. An example of this is certain facial recognition systems trained primarily on images of white men. These models have considerably lower levels of accuracy with white women and people of different ethnicities.

■ Exclusion bias: Exclusion bias is the case of deleting valuable data thought to be unimportant. However, it can also occur due to the systematic exclusion of certain information. For example, imagine you have a data set of customer sales in the United States and Canada: 98% of the customers are from the United States, so you choose to delete the location data thinking it is irrelevant. However, this means your model will not pick up on the fact that your Canadian customers spend three times more.

■ Measurement bias: This type of bias occurs when the data collected especially for training AI and analytics models differ from that collected in the real world. A good example of this bias occurs in image recognition data sets, where the training data is collected with one type of camera, but the production data is collected with a different camera. Measurement bias can also occur due to inconsistent annotation during the data labeling stage of a project.

■ Survivorship bias: It is easier to focus on the winners rather than the runners-up. Survivorship bias is the logical error of concentrating on the entities or events that made it past some selection process and overlooking those that did not, typically because of their lack of visibility. Survivorship bias influences us to focus on the characteristic of winners, due to a lack of visibility of other samples – confusing our ability to discern correlation and causation.

■ Confirmation bias: A confirmation bias involves insights that confirm previously existing data or hypotheses. This type of bias usually happens when the team prefers to play it safe by accepting the status quo.

■ Availability bias: Getting good quality data is challenging. Availability bias refers to the way in which the derived insights are carried out using only hypotheses and data that are easily and readily available.

■ Association bias: This bias is the tendency to be easily influenced by associations because the particular association has proven to be true in the past. For example, the data set may have a collection of jobs in which all men are doctors and all women are nurses. This does not mean that women cannot be doctors, and men cannot be nurses when applied to the population.

■ Framing bias: Framing bias refers to the observation that the manner in which questions are framed and the data is collected can affect decision making.

Again, biases in data can potentially result in misleading conclusions, especially while deriving insights from analytics. While it is impossible to eliminate bias completely, enterprises can strive to be aware and alert to situations where the bias can be damaging to the performance of the business.

Data Engineering

Data engineering is more than data cleansing or wrangling. Data engineering includes data formatting, removing duplicates, renaming, correcting, improving accuracy, populating empty data fields, data integration, aggregation, blending, and other data management activities, and more. The goal of data engineering is to make the quality data available in a canonical database like a data warehouse or data lake in a standardized format to perform analytics and derive insights, apart from using this standardized data to support operations and compliance. The ethical aspect of data engineering is making sure that the data is ethically managed in all the phases of the DLC, that is, in data collection, integration, testing, AI/ML model deployment, and so on. In addition, data ethics in data engineering is ensuring that the data managed is relevant to the organization's goals. For example, if insights are derived using data that is 10 years old to make decisions, those insights are not relevant today. In simple terms, if you need to derive actionable insights from data and analytics, the data needs to be relevant.

Stakeholder Management

Stakeholder management is enabling the stakeholders or the data consumers to have access to the right data at the right time. Data ethics in stakeholder management is refraining from fabricating data or falsifying data and insights that might potentially lead to misleading or manipulating the stakeholders.

- Fabrication is making up data or results; it is intentional misrepresentation of data. It is commonly referred to as the act of making up data and reporting the made-up data as the correct data.
- Falsification is manipulating equipment, or processes, or changing or omitting data or results such that the data is not accurately represented. It is the practice of changing or omitting the collected data to present an incorrect research result.

Overall, ethical data management includes defining ownership of data, obtaining consent from users to collect and share data especially their personal identifying information (PII), reducing model and data drifts, working on relevant data, and last but not least validating the AI/ML algorithms, the training data, and the insights produced by engaging the right business stakeholders.

 ## KEY TAKEAWAYS

So, what did we learn in this chapter? The following are the key takeaways from this chapter.

- Data is an important enabler for businesses to build trust with stakeholders. Getting data ethics wrong has greater consequences than ever before, as laws are much more stringent today and stakeholders are much more informed on the appropriate use of data.
- Fundamentally, data ethics is the responsible and sustainable use of data. As enterprises today are realizing a new reality where customers and other stakeholders want to have good understanding of what companies are doing with their personal data.
- A key ethical responsibility that comes with handling data these days is handling personal identifiable information (PII) data. Given that handling PII data is risky and complex, it is always better to collect and manage minimal amounts of PII data.
- Data clean rooms, known as the "Switzerland of data," are a secure environment that enables the connection of distributed, aggregated, and non-personal identifiable data across multiple platforms and parties.
- Implementing a sound ethical data framework has five key components: data sensitivity, explainability, bias, data engineering, and stakeholder management.
- Ethical data management includes defining ownership of data, obtaining consent from users to collect and share data especially their PII data, reducing model and data drifts, working on relevant data, and last but not the least validating the AI and ML algorithms, by engaging the right business stakeholders.

 ## CONCLUSION

Companies today are more regulated than ever before, and the number of regulations will only increase in the coming years. Companies that collect personal information about people's lives and homes at the most granular level are increasingly under pressure to protect data and ensure it is used responsibly and ethically. Discussions on the ethical use of data are increasing in frequency and intensity due to issues such as bias in data and AI algorithm design, lack of transparency, potential monetization of personal data, and so on. To hold themselves accountable, companies need a formalized data program that covers data ethics thereby building trust with business stakeholders. And to build trust companies must ensure that they have the right leadership, culture, organizational design, operating model, skills, technology, and processes to manage data ethically.

REFERENCES

Akselrod, O. (July 2021). How artificial intelligence can deepen racial and economic inequities. https://www.aclu.org/news/privacy-technology/how-artificial-intelligence-can-deepen-racial-and-economic-inequities.

Deloitte. (May 2017). Breach of trust measured in loss of business. https://www2.deloitte.com/ca/en/pages/press-releases/articles/breach-of-trust-measured-in-loss-of-business-deloitte-reports.html.

Fletcher, C. (February 2022). Why the ethical use of data and user privacy concerns matter. https://venturebeat.com/datadecisionmakers/why-the-ethical-use-of-data-and-user-privacy-concerns-matter/.

Gartner. (2022a). ModelOps. https://www.gartner.com/en/information-technology/glossary/modelops.

Gartner. (2022b). DataOps. https://www.gartner.com/en/information-technology/glossary/dataops.

Korolov, M. (November 2022). Why ethical use of data is so important to enterprises. https://www.techtarget.com/searchbusinessanalytics/feature/Why-ethical-use-of-data-is-so-important-to-enterprises.

NIST. (2022). Personally identifiable information (PII). https://csrc.nist.gov/glossary/term/personally_identifiable_information.

ODI. (June 2021). Data ethics canvas. https://theodi.org/article/the-data-ethics-canvas-2021/.

OGL (Open Government Licence). (2020). Data ethics framework. https://assets.publishing.service.gov.uk/government/uploads/system/uploads/attachment_data/file/923108/Data_Ethics_Framework_2020.pdf.

Appendix 1:
Abbreviations and Acronyms

- 3NF — third normal form
- ACID — atomicity, consistency, isolation, durability
- ADC — automatic data capture
- AI — artificial intelligence
- API — application programming interface
- B2B — business to business
- BI — business intelligence
- BP — best practices
- CCPA — California Consumer Privacy Act
- CDE — critical data elements
- CDO — chief data officer
- CIO — chief information officer
- COTS — commercial off the shelf
- CRM — customer relationship management
- CRUD — create, read, update, and delete
- DAG — direct acrylic graphs
- DAMA — Data Management Association
- DARS — define, assess, realize, and sustain
- DBMS — database management system
- DCR — data clean room
- DLC — data lifecycle
- DLP — data loss prevention
- DMBOK — data management body of knowledge
- DMMM — data management maturity model
- DR — disaster recovery
- DV — data visualization
- DWH — data warehouse
- EAI — enterprise application integration
- ECM — enterprise content management
- EDI — electronic data interchange

- EDIFACT   Electronic Data Interchange for Administration, Commerce and Transport
- EDW   enterprise data warehouse
- ERP   enterprise resource planning
- ETL   extract, transform, and load
- FCF   free cash flow
- GDPR   General Data Protection Regulation
- IAM   identity and access management
- ISO   International Organization for Standardization
- IT   information technology
- IoT   internet of things
- JSON   JavaScript Object Notation
- KPI   key performance indicator
- LDAP   lightweight directory access protocol
- LoB   line of business
- MDC   manual data capture
- MDM   master data management
- MELT   metrics, events, logs, and traces
- ML   machine learning
- OLAP   online analytical processing
- OLTP   online transaction processing
- PCI DSS   Payment Card Industry Data Security Standard
- PII   personal identifiable information
- RBAC   role-based access control
- RCA   root cause analysis
- REST   representational state transfer
- RPA   robotic process automation
- RPN   risk priority number
- ROI   return on investment
- SaaS   software as a service
- SME   subject-matter expert
- SOC   service organization control
- SoR   system of record
- SOX   Sarbanes-Oxley Act
- SQL   structured query language
- SSN   social security number
- SVOT   single version of truth
- TCO   total cost of ownership
- TDWI   The Data Warehousing Institute

- TTO   transfer, transpose, and orchestrate
- VSM   value stream mapping
- WORM   written once, read many
- XAI   explainable artificial intelligence
- XML   extensible markup language
- ZB   Zettabytes

Appendix 2: Glossary

3NF. Third normal form (3NF) is a database schema design approach for relational databases which uses normalizing principles to reduce the duplication of data, avoid data anomalies, ensure referential integrity, and simplify data management.

ACID model. A model applied to data for atomicity, consistency, isolation, and durability.

aggregation. Collecting data from various databases for the purpose of data processing or analysis.

algorithm. A mathematical formula placed in software that performs analysis on a set of data.

analytics. Use of statistical algorithms to derive insights from data.

API (application program interface). A set of programming standards and instructions for accessing or building web-based software applications.

big data. A term for data sets that is so large or complex that traditional data processing applications are inadequate to deal with them.

business intelligence (BI). The general term used for the identification, extraction, and analysis of data.

CDO. The senior executive who bears responsibility for the firm's enterprise-wide data.

cloud computing. A broad term that refers to any internet-based application or service that is hosted remotely.

data. A set of values of qualitative or quantitative variables.

data catalog. An organized inventory of data assets in an organization.

data custodian. The person responsible for the database structure and the technical environment, including the storage of data.

data democratization. Ensuring that everyone in the organization has secure access to data when required.

data element (or object). Any data structure (like the database or table or views or field) that can capture data.

data governance. A set of processes or rules that ensure the integrity of the data and that data management best practice are met.

data integration. It is the process of combining data from different sources and presenting it in a single view.

data integrity. The measure of trust an organization has in the accuracy, completeness, timeliness, and validity of the data.

data lake. A storage repository that holds a vast amount of raw data in its native format, including structured and unstructured data. In the data lake, the data structure and requirements are not defined until the data is needed for processing.

data lineage. It is the process of understanding, recording, and visualizing data as it flows in the data lifecycle from origination to consumption.

data mart. The access layer of a data warehouse used to provide data to users.

data mining. The process of deriving patterns or knowledge from large data sets.

data model. Defines the structure of the data for the purpose of communicating between functional and technical people, to show data needed for business processes, or for communicating a plan to develop how data is stored and accessed among application-development team members.

data observability. A term that covers an umbrella of activities and technologies to identify, troubleshoot, and resolve data issues in near real time.

data product. An outcome of the data and analytics activity to generate new revenue sources, enhance customer service, improve business efficiency, and offer new solutions to problems that span across the industry.

data pipeline. A set of tools and processes used to automate the movement and transformation of data between the source systems and the target repository, which could be a transactional system or a unified data store like the data warehouse or data lake.

data profiling. The process of collecting statistics and information about data in an existing data repository.

data quality. The measure of data to determine its worthiness for decision making, planning, or operations.

data science. A discipline and a stage in the data lifecycle that incorporates statistics, data visualization, computer programming, data mining, machine learning, and database engineering to solve complex problems.

data security. The practice of protecting data from destruction or unauthorized access.

data steward. A person who is responsible for the management and oversight of an organization's data assets, and providing business users with high-quality data that is easily accessible in a consistent manner.

data subject. An individual person who can be identified, directly or indirectly, via an identifier such as a name, ID number, location data, or via factors specific to the person's physical, physiological, genetic, mental, economic, cultural, or social identity.

data visualization. A software tool that provides visual abstraction of data for deriving meaning or communicating information more effectively.

data virtualization. A term used to describe any approach to data management that allows an application to retrieve and manipulate data without requiring technical details about the data, such as how it is formatted or where it is physically located.

data warehouse (DWH). A database that stores data for the purpose of reporting and analysis.

data wrangling. The process of cleaning and unifying messy and complex data sets for easy access and analysis.

database. A digital collection of data and the structure around which the data is organized. The data is typically entered into and accessed via a database management system (DBMS).

database management system (DBMS). Software that collects and provides access to data in a structured format.

deduplication. A method of eliminating a data set's redundant data.

enterprise resource planning (ERP). A software system that allows an organization to coordinate and manage all its resources, information, and business functions.

extract, transform, and load (ETL). A process used in data warehousing to prepare data for use in reporting or analytics.

feature. A measurable property of the data you are trying to analyze. In data sets, features appear as columns or attributes.

Gartner. A multinational research and advisory firm providing information-technology-related insight for IT and other business leaders.

golden record. A fundamental concept in data management that identifies and defines the single version of truth, where truth is understood to be data that is trusted to be both accurate and correct. When building database tables from disparate data sources, there commonly are issues of duplication of records, incomplete values within a record, and records with poor data quality. The golden record solves these issues by correcting duplications, by providing values when a value may not exist, and by improving data quality within a record.

MAD framework. A framework that allows the business user to view data and insights at three levels of detail (Monitor-Analyze-Detail) as required.

machine learning. The use of algorithms to allow a computer to analyze data for the purpose of "learning" what action to take when a specific pattern or event occurs.

master data management (MDM). Master data is any non-transactional data that is critical to the operation of a business – for example, customer or supplier data, product information, or employee data. MDM is the process of managing that data to ensure consistency, quality, and availability.

metadata. Any data used to describe other data – for example, a data file's size or date of creation.

microservices. An architectural approach to software development where software is composed of small independent services that communicate over well-defined APIs. REST APIs is a typical architectural pattern used for microservices.

middleware. Software that bridges gaps between other applications, tools, and databases in order to provide unified services to users. It is commonly characterized as the glue that connects different IT platforms together.

ModelOps. Model operationalization is focused primarily on the governance and life-cycle management of a wide range of operationalized artificial intelligence (AI) and decision models.

NoSQL. A class of database management systems that do not use the relational model. NoSQL is designed to handle large data volumes that do not follow a fixed schema, and this is usually unstructured data. The most popular NoSQL database is Apache Cassandra.

online analytical processing (OLAP). The process of analyzing multidimensional data using three operations: consolidation (the aggregation of available data), drill-down (the ability for users to see the underlying details), and slice and dice (the ability for users to select subsets and view them from different perspectives).

online transactional processing (OLTP). The process of providing users with access to large amounts of transactional data in a way that they can derive meaning from it.

privacy. The need and/or requirement to control access to and dissemination of sensitive, personal, and personally identifiable information in an organization's data stores.

reference data. Data that reflects the business categorization.

risk priority number (RPN). A numeric assessment of risk assigned as part of failure modes and effects analysis (FMEA) where each failure is quantified based on the likelihood of occurrence, likelihood of detection, and severity of the problem.

root cause analysis (RCA). A problem-solving method used for identifying the root causes of faults or problems.

schema. The structure that defines the organization of data in a database system.

service-oriented architecture (SOA). A style of software design where a number of services communicate with each other, in one of two ways: through passing data or through two or more services coordinating an activity.

structured data. Data that is organized by a predetermined structure.

structured query language (SQL). A programming language designed specifically to manage and retrieve data from a relational database system.

system of record (SoR). The authoritative data source for a given data element. To ensure data integrity in the enterprise, there must be one – and only one – system of record for a given data element.

telemetry data. The time-series data from IoT devices, which are used to observe and monitor the performance of the IoT devices.

transactional data. Data describing a business event; usually described with verbs. Transactional data always has a time dimension. Examples include accounts payable and receivable data, or data about product shipments.

unstructured data. Data that has no identifiable structure. Here the data is not arranged according to a pre-set data model or schema.

Appendix 3: Data Literacy Competencies

THE FOLLOWING ARE THE 10 data literacy competencies discussed in the BP 2 section of Chapter 8.

Data architecture Data architecture is the models, policies, rules, and standards that govern which data is managed in the data lifecycle in organizations.

Data acquisition Data acquisition is the process of digitizing data from the world around us so it can be stored and processed in an IT system.

Master data management Master data management (MDM) is a technology-enabled discipline in which business and IT work together to ensure the uniformity, accuracy, stewardship, semantic consistency, and accountability of the enterprise's official shared master data assets. Master data is the consistent and uniform set of identifiers and extended attributes that describe the core entities of the enterprise including customers, prospects, citizens, suppliers, sites, hierarchies, and chart of accounts.

Data engineering This is the practice of designing and building systems for collecting, storing, and analyzing business data and metadata at scale. It also includes the knowledge and skills to determine if data are clean and if they use the best method and tools to take necessary actions to resolve any problems to ensure data is in a suitable form for analysis.

Data ethics The knowledge that allows a person to acquire, use, interpret, and share data in an ethical manner including recognizing legal and ethical issues (e.g., biases, privacy).

Statistical modeling Statistical modeling is the use of mathematical models and statistical assumptions to derive insights. This covers the knowledge and skills required to ask and answer a range of questions by analyzing data including developing an analytical plan; selecting and using appropriate statistical techniques and tools; and interpreting, evaluating, and comparing results with other findings.

Data storytelling The knowledge and skills required to describe key points of interest in statistical information (i.e., data that has been analyzed). This includes identifying the desired outcome of the presentation, identifying the audience's needs and level of familiarity with the subject, establishing the context, and selecting effective visualizations.

3DM   Data-driven decision making (DDDM) is defined as using facts, metrics, and data to guide strategic business decisions that align with your goals, objectives, and initiatives. Also known as evidence-based decision making, 3DM is the knowledge and skills required to use data to help in the decision-making and policy-making process. This includes thinking critically when working with data; formulating appropriate business questions; identifying appropriate data sets; deciding on measurement priorities; prioritizing information garnered from data; converting data into actionable information; and weighing the merit and impact of possible solutions and decisions.

Data stewardship   Knowledge and skills required to effectively manage data assets. This includes the oversight of data to ensure fitness for use, the accessibility of the data, and compliance with polices, directives, and regulations.

Data governance   Data governance is the specification of decision rights and an accountability framework to ensure the appropriate behavior in the valuation, creation, consumption, and control of data and analytics

These 10 competencies are hard skills that can be measured, quantified, and can be learned quickly through training. While these hard skills are important, soft skills such as an individual's personality, people skills, and work ethic are also very important skills as part of data literacy. Soft skills are essentially habits and characteristics that shape how one works with others. So, what are the desired soft skills of a data professional? While every company's soft skill needs in a data analytics professional are different, there are still some common soft skills that can be applied to almost every data analytics role in every company. The 5Cs of soft skills pertaining to data analytics that are often interrelated are: communication, collaboration, critical thinking, curiosity, and creativity. The following section has more details on these 5Cs, including strategies to develop them.

1. *Good communication skills are essential to allow oneself and others to understand information accurately and quickly.* Communication in a data analytics project is not just about writing and speaking, it also includes listening. Listening skills are important because one has to pay close attention to what others, especially data and insight consumers, are saying to understand their insight requirements and decision needs. Due to business and technical complexities, often data and insight consumers are ambiguous in expressing their requirements. Actively listening and asking the right probing questions help clarify and frame consumers' real requirements and needs. Active listening by the data analytics professional helps business stakeholders (i.e., the data and insight consumers) to open up, avoids misunderstandings, and builds mutual trust.

2. *Data and analytics is a team endeavor where business, IT, and data teams need to work together.* Collaboration skills enable the data analytics professional to successfully work toward realizing the common goal with other teams. Collaboration can be further improved by inculcating two key aspects: (1) open-mindedness, that is, being open to appreciating and accepting novel ideas, and (1) respect for other team members when you value their opinions and ask for their ideas and views on various issues and problems.

3. *The third C of soft skills in data and analytics is critical thinking.* Critical thinking is the ability to think rationally and logically and solve problems in a consistent and systematic manner. At the core, data analytics is asking questions to gain insights for decision making. Critical thinking skills in data analytics involves questioning the hypothesis, identifying biases associated with framing the questions, validating the assumptions, selecting the appropriate models, critiquing the accuracy of the analysis and results, deriving and communicating actionable insights, assessing the ethical aspects in using insights for decision making, and more.

4. *Being curious is an important soft skill in data analytics.* This is because data and analytics projects are fraught with uncertainties, ambiguities, and numerous challenges such as unclear decision objectives, time and resource constraints, lack of expertise, poor-quality data, ethical and privacy issues in data, and more. The business and data analytics fields are constantly evolving, and curiosity enables analytics professionals to continuously learn and expand their knowledge and diversify their techniques. Curiosity in the data analytics project also enhances a person's ability to quickly overcome obstacles by asking powerful questions. Powerful questions are open-ended, create possibilities, and encourage deeper understanding and discovery.

5. *The fifth C of soft skills in data and analytics is creativity.* Data analytics is about discovering insights and successful analytics professionals will continuously explore to ensure that the insights are always timely, accurate, and relevant for business. Creativity in data analytics is the process of generating new and useful insights for improved business performance. As there will often be multiple approaches to solving user requirements and needs, being creative allows analytics professionals to consider and explore divergent possibilities and perspectives before converging on a specific analytics solution. It is closely associated with experimentation, that is, identification of the causal relationship between the variables. Overall creativity and experimentation with data and analytics is the vehicle for business innovation.

About the Author

D R. PRASHANTH SOUTHEKAL IS a consultant, author, and professor. He has consulted for over 80 organizations including Procter & Gamble, GE, Shell, Apple, FedEx, and SAP. Dr. Southekal is the author of two books – *Data for Business Performance* and *Analytics Best Practices* – and writes regularly on data, analytics, and machine learning in *Forbes* and CFO University. His second book, *Analytics Best Practices*, was ranked the number-one analytics book of all time in May 2022 by BookAuthority. He serves on the editorial board of MIT's CDOIQ Symposium, and is an advisory board member at BGV (Benhamou Global Ventures), a Silicon Valley-based venture capital firm, and a data and analytics advisor at Evalueserve (CH), Grihasoft (IN), uArrow (SG), Illumex (IL), Astral Insights (United States), and Miles Education (IN). Apart from his consulting and advisory pursuits, he has trained over 3,000 professionals worldwide in data and analytics. Dr. Southekal is also an adjunct professor of data and analytics at the IE Business School (Madrid, Spain) and *CDO Magazine* included him in the top 75 global academic data leaders of 2022. He holds a PhD from ESC Lille (France) and an MBA from the Kellogg School of Management (United States). He lives with his wife, two children, and a high-energy Goldendoodle dog in Calgary (Canada). Outside work, he loves juggling and cricket.

Index

Page numbers followed by *f* refer to figures.

A

Access control, 219
Accessibility of data, 44–45, 50*f*, 213
Accountability, 196, 225, 226
Accounting, transactional data in, 96
Accuracy of data, 43, 44*f*, 50*f*, 104
ACID (atomicity, consistency,
     isolation, and durability)
     model, 74, 241
ADC (automated data capture), 83, 169
Affinity Diagram, 67, 67*f*, 71*f*
Aggregation:
   for data sharing, 230
   defined, 241
   in OLAP systems, 57
   of third-party data, 19
Aggregation stage, 85
Agile, 119, 119*f*
AI, *see* Artificial intelligence
AIDC (automatic identification and data
     capture), 83
AIIM (Association for Intelligent
     Information Management), 171
Algorithms, 232, 241
Algorithm drift, 227
Amortization, 54
Analytics, 4–6
   and artificial intelligence, 5–6
   data enrichment for, 126
   data integration in, 161–162

defined, 241
to derive insights, 51–52
in driving decisions and
     performance, 227
insight consumption reports from, 184
real-time, 46
semantic layer as system of record for,
     181–183, 183*f*
types of, 23
Analytics view, 30–31
Analyze phase, 65. *See also specific focus
     areas and topics*
Anonymization, 219–220
API (application program interface),
     176–177, 241
Application security testing, 173
Arithmetic mean, 99, 100
Artificial intelligence (AI), 5–6
   bias in models of, 232–234
   and big data, 10
   carbon emissions in training
        algorithms, 148
   data overlooked in research on, 195
   defined, 5
   ethical use of, 225, 226
   explainability or
        interpretability of, 232
   model drift in, 226–228
   patterns in, 5, 6
   quality of data for, 44

Assessment of data quality, 95, 142.
    See also Data profiling
Assess phase, xxiii, xxiv*f*. *See also specific*
    focus areas and topics
Asset(s):
    data as, 6–7
    data for better use of, 17
    depreciation of, 54
    tangible and intangible, 3
Association bias, 233
Association for Intelligent Information
    Management (AIIM), 171
Atomicity, consistency, isolation,
    and durability (ACID) model,
    74, 241
Audit trials, data lineage in, 89
Authentication, 172, 218, 231
Authorization, 172, 218, 231
Automated data capture (ADC),
    83, 169
Automatic identification and data
    capture (AIDC), 83
Automation:
    artificial intelligence and analytics
        supporting, 6
    with artificial intelligence and
        big data, 10
    of critical data elements integration,
        162–168, 163*f*–168*f*, 187
    of data observability, 205
    with DataOps, 118
    data pipeline in, 162
    and interface feeds, 77
Availability bias, 233
Availability of data, 47–48, 50*f*
    data searching and retrieval
        challenges, 73
    in hot or cold storage, 217
    limited, 51
    and non-value-added tasks,
        11, 11*f*
    timing of, 75–76
    and tolerance for unavailability, 211

B
Batch Processing, 84
Best practices (BP), xxiii, 133–158,
    161–189
    acceptance of, 134
    build and improve data culture
        and literacy, 138–142,
        141*f*, 156
    build and manage robust data
        integration capabilities, 173–181,
        174*f*, 178*f*, 180*f*, 188
    capture and manage critical data with
        data standards in MDM systems,
        152–155, 157
    in data life cycle, 135–136, 135*f*
    define current and desired state of data
        quality, 142–145, 144*f*, 156
    defined, 134
    define SoR and securely capture
        transactional data in SoR/OLTP
        system, 168–173, 188
    distribute data sourcing and insight
        consumption, 181–186,
        183*f*, 185*f*, 188
    follow minimalistic approach to data
        capture, 145–148, 147*f*, 157
    identify business KPIs and ownership
        of KPIs and pertinent data,
        136–138, 156
    overlap of data governance, data
        management, and, 135
    overview, 133–134, 161–162
    rationalize and automate integration
        of critical data elements,
        162–168, 163*f*–168*f*, 187
    select and define data attributes for
        data quality, 148–151, 151*f*, 157
    sequential implementation
        of, 135, 135*f*
BI (business intelligence), 185, 241
Bias:
    defined, 232
    discriminatory, 224

in ethical data management,
231*f*, 232–234
and ethical data practices, 225
human vulnerability to, 226
IKEA effect, 74–75
types of, 233
Big Data, 10
BP, *see* Best practices
Build and improve data culture and
literacy (best practice #2),
138–142, 141*f*, 156
Build and manage robust data
integration capabilities (best
practice # 9), 173–181, 174*f*,
178*f*, 180*f*, 188
Business data, 17–35
critical data elements, 32–34
deriving value from, 38, 38*f*
first-party, 18, 20–21, 20*f*
key characteristics of, 31–32
key stages for, *see* Data lifecycle (DLC)
main perspectives/views on, 24–31
metrics, 21–22
purpose of, 22–24, 55, 181
second-party, 18–21, 20*f*
telemetry data, 21–22
third-party, 19–21, 20*f*
types of, 18–21, 20*f*
varied systems and formats for, 161
zero-party, 18, 20–21, 20*f*
Business entities:
constant evolution of, 227
definitions for, 182
main objectives of, 10
master data on, 25–26
Business function-owned
business data, 214
Business integrity, 49, 78
Business intelligence (BI), 185, 241
Business metadata, 28, 28*f*
Business performance, 4–6
artificial intelligence and analytics
supporting, 6

data analytics models driving, 227
data cardinality and, 42–43
and data ethics, 225
data quality impact on, 10–12, 11*f*
linking data governance to, 10–12
transactional data promoting, 96
Business processes:
critical data elements impacting, 34
differences in, 150
in 3Ps – Policy, Process, and
Procedures, 198–199, 199*f*
variation in, 101–102
Business results, 9, 9*f*
Business rules, 75, 78, 97
Business strategy:
as data management driver, 9, 9*f*
and data strategy, 8, 153–154
formulating, 134
model drift from changes in, 227
Business value, of data profiling, 95
Business value chain, 17
Business vision, 9, 9*f*

C
Cambridge Analytica, 7, 137, 224
Canonical databases, 57
Capital expenditures (CAPEX), 12, 154
Capture and manage critical data with
data standards in MDM systems
(best practice #6), 152–155, 157
Capture stage, 82–83. *See also*
Data capture
Cardinality:
data, 42–43, 50*f*
relationship, 43
Cash conversion cycle (CCC), 154
Categorizing business data, 25–31.
See also Classification of data
from analytics perspective, 30–31
from compliance perspective, 29–30
from integration perspective, 25–29
from storage perspective, 24–25
Cause-and-effect diagram, 68–69, 69*f*

Causes of poor data quality, 65–79
  data conversion and migration, 76
  data rules affecting business
    operations, 75
  data searching and retrieval
    challenges, 73
  data silos resulting from organization
    silos, 71–72
  differing interpretation and
    consumption of data, 72
  frequency of use and number
    of users, 73
  improper data purging and
    cleansing, 78
  interface feeds, 76–77
  manual errors, 77–78
  poor business case for data origination
    and capture, 73
  poor database design, 78
  root cause analysis of, 66–71
  system proliferation and integration
    issues, 74
  system upgrades, 77
  time-sensitivity of data quality, 75–76
  transient results of data quality
    improvement, 76
  varied value propositions
    between consumers and data
    originators, 74–75
  visible and hidden, 94–95, 94*f*
CCC (cash conversion cycle), 154
CDEs, *see* Critical data elements
CDO (chief data officer), 241
Centrality measures, 97–98, 143
  integrating variation KPIs and,
    109–111, 110*f*, 111*f*
  mean, 99–100, 101*f*
  median, 98–100, 101*f*
  mode, 98–100, 101*f*
Change management, 155, 227–228
Channels, for data product
  delivery, 122–123

Chief data officer (CDO), 241
Classification of data, 212–215, 215*f. See
  also* Categorizing business data
  by data life cycle stage, 214, 215*f*
  by data movement or data loss
    protection, 215, 215*f*
  by origination, 212, 215*f*
  by ownership, 213–214, 215*f*
  by sensitivity, 29, 213, 215*f*
  structured data, 24–25, 212
  unstructured data, 24–25, 212
Cloud computing, 31, 87, 148, 241
Coefficient of variation (CV),
  97, 104
Coexistence style MDM implementation,
  165–168, 165*f*, 167*f*, 168*f*
COGS (cost of goods sold), 12, 13
Cold data storage, 217
Cold deck imputation, 130
Cold storage repositories, 216
Collaboration skills, 247
Collection of data:
  in building data product, 121
  without purpose, 6
Collective outliers, 108
Commercialization of data product, 123
Common causes variation, 102
Communication skills, 246
COMPAS (Correctional Offender
  Management Profiling for
  Alternative Sanctions), 224
Competencies for data literacy, 140,
  141*f*, 245–247
Competitive advantage, 4
Completeness of data, 39–40, 40*f*, 50*f*
Compliance, 11–12
  data, 205–206
  and data ethics, 225
  data for, 22–23
  data lineage in, 89
  data origination and capture
    for, 23–24

of data products, 122
and data profiling, 95, 96
to data quality dimensions, 51
master data management as
    system of record for, 182
master data management for, 118
poor data quality impacts on, 53
privacy, 7
regulatory, *see* Regulatory
    compliance
requirements for, 121
Compliance view, 29–30
Concept drift, 227
Confidential data, 30, 152
    defined, 231
    in systems of record, 172
    types of, 213
Confidentiality, for data security, 218
Confirmation bias, 233
Conformity of data, 41, 50*f*
Consensus culture, 140
Consent, obtaining, 226
Consequences of poor data quality,
    52–54, 54*f*
Consistency of data, 41, 50*f*
Consolidation style MDM
    implementation, 164–165, 164*f*,
    167–168, 167*f*, 168*f*
Consumer behavior:
    and ethical use of data, 223
    leveraging data about, 10
Consumers of data:
    discriminatory outcomes
        experienced by, 224
    potential, 120–121
    varied value propositions between
        data originators and, 74–75
Consumption of data, xxii, 72–73
    in building data product, 122
    distributing data sourcing and
        insight consumption, 181–186,
        183*f*, 185*f*, 188

poor data quality resulting
    from differences in
    interpretation and, 72
responsibility for, 137
Consumption stage, 86
Context:
    in data quality, 51–52, 55
    key aspects of, 59
    and trust, 59–60
Contextual outliers, 108
Continuous improvement:
    in data quality management, xxii
    in performance, 139
Controls, data-related, 196
Control charts, 143
Control limits, 143, 144*f*
Cookies, third-party, 19
Correctional Offender Management
        Profiling for Alternative Sanctions
        (COMPAS), 224
Correctness of data, 44, 50*f*
Costs:
    of data storage, 216–217
    leveraging data to reduce, 10
    of poor data quality, 38, 52–55, 54*f*
Cost of goods sold (COGS), 12, 13
Coverage (fit for purpose), 48, 50*f*
Creativity, 247
Critical data, capturing and managing
        with data standards in MDM
        systems, 152–155, 157
Critical data elements (CDEs), 32–34
    defined, 33
    determining, 137
    governance of, 198
    identifying, 33–34
    in master data management, 116
    rationalizing and automating
        integration of, 162–168,
        163*f*–168*f*, 187
    standardization of, 196
Critical thinking skills, 247

Cross-sectional data analysis, 27
Curiosity, 247
Currency of data, 45–47, 50*f*
Customers, 18
Customer service, optimizing, 17
CV (coefficient of variation), 97, 104
Cybercrimes, 6–7
Cybersecurity, *see* Data security

D
DAMA (Data Management
  Association), 39, 88
Dark data, 6, 145–146, 148
DARS model, *see* Define-Assess-Realize-
  Sustain model
DAS (direct area storage), 216
Dashboards, insight consumption
  reports from, 184
Data, 3–7. *See also specific types of data*
  artificial intelligence,
    analytics and, 5–6
  as business asset or liability, 6–7
  in business value chain, *see*
    Business data
  classification of, 212–215, 215*f*
  for competitive advantage, 4
  as critical business resource, 3–4
  dark, 6, 145–146, 148
  defined, 241
  depreciation of, 54–56
  identify ownership of, 136–138, 156
  intended vs. actual use of, 72
  missing, 130
  status changes in, 81
  trust in, 60
Data acquisition:
  competency in, 245
  integrating acquired data,
    128, 129*f*
Data analysis. *See also* Analytics
  cross-sectional, 27
  longitudinal, 26–27

Data architecture, competency in, 245.
    See also Reference architecture
Data archiving, for data safety, 218
Data at rest, 215, 219
Data attributes, selecting and defining,
    148–151, 151*f*, 157
Data backup:
  for data safety, 217
  to solve physical data decay, 66
Database(s):
  canonical, 57
  cardinality in, 42
  defined, 243
  legacy, 76
  relational, 24
Database design, 78. *See also* Reference
    architecture
Database management system (DBMS),
    48–49, 243
Data breaches:
  cost of, 11
  with large databases, 6–7
Data capture:
  for analytics to derive insights, 52
  best practices for, 133–158
  from data conversion or migration, 76
  in data lifecycle, 82–83
  in enterprise content management
    systems, 171
  manual vs. automatic, 83, 169
  minimalistic approach to,
    145–148, 147*f*, 157
  for operations and compliance, 23–24
  poor business case for, 73
  telemetry data, 21
  without defined purpose, 6
Data cardinality, 42–43, 50*f*
Data catalogs:
  defined, 150, 241
  leveraging, 203
  and semantic layer, 150–151, 151*f*
  value of, 150

Data clean rooms (DCRs), 230
Data cleansing, 78, 117
Data compliance standards, 205–206.
    See also Compliance
Data conversion and migration, poor
    data quality resulting from, 76
Data culture, 138–142, 141*f*, 156
Data custodian, 200, 201, 201*f*, 241
Data decay, 54–55
    logical, 65, 66, 94
    physical, 66
    reasons for, *see* Causes of poor
        data quality
Data definitions, 148–150, 182
Data delivery, 171
Data democratization, 196, 241
Data dictionary, 27, 80–89
Data downtime, 204, 211
Data drift, 227
Data-driven culture, 139
Data-driven decision making
    (DDDM; 3DM):
    business data for, 23
    competency in, 246
Data-driven organizations, 4, 10
Data economy, 4
Data element (or object):
    critical, *see* Critical data
        elements (CDEs)
    for data governance, 197–198
    defined, 241
    for measurement, identifying, 95
    metadata describing, 27
    perspectives or views of, 24–31
Data engineering:
    competency in, 245
    in ethical data management, 231*f*, 234
Data enrichment, 126–131
    data imputation, 130–131
    feature engineering, 127–128, 127*f*
    synthetic data, 129
    third-party data integration, 128, 129*f*

Data ethics, 223–236
    AI model drift in, 226–228
    and bias, 231*f*, 232–234
    competency in, 245
    data engineering in, 231*f*, 234
    in data management, 230–235, 231*f*
    data privacy in, 228–230
    data sensitivity in, 231–232, 231*f*
    defined, 224
    and explainability or
        interpretability, 231*f*, 232
    important business benefits
        of, 224–225
    principles of, 225–226
    in stakeholder management,
        231*f*, 234–235
Data fabric, 124–126, 125*f*
Data footprint, 148
Data governance (DG), 8, 193–209
    barriers to achieving, 194–195,
        195*f*, 195*t*
    benefits of, 194
    competency in, 246
    data compliance in, 205–206
    and data management, 7
    data objects to govern in, 197–198
    data observability in, 203–205
    data quality in, 56
    defined, 8, 194, 241
    design components for, 197–202
    goal of, 194
    implementing program for, 202–203
    key principles of, 195–197
    listing of critical data
        elements in, 33–34
    organizational mechanisms
        for, 199–202
    overlap of data management, best
        practices and, 135
    overlap of data management, data
        quality, and, 7–9, 9*f*
    procedural mechanisms for, 201

Data governance (DG) (*Continued*)
  relational mechanisms for, 201–202
  structural mechanisms for,
      199–201, 201*f*
  success criteria for, 8–9
  3Ps – Policy, Process, and Procedures
      for, 198–199, 199*f*
  use of term, 7
  value of, 194
Data imputation, 130–131
Data in motion/transit, 215, 219
Data integration, 25
  best practices for, 161–189
  building and managing robust
      capabilities for, 173–181, 174*f*,
      178*f*, 180*f*, 188
  and data governance, 9
  defined, 85, 241
  defining SoR and securely capturing
      transactional data in SoR/OLTP
      system, 168–173, 188
  distributing data sourcing and
      insight consumption, 181–186,
      183*f*, 185*f*, 188
  interface feeds, 76–77
  issues with, 74
  for OLTP systems, 57
  primary objective of, 162
  rationalizing and automating
      integration of critical
      data elements, 162–168,
      163*f*–168*f*, 187
  for remediation of data
      quality, 117, 118
  third-party, 128, 129*f*
Data integrity, 48–49, 50*f*
  and database design, 78
  of data structures, 57
  in data warehouse, 186
  defined, 242
  enabling, 78
  enforcing, 48–49
  types of rules for, 49

Data lakes, 57
  data pipeline to, 162
  defined, 242
  diverse data sets in, 88
Data lakehouses, 57, 162
Data lifecycle (DLC), 8, 81–88, 90
  aggregation stage of, 85
  best practices in, 135–136, 135*f*
  capture stage of, 82–83
  consumption stage of, 86
  data classification by stage
      in, 214, 215*f*
  data governance throughout, 196
  data observability throughout, 204
  data quality impacted during, 55
  and data security, 87, 88*f*
  and data storage, 87, 88*f*
  defined, 82
  distribution stage of, 85
  interpretation stage of, 86
  IT business-enabled stages, 86–87, 88*f*
  origination stage of, 82
  processing stage of, 83–85
  validation stage of, 83
Data lineage, 88–89
  in data observability, 204
  defined, 88, 242
  importance/value of, 89
Data literacy:
  building and improving, 138–142,
      141*f*, 156
  competencies for, 140, 141*f*, 245–247
  with data governance, 194
  defined, 138
  for leaders, 137–138
Data loss, 211
Data loss protection (DLP), 215, 215*f*
Data management, 8
  architectural frameworks for, *see*
      Reference architecture
  data ethics in, 230–235, 231*f*. *See also*
      Ethical data management
  with data governance, 194

in data lifecycle stages, 214
data standards in MDM systems,
   152–155, 157
defined, 8
in enterprise content management
   systems, 171
metadata, 28
overlap of data governance, best
   practices and, 135
overlap of data governance, data
   quality, and, 7–9, 9*f*
privacy compliance in, 7
stakeholder needs in, 37
of structured and unstructured
   data, 24–25
transparency of, 226
types of data for, 115–116
use of term, 7
Data Management Association
   (DAMA), 39, 88
Data mart, 85, 117, 242
Data mesh, 124–126, 125*f*
Data minimization, 145–148,
   147*f*, 157, 230
Data mining, 242
Data model:
   defined, 242
   enterprise-wide, 74
   model drift, 89, 226–228
Data movement:
   archiving data, 218
   data classification by, 215, 215*f*
Data object, *see* Data element (or object)
Data observability, 203–205, 242
DataOps (data operations), 118–120,
   119*f*, 228
Data origination, 133
   for analytics to derive insights, 52
   data classification by, 212, 215*f*
   from data conversion or migration, 76
   in data lifecycle, 82–83
   for operations and compliance, 23–24
   poor business case for, 73

Data originators, varied value propositions
   between consumers and, 74–75
Data owners, 200, 201, 201*f*
Data ownership, 136–138, 156
   classification by, 213–214, 215*f*
   in data ethics, 225–226
   defined, 213
Data pipeline:
   in data integration, 162
   in DataOps, 120
   defined, 162, 242
   getting visibility into, 204, 205
   key characteristics of, 120
Data preservation, 171
Data privacy:
   confidential data, 30, 152, 172, 213
   in data ethics, 228–230
   personally identifiable information,
      228–230
   regulations for, 22
   sensitive data, 30, 152, 225
Data processing, 83–84, 226
Data products, 120–123
   channels for delivering, 122–123
   collection of, 121
   commercialization of, 123
   compliance of, 122
   compliance requirements for, 121
   consumption of, 122
   defined, 242
   potential consumers of, 120–121
Data profiling, 93–112
   best practice for, 142–145, 144*f*
   business value of, 95
   centrality measures in, 98–100, 101*f*
   criteria for, 95–98
   defined, 95, 143, 242
   integrating centrality and variation
      KPIs in, 109–111, 110*f*, 111*f*
   key performance indicators in, 93–94
   process states in, 111, 111*f*
   sample of, 110*f*
   variation measures in, 100–109

Data protection, 211–221
  classification of data in,
      212–215, 215*f*
  and data governance, 196
  data safety, 216–218
  data security, 218–220
  elements of, 211
  General Data Protection
      Regulation, 11
Data purging, 78
Data quality, xxi, 37–61. *See also*
      individual topics
  best practices for, *see* Best
      practices (BP)
  for business growth, 10–12, 11*f*
  context in, 51–52
  with data governance, 194
  in data warehouse, 186
  defined, 242
  defining current and desired state of,
      142–145, 144*f*, 156
  definitions of, 38–39
  depreciation of data, 54–56
  dimensions of, 39–51, 50*f*. *See also*
      Dimensions of data quality
  high quality, 8–9
  issues with, 37–38, 38*f*
  in IT systems, 56–58
  lack of high-quality data, 4
  leadership commitment to, 10–12
  overlap of data management, data
      governance, and, 7–9, 9*f*
  poor, 52–54, 54*f*. *See also* Poor
      data quality
  relevance of, xxiii
  selecting and defining data attributes
      for, 148–151, 151*f*, 157
  time-sensitivity of, 75–76
  and trusted information, 59–60
  use of term, 7
Data Quality Assessment
      (Maydanchik), 71, 76

Data quality improvement, transient
      results of, 76
Data rules:
  business operations affected by, 75
  for data integrity, 49
Data safety, 216–218
  data archiving, 218
  data backup, 217
  data storage, 216–217
  disaster recovery, 218
Data science, 135*f*, 148–149,
      151*f*, 183*f*, 242
Data scrambling, 229
Data searching and retrieval
      challenges, poor data quality
      resulting from, 73
Data security, 45, 50*f*, 218–220
  application security testing, 173
  and data governance, 9
  with data movement, 215
  in data warehouse, 186
  defined, 211, 242
  in IT systems, 87, 88*f*
  for personally identifiable
      information, 229–230
Data sensitivity:
  data classified by, 29, 213, 215*f*
  in ethical data management,
      231–232, 231*f*
  types of, 231–232
Data silos, 71–72, 140
Data sourcing, distributing, 181–186,
      183*f*, 185*f*, 188
Data standards:
  compliance to, 205–206
  in MDM systems, capture and
      manage critical data with,
      152–155, 157
  for metadata management, 28
  typical components of, 198
Data stewards, 200, 201, 201*f*, 242
Data stewardship, competency in, 246

Data storage, 24–25
    backup, 217
    costs of, 216–217
    for data safety, 216–217
    energy required for, 6
    in enterprise content management
        systems, 171
    in IT systems, 87, 88*f*
    media for, 31
Data storytelling, competency
    in, 245
Data strategy:
    and business strategy, 9, 153–154
    for ethical data use, 225–226
Data subject, 225, 242
Data traceability consistency, 41
Data values:
    consistency of, 41
    missing, 130
Data vendors, 75
Data virtualization (DV), 177, 242
Data visualization, 89, 242
Data warehouse (DWH), 57–58
    collecting data in, 161
    data pipeline to, 162
    defined, 243
    fixing data quality in, 198
    regulatory reports from, 186
The Data Warehousing Institute (TDWI),
    38, 184
Data wrangling, 117, 118, 243
DBMS (database management system),
    48–49, 243
DBP Institute, 37
DCRs (data clean rooms), 230
DDDM, *see* Data-driven decision making
Decision making:
    business data for, 17, 23
    data analytics models driving, 227
    data-driven, 23, 246
    data-related, 196
    deriving insights for, 51–52, 139

leveraging data in, 10
    transactional data promoting, 96
Deduplication, 47, 243
Deep learning, 148
Define-Assess-Realize-Sustain (DARS)
        model, xxiii, xxiv*f,* 193. *See also*
        individual phases
Define current and desired state of
        data quality (best practice #3),
        142–145, 144*f,* 156
Define data attributes for data quality
        (best practice #5), 148–151,
        151*f,* 157
Define phase, xxiii, xxiv*f,* 3–12. *See also*
        specific focus areas and topics
Define SoR and securely capture
        transactional data in SoR/
        OLTP system (best practice #8),
        168–173, 188
Degrading of data, 54–55. *See also*
        Data decay
Deming, Edwards, 101
Denormalization, 57
Depreciation of data, 54–56. *See also*
        Data decay
Descriptive analytics, 23, 141–142
Design components, for data
        governance, 197–202
Destruction of data, 214
DevOps, 119, 119*f*
DG, *see* Data governance
Differential backup, 217
Digitally mature firms, 4
Dimensions of data quality, 39–51, 50*f*
    accessibility, 44–45, 50*f*
    accuracy and precision, 43, 44*f,* 50*f*
    completeness, 39–40, 40*f,* 50*f*
    conformity or validity, 41, 50*f*
    consistency, 41, 50*f*
    correctness, 44, 50*f*
    coverage (fit for purpose), 48, 50*f*
    currency and timeliness, 45–47, 50*f*

Dimensions of data quality (*Continued*)
  defined, 39
  integrity, 48–49, 50*f*
  redundancy or availability, 47–48, 50*f*
  security, 45, 50*f*
  uniqueness or cardinality, 42–43, 50*f*
Direct area storage (DAS), 216
Dirty data, 54
Disaster recovery (DR), 218
Discrimination, 224
Distribute data sourcing and insight
    consumption (best practice #10),
    181–186, 183*f*, 185*f*, 188
Distributed Processing, 84
Distribution of data, 204
Distribution stage, 85. *See also* Data
    integration
DLP (data loss protection), 215, 215*f*
Domain integrity, 49, 78
DR (disaster recovery), 218
Drucker, Peter, 136
Duplicated data, 47–48
DV (data virtualization), 177, 242
DWH, *see* Data warehouse

E
EAI (enterprise application
    integration), 178–179
EBITDA (earnings before interest, taxes,
    and depreciation), xxi, 10
ECM (enterprise content management)
    systems, 171–172
Ecosystem, 123
EDIFACT data standard, 205
Encryption, 219, 230
Energy consumption, of data centers, 6
Engagement, artificial intelligence and
    analytics supporting, 6
Enterprise application integration
    (EAI), 178–179
Enterprise content management (ECM)
    systems, 171–172

Enterprise-owned data, 214
Enterprise resource planning (ERP),
    41, 142, 243
Enterprise service bus (ESB),
    179–180, 180*f*
Enterprise-wide data model, 74
Entity integrity, 49, 78
Environmental, social, and governance
    (ESG), 6, 148
Equifax, 7
ERP, *see* Enterprise resource planning
ESB (enterprise service bus),
    179–180, 180*f*
ESG (environmental, social, and
    governance), 6, 148
Ethical data management, 230–235,
    231*f*. *See also* Data ethics
  bias, 231*f*, 232–234
  data engineering, 231*f*, 234
  data sensitivity, 231–232, 231*f*
  explainability or
      interpretability, 231*f*, 232
  stakeholder management,
      231*f*, 234–235
ETL (extract, transform, and load),
    178, 178*f*, 243
Event data, 22
Exclusion bias, 233
Experian Data Quality, 4, 38
Explainability, in ethical data
    management, 231*f*, 232
Explainable Artificial Intelligence
    (XAI), 232
Extensible Markup Language
    (XML), 175
Extract, transform, and load (ETL),
    178, 178*f*, 243
Extrapolation imputation, 131

F
Fabrication, 234, 241
Facebook, 4, 7, 137, 224

Failure Mode and Effects Analysis
    (FEMA), 67, 68, 68*f*, 71*f*
Fairness, in data ethics, 226
Falsification, 234
FCF (free cash flow), 154
Feature(s):
    of data fabric solutions, 123, 124*f*
    of data mesh solutions, 124, 125*f*
    defined, 243
Feature engineering, 127–128, 127*f*
FEMA, *see* Failure Mode and
    Effects Analysis
Feravich, Stuart, 45
Financial impacts of poor data
    quality, 53
Financial Industry Regulatory Authority
    (FINRA), 23
Financial regulation, 23
FINRA (Financial Industry Regulatory
    Authority), 23
Firefox, 19
First-party data, 18, 20–21, 20*f*, 129
Fishbone diagram, 68–69, 69*f*, 71*f*
Fit for purpose, 48
5Cs of soft skills, 246–247
5-Whys method, 69–70, 70*f*, 71*f*
Flawed data, xxi
Follow minimalistic approach to data
    capture (best practice #4),
    145–148, 147*f*, 157
Framing bias, 233
Free cash flow (FCF), 154
Frequency of use, poor data quality
    resulting from, 73
Freshness of data, 204
Full backup, 217
Fuzzy logic, 47

G
Gartner:
    on cost of poor quality data, 55
    on data downtime, 204

on data governance, 194
on data literacy, 138–139
on data management, 8
on data products, 120
defined, 243
on master data, 25–26
General Data Protection Regulation
    (GDPR), 11
Geometric mean, 99–100
Global outliers/global anomaly, 108
Goals, 96–97, 143–145, 144*f*
Golden record, 47, 243

H
Hamilton Insurance Group, 4
Harmonic mean, 99, 100
Hidden data quality issues,
    94–95, 94*f*
Hierarchical culture, 140
HL7, 153
Home Depot, 11
Hot data storage, 217
Hot deck imputation, 130
Hot storage repositories, 216

I
IBM, 38, 136
Identify business KPIs and ownership
    of KPIs and pertinent data
    (best practice # 1), 136–138, 156
IKEA effect, 74–75
Improper data purging and
    cleansing, poor data quality
    resulting from, 78
Insight consumption:
    for decision making, 51–52, 139
    distributing, 181–186, 183*f*,
        185*f*, 188
Intangible assets, 3
    and data as liability, 6–7
    depreciation of, 54
Integration systems, 56–58, 58*f*

Integration view, 25–29. *See also* Data integration
Integrity of data, *see* Data integrity
Interface feeds, 76–77
Internet of things (IoT), 21, 82
Interoperability, of business data, 32
Interpolation imputation, 131
Interpretability, in ethical data management, 231*f*, 232
Interpretation, poor data quality resulting from differences in consumption of data and, 72
Interpretation stage, 86
Interquartile range (IQR), 106
Interval data, 30, 31
Invisible data quality issues, 94–95, 94*f*
IoT (internet of things), 21, 82
IQR (interquartile range), 106
IQR rule, 108–109, 108*f*
Ishikawa diagram, 68–69, 69*f*
ISO 15926, 153
ISO 27001, 205, 206
ISO/IEC 11179, 28
IT systems:
 data lifecycle stages in, 86–87, 88*f*
 data quality in, 56–58
 specialized and fit-to-purpose, 173

J
JSON (JavaScript Object Notation), 175

K
Key performance indicators (KPIs):
 cash conversion cycle, 154
 of centrality, 98–100, 101*f*
 data profiling with, 93–94
 defined, 93
 goals based on, 143–145, 144*f*
 identifying, 136–138, 156
 in identifying critical data elements, 33
 integrating centrality and variation KPIs, 109–111, 110*f*, 111*f*

in managing model drift, 228
 to measure accuracy and precision, 43, 44*f*
 ownership of, 94, 136–138, 156
 of variation or spread, 102–109.
  See also Variation measures
KPIs, *see* Key performance indicators
Kurtosis, 106–107

L
Lakehouses, 57, 162
Latency, 31, 46
Leaders:
 commitment to data quality by, 10–12
 in data governance, 10–12
 data ownership by, 137–138
Lean manufacturing, 119, 119*f*
Legal implications of data, 32, 96
Liability, data as, 6–7
Line of businesses (LoB)-owned data, 214
Linkable information, 229
Linked information, 229
LoB (line of businesses)-owned data, 214
Logs, 22
Logging, 172
Logical data decay, 65, 66, 94
Log metadata, 28, 28*f*
Longitudinal data, 27
Longitudinal data analysis, 26–27
Loshin, David, 45, 52–53

M
Machine-generated data, 82
Machine learning (ML):
 bias in models of, 232–234
 data lineage in, 89
 defined, 243
 ethical use of data in, 226
 explainability or interpretability of, 232
 increasing maturity of, 227
MAD framework, 184–185, 185*f*, 243

Manual data capture (MDC), 83, 169
Manual errors, poor data quality
  resulting from, 77–78
Marketplace impacts of poor data
  quality, 53
Masking, 219, 229
Master data, 25–26, 152
  business value of, 168
  coverage of, 48
  critical data elements, 33
  and data profiling or
    assessment, 95–96
  ensuring availability of, 9
  governing, 197, 198
  key characteristics of, 29
  management of, 152–153, 162
  types of, 26
Master data management
    (MDM), 116, 118
  capturing and managing critical
    data with data standards in,
    152–155, 157
  competency in, 245
  defined, 243
  implementation styles for, 163–168,
    163f–168f
  for operations and compliance,
    181, 182
  in rationalizing and automating
    data integration, 162–168,
    163f–168f
  reusing data with, 147
Maydanchik, Arkady, 71, 76
McKinsey, 120
MDC (manual data capture), 83, 169
MDM, see Master data management
Mean, 99–100, 101f
Measurement bias, 233
Median, 98–100, 101f
MELT (metrics, event, logs, traces)
    data, 21–22
Message-based integration, 179

Metadata, 27–29, 28f
  in data lineage solutions, 80–89
  defined, 243
  definitions of, 74
  semantic layer as, 183
  types of, 28, 28f
Metrics, 21–22
Metrics, event, logs, traces (MELT)
    data, 21–22
Microservices, 243
Middleware:
  defined, 176, 243
  for delivering data product,
    122–123
  IT system compatibility with, 176
Middleware systems, 56–58, 58f
Minimum viable data (MVD),
    146–148, 147f, 225, 230
Missing data/values, 130
ML, see Machine learning
Mode, 98–100, 101f
Model drift, 89, 226–228
ModelOps, 228, 244
Moderna, 4
Monitoring governance initiatives, 203
Moral obligations, 224. See also
    Data ethics
Moses, Barr, 204
Multidimensionality, 57
Multi-Processing, 84
MVD, see Minimum viable data

N
NAS (network-attached storage), 216
National Association of Insurance
    Commissioners (NAIC), 23
National Institute of Standard
    Technology (NIST), 136, 228
Netflix, 4
Network-attached storage (NAS), 216
Network-based storage, 216
Nexen, 11–12, 171

Ng, Andrew, 195
NIST (National Institute of Standard
    Technology), 136, 228
Noise, adding, 229
Nominal data, 30
Normal distribution, 106–107
Normalization of data, 47, 78
Norvig, Peter, 4
NoSQL, 25, 244
Noun-modifier-attribute(s) format, 41
NULL, 40
Number of users, poor data quality
    resulting from, 73

O
ODI (Open Data Institute), 224
OLAP (Online Analytical Processing)
    systems, 56–58, 58*f*, 184, 244
OLTP (Online Transactional Processing)
    systems, 56–58, 58*f*
    capturing transactional data in SoR/
        OLTP system, 168–173, 188
    changes in, 76–77
    defined, 244
    defining SoR and securely capturing
        transactional data in SoR/OLTP
        system, 244
    defining system of record as, 170–171
    insight consumption reports from, 184
1-10-100 rule, 53–54, 54*f*, 95, 204
Online Analytical Processing systems, *see*
    OLAP systems
On-line Processing, 84
Online Transactional Processing
    systems, *see* OLTP systems
Open data, 29, 213, 231
Open Data Institute (ODI), 224
Operating expenses (OPEX):
    and data quality, 12, 13
    and free cash flow, 154
Operations:
    data for, 22

data origination and capture for,
    23–24
data rules affecting, 75
master data management as system of
    record for, 182
master data management for, 118
OPEX, *see* Operating expenses
Orchestration of data, 57, 85, 175
Ordinal data, 30
Organizational mechanisms, for data
    governance, 199–202
Organization silos, data silos resulting
    from, 71–72
Origination stage, 82. *See also* Data
    origination
Outliers, 107–109, 108*f*
Ownership:
    of data, *see* Data ownership
    of KPIs, 94, 136–138, 156

P
Panel data, 27
Patterns, 133
Payment Card Industry Data Security
    Standard (PCI DSS), 23
Performance, *see* Business
    performance
Personal data, 29
    defined, 231
    ethical conduct in relation to, 224
    ownership of, 225–226
    types of, 213
Personally identifiable information (PII),
    29, 228–230
Physical control, 219
Physical data decay, 65, 66
PII (personally identifiable information),
    29, 228–230
Policy:
    defined, 198
    in 3Ps – Policy, Process, and
        Procedures, 198–199, 199*f*

Poor business case for data origination and capture, poor data quality resulting from, 73
Poor database design, poor data quality resulting from, 78
Poor data quality, 65–79
  consequences and costs of, 52–54, 54*f*
  cost of, 38, 52–55, 54*f*
  root cause analysis of, 66–71. *See also* Root cause analysis (RCA)
  types of data decay, 65–66
  typical causes of, 71–78. *See also* Causes of poor data quality
Porter, Brian, 3–4
Precision of data, 43, 44*f*, 50*f*
Predictive analytics, 23
Prescriptive analytics, 23
Primary data storage, 87
Principles, 133
Prioritizing data quality improvement, 12
Privacy, 244. *See also* Data privacy
Problem solving, 66, 71
Procedural mechanisms, for data governance, 201
Procedures:
  defined, 199
  in 3Ps – Policy, Process, and Procedures, 198–199, 199*f*
Processes:
  data-related, 196
  defined, 199
  in 3Ps – Policy, Process, and Procedures, 198–199, 199*f*. *See also* Business processes
Processed data, 31–32
Processing stage, 83–85
Process states, 111, 111*f*
Productivity, 10–11, 11*f*, 53
Profit growth, 10
Public data, 29, 213
Pull integration, 175, 175*f*

Purpose:
  collecting data without, 6
  coverage (fit for purpose) data quality dimension, 48, 50*f*
  of data in business, 22–24, 55, 181
Push integration, 175, 175*f*

R
Range, 106
Ranked data, 30
Rationalize and automate integration of critical data elements (best practice # 7), 162–168, 163*f*–168*f*, 187
Ratio scale, 30, 31
Raw data, 31
RCA, *see* Root cause analysis
RDBMS (relational database management system), 24
Realize phase, xxiii, xxiv*f*, 115. *See also* *specific focus areas and topics*
Real-time analytics, 46
Real-time Processing, 84
Recovery Point Objective (RPO), 218
Recovery Time Objective (RTO), 218
Redman, Tom, 171
Redundancy of data, 47–48, 50*f*
Reference architecture, 115–132
  data enrichment, 126–131
  data fabric, 124–126, 125*f*
  data mesh, 124–126, 125*f*
  data product, 120–123
  for data quality, 116
  for remediation of data quality, 116–120
Reference data, 25, 152
  business value of, 168
  coverage of, 48
  critical data elements, 33
  and data profiling or assessment, 95–96
  defined, 244

Reference data (*Continued*)
  governing, 197, 198
  key characteristics of, 29
  management of, 152–153, 162
Referential integrity, 49, 78
Registry style MDM implementation,
     163–164, 163*f*, 167–168,
     167*f*, 168*f*
Regression imputation, 130
Regulatory compliance, 11–12
  and data ethics, 225
  data for, 22–23
  with data governance, 194
  data lineage in, 89
  and listing of critical data elements,
    33–34
  use of data for, 17
Relational database, 24
Relational database management system
    (RDBMS), 24
Relational mechanisms, for data
    governance, 201–202
Relationship cardinality, 43
Relevance of data quality, xxiii
Remediation of data quality, 116–120
  data integration, 117, 118
  DataOps, 118–120, 119*f*
  data wrangling, 117, 118
  master data management,
    116, 118
  1-10-100 rule in preventing need for,
    53–54, 54*f*
  semantic layer, 117–118
Representational state transfer
    (REST), 176, 177
Resource constraints, 95
REST (representational state
    transfer), 176, 177
Restricted data, 30, 213, 232
Retention mindset, 146
Reusing data, 31
Revenue growth, 10

Risk:
  critical data elements dealing
    with, 33–34
  in handling personally identifiable
    information, 230
  poor data quality impacts on, 53
Risk priority number (RPN), 68, 244
Risk reduction, 11, 226
Risk-to-reward ratio, 104
Robotic process automation (RPA),
    180–181
Root cause analysis (RCA), xxii,
    66–71, 71*f*
  Affinity Diagram, 67, 67*f*, 71*f*
  defined, 244
  Failure Mode and Effects Analysis, 71*f*
  fishbone or cause-and-effect
    diagram, 71*f*
  5-Whys method, 71*f*
  as key to data quality solutions, 107
Rosansky, Victor, 54
RPA (robotic process
    automation), 180–181
RPN (risk priority number), 68, 244
RPO (Recovery Point Objective), 218
RTO (Recovery Time Objective), 218

S
Sample bias, 233
SAN (storage area network), 216
SAP Vendor Master, 40*f*
Schema, 204, 244
Scotiabank, 3–4
SD (standard deviation), 103–105
SDI (stream data integration), 180
SE (standard error), 104–105, 105*f*
SEC (Securities and Exchange
    Commission), 23
Secondary data storage, 87
Second-party data, 18–21, 20*f*, 129
Securities and Exchange
    Commission (SEC), 23

Select and define data attributes for
data quality (best practice #5),
148–151, 151*f*, 157
Selection bias, 233
Semantically defining data, 149–150
Semantic layer, 117–118, 147
for analytics, 181–183, 183*f*
and data catalogs, 150–151, 151*f*
Sensitive data, 30, 152, 225, 231–232.
See also Data sensitivity
Service culture, 139
Service-oriented architecture (SOA), 244
Sharing data:
among stakeholders, 33
data clean rooms for, 230
data coverage promoting, 48
and number of data consumers, 73
"Silent killer of data," 66
Silos, 71–72, 140, 146
Silos, Politics and Turf Wars (Lencioni), 72
Simple Object Access Protocol
(SOAP), 176, 177
Single Version of Truth (SVOT),
116, 155, 168
6Ms assessment, 69, 69*f*
Skewness, 106–107
SOA (service-oriented architecture), 244
SOAP (Simple Object Access
Protocol), 176, 177
SOC1, 205–206
SOC2, 205, 206
Soft skills, 246–247
SoI (System of Insights) systems, 57.
See also OLAP (Online Analytical
Processing) systems
SoR, *see* System of record
Special cause variation, 102
Specification limits, 143, 144*f*
Spread, *see* Variance
SQL (structured query language), 244
Stakeholders:
data shared by, 33

diverse views of, 159
needs of, 37
work of data governance team with, 9
Stakeholder engagement, artificial
intelligence and analytics
supporting, 6
Stakeholder management, in ethical data
management, 231*f*, 234–235
Standards. *See also* Data standards
compliance with, 22
financial, 22
for metadata management, 28
Standard deviation (SD), 103–105
Standard error (SE), 104–105, 105*f*
Standardization of enterprise data, 196
Statistical modeling, competency in, 245
Stibo, 162
Stochastic substitution, 229
Storage area network (SAN), 216
Storage view, 24–25. *See also*
Data storage
Stream data integration (SDI), 180
Structural mechanisms, for data
governance, 199–201, 201*f*
Structured data, 24–25
defined, 212, 244
processing, 84
protection of, 212
Structured query language (SQL), 244
Structuring data, 148
Survivorship bias, 233
Sustain phase, xxiii, xxiv*f*, 193. *See also*
specific focus areas and topics
SVOT, *see* Single Version of Truth
Synthetic data, 129
System of Insights (SoI) systems, 57.
See also OLAP (Online Analytical
Processing) systems
System of record (SoR):
define, and securely capture
transactional data in SoR/OLTP
system, 168–173, 188

System of record (SoR) (*Continued*)
defined, 169, 244
defining OLTP as, 170–171
issues with, 74
for operations, compliance, and
analytics, 182
System proliferation and integration
issues, poor data quality
resulting from, 74
System upgrades, poor data quality
resulting from, 77

T
Tangible assets, 3
Target value, 143, 144*f*
TDWI (The Data Warehousing
Institute), 38, 184
Technical metadata, 28, 28*f*
Telemetry data, 21–22, 244
Theory of Constraints (ToC), 119
Third-party data, 19–21, 20*f*, 128, 129*f*
3DM, *see* Data-driven decision making
3Ps – Policy, Process, and Procedures,
198–199, 199*f*
Timeliness of data, 45–47, 50*f*, 186
Time-sensitivity of data quality, 75–76
Time-sharing Processing, 84
ToC (Theory of Constraints), 119
Tokenization, 229
Tolerance limits, 143, 144*f*
Toyoda, Sakichi, 69
Traces, 22
Transactional data, 26–27
in building data product, 122
coverage of, 48
critical data elements, 33
in data profiling or assessment,
95–97
defined, 244
governing, 197
main characteristics of, 26, 29

secure capture of, in SoR/OLTP system,
168–173, 188
trust in, 59–60
Transaction/centralized style
MDM implementation,
166–168, 166*f*–168*f*
Transfer of data, 57, 85, 175
Transformation of data, 57
Transient results of data quality
improvement, poor data quality
resulting from, 76
Transparency, 196, 226
Transpose of data, 85, 175
Trust:
and data ethics, 225
in data governance, 196
importance of, 223
Trusted information, 59–60
TTO capabilities, 85, 175

U
Uber, 4
Unfairness, 226
Uniqueness of data, 42–43, 50*f*
UNSPSC, 153
Unstructured data, 24–25
defined, 212, 244
processing, 84
protection of, 212
Unused data, 6, 145–146, 148
Use of data:
data governance on, 196
frequency of, 73
intended vs. actual, 72
responsible and sustainable, 224. *See
also* Data ethics
User integrity, 49

V
Validation stage, 83
Validity of data, 41, 50*f*

Value chain, 17, 149–150
Value propositions, variation in,
    between consumers and data
    originators, 74–75
Value stream maps (VSM), 147, 147*f*
Variability, 102
Variance, 106
Variation (spread):
  across and within samples, 104, 105*f*
  causes of, 102
  key performance indicators
    of, 102–109
Variation measures, 97–98,
    100–109, 143
  coefficient of variation, 104
  common KPIs, 102–109
  integrating centrality measures and,
    109–111, 110*f*, 111*f*
  interquartile range, 106
  kurtosis and skewness, 106–107
  outliers, 107–109, 108*f*
  range, 106
  standard deviation, 103–105, 105*f*

standard error, 104–105, 105*f*
variance, 106
Varied value propositions between
    consumers and data originators,
    poor data quality resulting
    from, 74–75
Visible data quality issues, 94–95, 94*f*
Volume of data, 204
VSM (value stream maps), 147, 147*f*

W
Weighted average mean, 99
Wheeler, Donald, 111
WorldCom, 224

X
XAI (Explainable Artificial
    Intelligence), 232
XML (Extensible Markup Language), 175

Z
Zero-party data, 18, 20–21, 20*f*
Z-score rule, 108, 109